GOLF AND THE SPIRIT

Also by M. Scott Peck, M.D.

The Road Less Travelled

People of the Lie

What Return Can I Make?
(with Marilyn von Waldner and Patricia Kay)
(reissued as *Gifts for the Journey,* with Marilyn von Waldner)

The Different Drum

A Bed by the Window

The Friendly Snowflake
(illustrated by Christopher Peck)

A World Waiting to Be Born

Meditations from the Road

Further Along the Road Less Travelled

In Search of Stones
(illustrated by Christopher Peck)

In Heaven as on Earth

The Road Less Travelled and Beyond

Denial of the Soul

GOLF
AND THE
SPIRIT

LESSONS FOR THE JOURNEY

M. SCOTT PECK, M.D.

Illustrated by Christopher Peck

SIMON & SCHUSTER
A VIACOM COMPANY

1 3 5 7 9 10 8 6 4 2

Simon & Schuster UK Ltd
Africa House
64-78 Kingsway
London WC2B 6AH

Simon & Schuster Australia
Sydney

A CIP catalogue record for this book is available from the British Library

ISBN 0-684-86161-5

Typeset by
Printed and bound in Great Britain by the Bath Press

TO

BARB AND WALLY WEITZ,

WONDERFUL FRIENDS,

FINE PHILANTHROPISTS,

AND

GOLFING PARTNERS EXTRAORDINAIRE

ACKNOWLEDGMENTS

I thank thousands, golfers and nongolfers alike, for significant direct or indirect contributions to this work. Brevity, however, dictates special mention of several for their special service.

Leslie Meredith, who first proposed the book and both became its acquisition editor and made valued suggestions for its second draft.

Peter Guzzardi, who then took over, editing the third, fourth, and fifth drafts with obvious patience as well as tolerance for my stubbornness.

Jonathan Dolger, my beloved agent, who held my hand while overseeing all the above.

For braving the book's first draft so as to provide technical assistance to this amateur on the finer details of golf's rules, Wallace Weitz, who could have been a professional golfer had he not found an easier way to make a living, and Dave Jensen, who actually was a golfing professional before moving on to even greener fairways.

Gail Puterbaugh, my executive director, who not only typed the whole thing but does indeed direct me with extraordinary wisdom in almost every aspect of my life, with considerable assistance, particularly in this regard, from her golfing husband, Earl.

And finally, as always, Lily, my wife of forty years, who is behind it all, praying each of us on, and who happens to be a far better putter than I.

A "How Not To" Book

and, therefore, one of

the Longest Golf Books Ever Written

—certainly the only one fully annotated with notes—

requiring no knowledge of the game,

to help you understand why some of your friends play it,

possibly even encouraging you to join them,

or at least experiment a bit;

Being, furthermore, the only illustrated interactive golf book

for the computer-ignorant as well as the computer-literate,

which can also be enjoyed by those already addicted

to the sport

and can be put to some good use

on the course and in the rest of life.

CONTENTS

INTRODUCTION

B ecause it's about the sport I most love, initially I thought this would be an easy book to write. As is typical of assumptions made about golf, I was wrong. Although this book has been a joy to write, it has also been very difficult.

Most golf books are written for those who are already enthusiasts of the game, and I hope they will be part of the audience for this one as well. But I also wanted to write for my traditional audience: women and men on a journey of spiritual growth, many of whom know nothing of golf or couldn't care less about it—indeed, some of whom, on the basis of unfortunate personal experience, actively despise the sport.

So from the outset I had a dilemma: How does one simultaneously address the sophisticated and the innocent? The experienced and the inexperienced? The passionate and the uninterested? The degree to which I have succeeded in my paradoxical aims remains to be seen. But I do ask an indulgence from the reader: Temporarily set aside some of your knowledge, prejudices, and preconceptions about golf. Specifically, I request experienced golfers not to think that you know all there is to know about the game or that spirituality is of little consequence to it. Of nongolfers, including those who have been "burned" by the game in the past, I ask that you not consider golf to be merely frivolous on the one hand or downright masochistic on the other.

One more thing I ask. A lot about golf strikes me as frankly funny—at least when I am in a good mood. Consequently, this is the most humorous of my books, while at the same time quite serious. On occasion I have been able to juxtapose these two levels in the text. At other times I have not and have therefore relegated my sometimes lengthy "humorous asides" to the notes. This is not to demean them, however, and I urge you not to skip the notes. Still, to simplify your experience of the text, I have placed them at the end of each chapter, or "hole." Nonetheless, I believe you will find the book more enjoyable and rewarding if you honor these notes as necessary devices to assist you in jumping back and forth between the different levels of the world's most many-leveled sport.

Because there are so many levels to golf, each chapter, or "hole," herein will function in many ways. Even on the course itself, the most experienced golfers often lose sight of the point of the game. To help you keep focused, I have begun each chapter with a brief aphorism that attempts to capture the chapter's most essential message. Some of these aphorisms may seem a bit cryptic at the start. Should this be the case, I suggest you return to the aphorism as soon as you have completed that particular chapter. If you still find it cryptic, then please take the time to meditate upon it.

Thank you.

Exotica Golf Course
and Country Club

Course Pro
Wallace R. Weitz

Hole	1	2	3	4	5	6	7	8	9	Front	10	11	12	13	14	15	16	17	18	Back	Total
Blue	420	355	130	535	350	410	370	175	623	3368	404	402	201	635	327	352	439	205	643	3608	6976
White	401	340	117	510	330	392	350	160	599	3199	385	375	182	602	299	330	420	183	610	3386	6585
Red	380	315	107	430	305	350	322	130	561	2900	337	348	150	547	269	301	382	169	574	3077	5977
Par	4	4	3	5	4	4	4	3	5	36	4	4	3	5	4	4	4	3	5	36	72
Handicap	5	7	18	13	9	6	12	15	3		10	11	4	1	17	16	14	8	2		

Attested to _____

Date _____

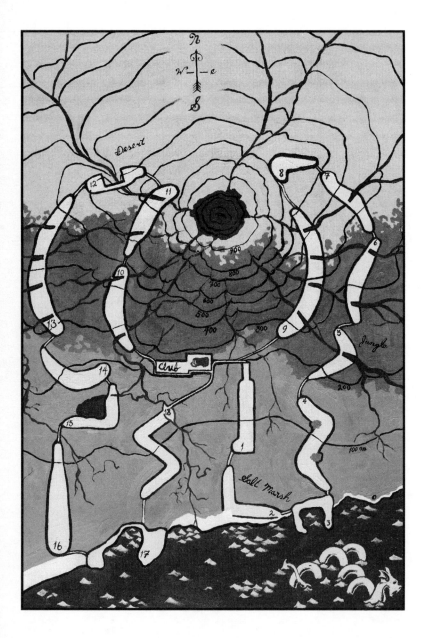

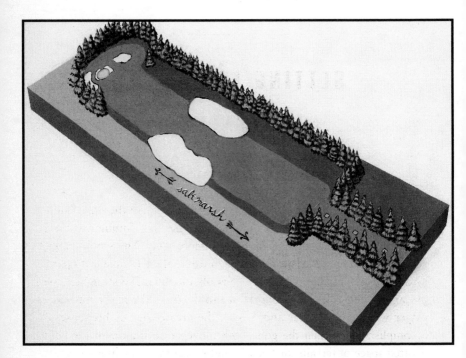

salt marsh

Once there was a man of limited imagination
who considered the progress of life to be straightforward.

H O L E   1

SETTING THE SCENE

To the proverbial man from Mars, golf would seem the most *linear* of all human activities. For example, it is the only common game I know where the player with the *lowest* score wins. The whole point, apparently, is to get the ball from here (a tee) to there (a hole in a green) as directly as possible. Generally, it is obvious that the straighter the passage of that little ball from the tee to the hole, the fewer times the player will have to hit it and, hence, the greater her or his sense of accomplishment. Then the golfer will move on to the tee of the next allotted space of terrain (or "hole") and repeat the same linear process all over again. And again. And again.

A few practicing human golfers actually do envision the game in this manner. Usually they are male. They are the "chargers." They advance directly along the course, their eyes only on the hole ahead, plowing forward with maximum speed, as if driven by a mule. They are generally not having much fun. They are also often not playing very well, either.

This is because the reality—unlike the appearance—is that golf is probably the most nonlinear pastime on the face of the earth. This book is devoted to that reality. Consequently, it will be the most nonlinear book I've ever written. For those of you who have trouble tolerating anything that isn't clearly straightforward, I suggest you stop now. Throw in the towel. Quit. And don't look for much from golf.

This is not a "how to" book. You will read herein almost nothing about how to grip a golf club properly, and very little about how to swing one. Or hit from a downhill lie. Or get out of a sand trap with dignity. Moreover, my lawyers have firmly advised me not to give you any guarantee whatsoever that anything I have to say will improve your game by a single stroke.

This is a "how not to" book.

Human beings have amazingly different personalities. Why this is so—to what degree it is a fact of nature (genes) or nurture (how their parents raised them)—even as an experienced psychiatrist, I don't have the foggiest idea. In any case, certain people—like the pros—seem almost to have been born to play golf well. Others have personalities that make them bound to play the game poorly.

Learning how to play golf with the slightest decency or pleasure has been for me a continual battle against my own personality. This is what has made me an expert. I am an expert on how not to play golf.

Why, you may naturally wonder, would anyone spend an enormous amount of time and money "playing" at something he will never be very good at, something that may often be humiliating? Ah, there you have it. The answer is in the question: I play golf precisely because it is humiliating. While I don't enjoy being humiliated, I do need it.

There's another word for what golfers go through that's even stronger than *humiliation*: *mortification*. It is derived from *mors*, the Latin word for "death," as is the term *mortician* for "undertaker." To be mortified is to feel so humiliated that you would rather bury yourself deep in the nearest sand trap than ever show your face on a golf course again.

In the good (or not so good) old days, certain Roman Catholic monks and nuns and a few others used to practice mortification as a discipline. They defined it as the discipline of "daily dying." Some of their techniques, such as wearing hair shirts, self-flagellation, and floor licking, were indeed masochistic. Yet I believe they were onto some-thing—something we have generally forgotten but still very much need.

They practiced mortification deliberately in order to learn humil-ity. Another word in theology gets more to the heart of the matter: *kenosis. Kenosis* is defined as "the process of the self emptying itself of self." In doing battle on the golf course against my own personality—against my ego, if you will—I am attempting to practice kenosis: get-ting myself out of my own way. It is what spiritual growth is all about.

In this book there will eventually be much more about kenosis, this struggle of self against self. For the moment let it suffice to say that, among other reasons, I play golf because it is for me a highly useful spir-itual discipline. Indeed, given the fact that it is so humiliating, I doubt I could play it at all unless I envisioned it as a spiritual discipline. And I am suggesting that you too might want to regard the game in this light.

So what you have here from me is yet one more "spiritual growth" book.

And while there are no guarantees, reading it might just enable you to take a dozen strokes or more off your score. Or at least persist in your attempt to do so. And for some of you, even to take up the game as a beginner.

What's so wrong with my personality that I need to empty myself of parts of it? My anger, just for starters. I am a very determined person. That's not all to the bad, but I tend to get very angry when things don't go just my way. Things like golf balls. Or family life. Ask Lily, my wife, or my children, and they will tell you that while I am generally a rea-sonable man, on occasion I get unreasonably angry at home as well as on the golf course. And that's when I start to blow it.

For much of my life, I have wanted to design a golf course, and I am profoundly grateful to my editor for finally giving me the oppor-tunity to do so. It is partly the job of a good designer to make his courses "challenging" to a greater or lesser degree. The fact that I have sometimes experienced the challenges to be humiliating does not nec-essarily mean that golf course designers are sadists or bullies. Or that getting back at them has been my motivation for designing the course herein.

My primary intent has been to accurately convey reality as I see it. For instance, were I to lecture an audience about the geology of Malaysia, there would be something unreal—and likely boring—about it if I did not bring along some maps and pictures. Or take the example of a mystery novel. Being fiction, it is not real in a sense, but the more colorful details the author can include, the more real it will seem to the reader. Indeed, a characteristic of good novels is their ability to involve the reader so that she feels herself to be an actual participant in the drama. So it is with this book. It is structured around a fictional golf course because I want you to participate. Imagine yourself into it as a participant on each specific hole.

Designing the course herein has been a rare personal opportunity because it came without responsibility. I have no responsibility for hiring bulldozers to shape the land. I don't have to learn about the different types of grass that grow in particular climates, to create tees and roughs and fairways and greens that actually *work*. Nor do I have to maintain them. This will be purely a golf course on paper.

Yet a golf course on paper is hardly real. You may have played on the more elegant courses where, when you pay your greens fees, they give you a two-dimensional map of the course. Invariably, no matter how elaborate, the map has relatively little relationship to reality. Golf is at least nine-dimensional.

However, in order to help as much as possible, I have once again called upon my son, Christopher, the only great visual artist I personally know, for his assistance. Not even the greatest of artists can capture a golf course, but his illustrations have provided a partial, more multidimensional view of every hole or its subject to help our imaginary course come to life.

One can construct a golf course virtually anywhere there is land. The easiest—and hence cheapest—way to do so is on about fifty acres of flat terrain with enough of a water supply to grow grass. Separate the eighteen holes (the standard number) by a single row of trees, keep some of the grass mowed (preferably at variable lengths), and voilà: You have a golf course!

Such courses need not be particularly aesthetic, and indeed the majority of them aren't. This is not to be decried. They are likely inexpensive and nearby. They are perfectly fine places to begin to learn the game. And if you don't have gobs of money and you do have good golfing companions, they can provide you with a lifetime of fulfillment.

In spots of great natural beauty, the owners have constructed golf courses to make maximum use of that beauty, carving them out of the land. These courses are usually in resorts and have been built at enormous expense with amazing ingenuity. Here playing golf is truly an aesthetic experience. The holes have been deliberately designed to be gorgeous and otherwise interesting (for *interesting*, read "challenging"; for *challenging*, read "nearly impossible to score well").

Needless to say, having the opportunity, I have designed my imaginary course to be one of this beautiful variety. I have chosen to locate it on a mythical tropical island we shall call Exotica. Islands tend to have the most varied landscapes, and I made Exotica a tropical island because I have a thing about coconut palms.

We need not concern ourselves with the grand Exotica Resort Hotel overlooking the ocean, save to know that every five minutes a van takes guests for the one-mile trip to the Exotica Golf and Tennis Club. The club sits a half mile inland at the base of Mount Intrepid, a thousand-foot-high, hopefully extinct volcano. Its tennis courts are of no consequence whatsoever. Once you've seen one tennis court, you've seen them all.

Now to the first hole.

From the map you will see it begins with three tiny squares. These designate the tees. Tees are, in fact, more or less square—little flat areas of well-mown grass from which one hits his or her first shot of the hole. It is the only place on a hole where one is allowed to *tee up*, or raise the ball an inch or so off the ground on a tiny sort of twig of wood or plastic.[1] Supposedly this elevation of the ball allows one to hit it better.[2] In any case, hitting the ball from the tee, particularly the tee of the first hole, is referred to as *teeing off*.[3]

The first of these three tees (the one farthest from the hole) is usually designated by blue markers. They signify "expert." Blue tees are used only by male professionals, by men reasonably close to being professionals, or by macho types with delusions of grandeur. We will never mention the blue tees again.

The middle tee is usually designated by white markers and is the one customarily used by normal male players.

The tee farthest in front (and closest to the hole) is usually designated by red markers. It is called the "ladies' tee" because it can be legally used only by the female of the species. Depending upon the nature of the hole and the chivalry of the course designer, using the red tees may give a player an absolutely extraordinary advantage.[4]

At the opposite end of the hole from the tee is the *green*. Unlike tees, the shape and size of greens is extremely variable. Although this variability may often be of considerable consequence, it cannot be captured on a map. So all map greens will simply be designated by a circle.

The grass of greens is usually of a different genus from that of tees or fairways and is invariably cut much shorter. In fact, the grass of many greens (unless we are speaking of golf courses in Arabia, where the "greens" may be pounded sand) is so short and smooth that their surface is almost as hard and fast as that of a bowling alley. Relatively speaking, however, bowling alleys are a snap because they are flat. Greens may be flat; they also may not be. Try bowling on an alley that undulates this way and that!

Somewhere in the green there is a hole (where exactly can vary from day to day depending upon the whims of those who go about maintaining golf courses at dawn). In size the hole is approximately two and a half times the diameter of a golf ball. The course from the tee to its hole is called a *hole* because the point of the game is to get the ball from the tee into this minuscule hole. *Hole* is a proper term. It can suggest the pits of hell. Sometimes it is euphemistically called a cup, as if to imply that it is a feminine, nurturing sort of spot. It is not. But then one of the underlying reasons for this book is the profound tendency of golf to mimic life, and some will recall that the author began his first book, *The Road Less Traveled*, with the sentence "Life is difficult."

Between the tee and the green lies an expanse of terrain of two types. One, composed of short grass like that of a tee, is called the *fairway*. The other type is called the *rough*. A point of golf is to try to keep your ball in the fairway. It is very nice. But since this is a book primarily about how not to play golf, we shall generally be speaking more about the rough.

As far as the rough is concerned, the word's origin seems clear: It is rough. As in the rough spots of life. Sometimes impossible. There are two distinct types of rough. One consists of grass mown higher than that of greens and fairways: perhaps three inches high. This rough is not easy to hit out of, but it is possible. The other type of rough may consist of anything: forest, jungle, cactuses, high hayfields, and salt marshes. If you can even find your ball in this kind of rough, you are theoretically allowed to try and hit it. I advise you not to, however. I advise you not to look for it in the first place. Take your prescribed penalty like a man. Better yet, like a woman, since women tend to be better at handling this sort of emotional stress.

On this first hole the designated rough to the left is a meandering salt marsh. The rough to the right consists of tropical pine trees and the houses of local landowners. Every ten yards along its edge there are white stakes, signifying that this rough is *out of bounds*. What this means is that you are not even allowed to hit your ball out of it. You must take your penalty whether you like it or not.

From the center, white-marked tee in an exactly straight line to the middle of the green of our first hole, it is precisely 401 yards. This means that it is a par-4 hole. It also means we must begin to speak about the deep, mystical subject of *par*.

The concept of par in golf is based upon certain wild assumptions. One of these assumptions is that after your ball has landed on the green, no more than two taps (with a club called a *putter*) should be required for you to knock it into the cup. The other wild assumption is the number of times (or *strokes*) one needs to hit the ball from the tee for it to land on the green. Not even a pro can drive 400 yards from the tee. On a hole of medium length, like this one, it is assumed you should be able to get your ball to the green by hitting it no more than twice, designating it as a par 4. On a "short" hole it is assumed you should be able to reach the green with a single stroke, making it a par 3. Long holes are par 5's.[5]

The word *par* was in use in the English language long before golf was ever invented. It was taken directly from the Latin word meaning "equal." It generally came to mean a standard of measure of equality, and golfers adopted it as a standard measure of their courses.

No expression from golf has become so deeply embedded in our everyday language as "par for the course." This expression is routinely used by people who have never been near a golf course and know nothing of the game. When they say, "Well, that's par for the course," what they generally mean is, "Well, that's to be expected." It has come to connote what's average or roughly equal to the average. As such, it is the most deceptive and fallacious expression in existence.

Let us talk about the truth. About reality. I would guess that approximately forty million people around the globe routinely play golf. I would further estimate that no more than ten thousand of them are capable of scoring par on the average. What this means, if my statistics are roughly correct, is that at best one regular player out of four thousand is a par golfer. In other words, over 99.9 percent of players are incapable of shooting par golf.

"Par for the course" should be reserved for almost outrageous good fortune, for the blatantly unequal, for performance beyond superior, for competence that is virtually superhuman.

So I would advise you to forget about par.

Only, the bastards won't let you. It is usually posted at every tee. It is plastered over every scorecard. And every golfer you meet will intone the word with reverence. So, far from being able to forget about par, you will dream of it, in daily reverie and when you are asleep. But I warn you: In the battle of self against self that is golf, you will likely find your greatest enemy to be your own enamorment with par. Your enamorment with score and superior performance. It will be one of your demons. You will need, as we shall repeatedly see, to practice kenosis, to empty yourself of this enamorment—if you can.

Although there are some variations, the standard first nine holes of a golf course (the front nine) contain two par-3 holes, five par-4 holes, and two par-5 holes. The same is true for the next nine holes (the back nine). Thus the standard eighteen-hole golf course is approximately seven thousand yards long and is a par 72. You will see from the scorecard preceding this chapter that Exotica is a standard course according to such dimensions. As we proceed, however, you will find it to have some most unique features.

You will also perceive a certain difference in tone between our discussions of the front nine and the back nine. On the front nine my focus will be primarily—although not exclusively—upon the more physical and external challenges of golf. But on the back nine my consideration will increasingly turn to the more internal, psychological, and spiritual challenges of the game.

Throughout, however, the major theme will be golf as a learning experience, with enormous potential for facilitating one's spiritual growth.

Back to this first "starting" hole. And to a bit more about deception.

There is no tradition to designing first holes. But many golf course designers harbor, like magicians, a desire to deceive with illusion. And they are not unlikely to work out this desire from the start.

For instance, one of the most difficult courses I know begins with a 320-yard par 4. The flat fairway is wide at the tee and gets even wider the closer it comes to the flat green. The hole's only hazard is a small sand trap behind the green, which means the only way one can get in the slightest trouble is by overhitting. Even I can par it almost half the time. It is probably the easiest hole I have ever played. But each successive hole gets more difficult. The eighteenth is a nightmare. The best score I ever had on the course—on Christmas Day, during a fourteen-day vacation, praise the Lord—was 95: a mere 23 over par.

Each day I played the course, the more obvious it was that its opening hole had been designed to suck me in, to deceive me with the illusion that the course would be easy.

I've proposed that the greatest illusion in golf is that it is a linear game. Consequently, I've designed our opening hole here to foster that illusion. The line from the tee to the green is as straight as an arrow. To reinforce the illusion of linearity, I have deliberately bordered the tees in a straight, narrow avenue of "Australian pines" (wispy casuarina trees native to the tropics). Christopher has contributed to this deception by drawing his illustration from behind the white tee, making the hole look as simply straightforward as the Champs-Elysées.

It is not, however, an easy hole. Indeed, it is quite difficult precisely because of its linearity.

First of all, there is this narrow little avenue of pines. If you do not hit your tee shot, or drive, dead straight out of the avenue, your ball will go crashing into pine branches or thud against one of their trunks. The result may well be that your first shot will end up behind the tee. Worse yet, it may end up at the foot of one of the tree trunks in such a manner that you will have to hit your second shot backward so that it lands behind the tee—or else take a penalty stroke.

But let's assume that your drive whips directly ahead and the ball begins to sail out over the fairway. Unfortunately, this does not necessarily mean that it will land in the fairway since, in its deceptive straightness, this particular fairway is quite narrow. But why? Why won't your straightly hit ball inevitably end up on the fairway to which the avenue of pines gives way?

The answer is a phenomenon called *slices* or *hooks*. It is somewhere between possible, common, probable, and inevitable that a golfer will swing the club on a long shot in such a way that he hits the ball straight but not squarely. The effect of this is to give the ball a spin that demonstrates the most extraordinary aerodynamics. When it happens, the ball will sail straight ahead and then, at its apogee over the fairway, veer as much as 90 degrees right or left. Someone who has not directly observed this phenomenon will find it hard to believe.

When the ball of a right-handed hitter turns left in midair, it is called a *hook*. If the player hooks on this particular hole, her ball will go plop into the salt marsh. If the ball turns to the right, it is called a *slice*. A slice here means that the ball will land out of bounds among the houses. Or on top of one of the houses. Or through a window. One waits with trepidation for the sound of shattered glass.

There are a host of reasons that a golfer may hook or slice a shot. In each case he is doing something wrong, making a type of mistake. The mistake may be in the way he is gripping his club, the placement of his feet, the nature of his backswing or his follow-through, or a combination thereof. Such mistakes that put an unwanted spin on the ball are often subtle. The subject is complex and belongs in the category I would call the "technology" of golf. It is properly addressed in "how to" books and not in this "how not to" book, which is based more upon my professional psychiatric expertise and therefore is focused primarily upon emotional mistakes. If you have a repetitive slice or hook, as is so often the case, I can only advise you to repair to one of the many technical "how to" books on the subject written by a golf professional or to one such professional himself.

In emphasizing the linearity of this hole, I have quite deliberately created another major problem for the golfer. You will note on the map that two large white globs protrude into each side of the fairway between 210 and 260 yards from the tee. These represent sand traps. For the moment, let's just say that it is not good when your ball lands in a sand trap.

You can see that the effect of these sand traps is to make an already-narrow fairway even more so at this point, reducing it from 25 yards in width to 15. Fifteen yards is not wide. My wife and I refer to such delicate passageways between sand traps or other hazards as "narrows." Narrows are fine places to build bridges over (as in the Verrazano Narrows Bridge that connects Brooklyn with Staten Island in New York City). For golfers, however, they are not fine places—particularly as they are situated on this hole. Let me explain why.

Using his longest-hitting club (called a *driver*), the average good male player will usually drive his ball somewhere between 210 and 260 yards from the tee. A great player can routinely drive well over 260 yards, so for him the narrows on this hole will not pose a problem. It is also not a problem for me. Because of my bad back, I can't hit any ball farther than 200 yards. But I have deliberately created a dilemma for the average good player.

He has two options. One is to *hit all out* in the hope that his ball will land in the fairway of the narrows and bounce straight. Perhaps half the time his hope will be fulfilled. But at least half the time it won't. His ball will either land directly in one of the sand traps or bounce in. So it is a high-risk option.

The low-risk option is to *lay up*—a term for deliberately hitting short, in this case approximately 190 yards from the tee. He will then have a longer but quite safe shot to the green. It is probable that he will score better than the player who hit all out.

Since golfers are obsessed with scoring well, you would think that the majority of them would take this low-risk option. Not so. Male golfers, generally obsessed by distance and length (sound familiar?), love to go all out and hate self-restriction. It is possible this book may eventually teach us, gentlemen, a bit about nurturing our feminine side—an aspect of our personalities that can forget about par and performance upon occasion, that can accept some limitations; a side that is not so obsessed with linearity as to prevent some sniffing of the flowers. In recent years I have learned a bit about this myself. Certainly it has not hurt my score and has improved my enjoyment of the game. Nowadays it is pure fun for me to simply be out on a golf course at all.

After God-knows-how-many strokes and penalties, we have finally arrived at an easy green and pull out our putters. Enough said for the present. Our big troubles are over. But how did we get here in the first place? I don't mean strokes. I don't mean by van from the Exotica Resort Hotel. I mean, how did we ever get on any golf course? How and why did we ever first start playing the least linear, most convoluted, frustrating, and challenging sport on the face of the earth? This question we will ponder as we proceed to the second hole and tee off toward the ocean over some very different terrain. One of the almost innumerable virtues of golf is that its transitions between holes can provide us—if we let them—with a little time and focus for contemplation of the Important.

NOTES

1. Although this "twig" is roughly the shape of a T, that is actually not the origin of the word *tee*. As far as I can ascertain from the most extensive scholarship, the teeing-off place was called a tee for centuries before the elevating device was invented. Even back then golfers would elevate their ball on a little mound of sand that in no way resembled a T. In truth, the origins of the word *tee* are lost in history.
2. If this supposition is correct, it is one of the only very few legal concessions I know to making the game of golf any easier.
3. I cannot help but wonder if the failure to tee off well—that is, flubbing your first shot—might possibly be the origin of the expression to get or to be "teed off." Certainly, teeing off badly is infuriating. If you do it so badly as to hit your partner, you will also tee him off.

There was a man who believed all his endeavors to be
the result of his self-determination and self-reliance.
He had very little gratitude.

H O L E   2

TAKING UP THE GAME

Many years ago Lily, my wife, took a course on the eighteenth-century English novel. By way of introduction her professor told the class that there are only thirty-seven basic plots in the novel, then and now.

I have no reason to doubt this statistic. But when I consider how I got out here as we proceed to the second tee of the Exotica golf course—how I took up golf in the first place—it strikes me that there are at least a thousand different plots for us human beings becoming engaged in such a strange game.

There is no space herein even to begin to describe a thousand different plots. The most I can do is describe but one, the one I know best: my own. So I shall speak of how it came to pass that I myself took up golf in my thirty-second year on the island of Okinawa.

At the age of ten, I decided to become a great tennis player. I took all the lessons I could. In the summers I hung around the local country club, waiting hours for the occasional adult kind enough to rally with me for a few minutes. I picked up words of advice, watched myself swing whenever I passed a mirror, and endlessly hit balls against the backboard.

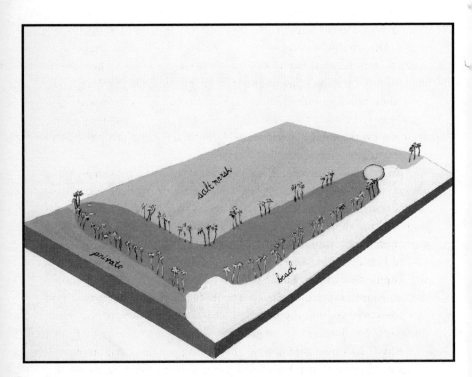

The result was that by the age of twelve, I had become the pre-teen scourge of the courts. I had a fine serve, a good net game, and a magnificent forehand. The only problem was that I had a relatively weak backhand, so I developed a pattern well known to many tennis players. It is called *running around your backhand*. What I would do was position myself a little bit to the left of the middle of the baseline so I could take every possible shot with my forehand. Using this pattern, I was able to wipe 95 percent of my opponents right off the court. The trouble was the other five percent who were better than I. Immediately recognizing that I had a weak backhand, they would consistently hit to it, drawing me farther and farther to my left; and then they would suddenly cross-court me to my magnificent fore-hand—only I couldn't get there fast enough to use it, and they would wipe *me* off the court. Nonetheless, I continued using this pattern for the next twenty years.

In 1967, as a psychiatrist in the U.S. Army Medical Corps, I was assigned to Okinawa. Quickly I became a member of the local army tennis team, but not quite the top player. Quickly I also made friends with Norm, an American businessman on the island. Norm was a golfer. He kept asking me to try my hand at playing golf with him. I turned him down flat every time. As far as I was concerned, golf was the stupidest of games. Either you hit the ball well and had to walk a mile to your next shot, or else—far more likely—you chopped it ahead but a few feet and felt disgusted with yourself. Tennis was fast, excit-ing. Golf? No thanks.

After I had been on Okinawa for a year, a weird thing happened. It occurred to me that if I was ever going to be the best tennis player I could be—perhaps the tennis player that God wanted me to be—if I was ever to have a "whole" game, I was going to have to work on my backhand. This meant doing the exact opposite of what I'd been doing for twenty years; it meant standing to the right of the center of the base-line and taking every possible shot that I could with my backhand. It was kenotic, meaning I was emptying myself of a long-established habit. It felt totally unnatural. It was also profoundly humiliating. It meant routinely losing to players I could easily beat. Worse were the onlookers who watched me hitting balls over the fence or three courts to the side or else dribbling them into the net. In my mind I could hear them sniffing, "I thought you told me that Scott Peck was a really good tennis player?"

Nevertheless, it worked, this exposure of my weak side. After three months I had developed a relatively good backhand. At that point I became far and away the best tennis player on the island. I no longer had any competition. For the first time in my life, the game bored me. After a month of boredom, I called Norm. "Do you still want to play golf with me?" I asked.

"You bet."

"Even though I haven't hit a golf ball for years and I can't play worth a damn?" I persisted.

"No problem," Norm said. "How 'bout this Sunday?"

"Okay," I replied.

"Great. I'll call you Friday with our tee time. The way the system works, to get a starting time one has to phone for it two days in advance," Norm explained, adding, "I'm looking forward to it."

I wasn't sure I was looking forward to it at all.

Even today, thirty years later, when I play a new course for the first time, I am mildly terrified. Where in relationship to the clubhouse is the pro shop? The bathrooms? Will there be bathrooms in the middle of the course? How does one sign in and pay the greens fees? Is there a practice range? How do you find your way to the first hole? Each course and its system is a little bit different, and one's initial encounter with it is a "going into the unknown." It is human to be frightened of going into the unknown. Being a particularly fearful person back then, I was frightened indeed.

On that Sunday morning thirty years ago, I was in fact so nervous, I can hardly remember anything. These are the few things I do remember: It was atrociously early, around seven A.M. Norm met me and shepherded me through the process of signing in, paying my greens fees, buying a glove and balls, and renting clubs; he introduced me to Terry, an army dentist, and Ned, a high school principal, who would round out our foursome; and finally, I remember how horrified I was that not only were we required to use caddies, but the caddies were middle-aged Okinawan women, their faces almost entirely hidden by scarves, who were to carry double.[1]

There are some specific things I do not remember. I don't remember Norm or Terry or Ned ever seeming the slightest bit impatient with all my practice swings, my totally missed shots, my balls going off at insane angles, or the fact that I took at least twice as many strokes as any of them. I don't remember them trying to hurry me up. I don't remember any of the three of them trying to teach me anything about how to do it better. Nor do I remember anyone telling me about penalty strokes when I counted up my score on each hole. I am the kind of person who remembers even a hint of criticism before anything else. Consequently, I am quite sure that the reason I don't remember any of these things is that none of them ever happened.

After I had paid off my caddie under their tutelage and the whole ordeal was over, my memory begins to improve. The four of us assembled in the bar and ordered beer. We added up our scores. The three of them had shot in the 90s. I had shot a 167 (not counting the penalty strokes, which I then didn't know anything about). I was feeling mortified, but we ordered more beer. We began to play an amusing game of dice called Ship, Captain, and Crew. I'd never played it before, but it required no intelligence whatsoever to learn and nothing but pure luck to win. I won the first round. We ordered some more beer. I confess I don't remember exactly how many rounds of beer we ordered, but after a lot of rounds of dice in which I continued to rake in our modest betting stakes, Norm said, "This has been fun. How 'bout we do it again next Sunday?"

"Sure," I answered without a moment's hesitation.

Ned and Terry also agreed.

The next Sunday went only a little differently. I lost a small bit on Ship, Captain, and Crew, but when I added up my golf score, it came to 144 (not counting penalty strokes). Wow! I'd knocked 23 strokes off my game in a single week! In another few weeks I'd be down with my new friends scoring in the 90s. We agreed to play again the following Sunday.

That third Sunday my score soared back up to 169 (still not counting penalty strokes). But it didn't matter. By then I was hooked.

You may think I was hooked on the beer, but I could drink beer anytime, anywhere. You might think I was hooked on the companionship, the camaraderie, and the kind of male bonding that's almost nonexistent in the killer game of tennis. In fact, that's part of the truth, and we'll have more to say about the camaraderie of golf later. But there are other reasons I'd become hooked, which I'll also be talking about in even greater depth in the chapters to come. Before I do, however, let me consider what seem to me to be the two major morals of the story to date.

I had played golf before that day in Okinawa. I had played it as a child and an adolescent, and I had hated it each and every time. I had hated it because I was terrible at it, and as an excruciatingly self-conscious youngster, I was invariably humiliated by the experience.

This is why I was so hesitant when I finally told Norm I would play golf with him on that first Sunday. It wasn't just my fear of a new course or the unknown; it was my fear of the known. I *knew* I was going to feel humiliated. But I agreed to do it anyway, partly because of my recent experience of working on my backhand. I do not think it an accident that it took me until the age of thirty-two to do such things. Only then did I have the maturity and self-confidence to display my weak sides. The fact that I no longer had any competition in tennis was the minor reason I took up golf at that point. The major reason was that I knew I could survive the humiliation of the game.

I have said there are a thousand or more plots to describe how people get lured into taking up golf. This doesn't mean, however, that certain themes don't repeatedly run through these plots. One is the theme of humiliation. I touched upon it in the very first chapter when I spoke of monks and nuns practicing the discipline of mortification or kenosis. I am speaking of it now, and I shall speak of it again in almost every chapter to come. How they deal with humiliation is a significant theme in the stories of the vast majority of golfers. It is also, I suspect, a theme in the stories of millions who choose not to take up golf.

Having taken up golf on Okinawa, I wish I could tell you I immediately submitted to the humiliation required to develop a "whole" golf game. But I cannot. The fact is, I immediately regressed to playing golf at thirty-two the same way I'd played tennis at twelve.

My "natural" golf swing on my long shots gave the ball a huge slice. It would sail out over the fairway, only to turn sharply right and infallibly land in the rough or the China Sea. I should have quickly sought out a pro to tell me what I was doing wrong and teach me how to hit the ball straight. But for deep-seated psychological reasons to be recounted later, the notion of taking lessons struck me as even more humiliating than being a poor golfer. So I began a pattern of what might be called *running around your slice*. From the tee, for instance, I would aim insanely to the left. I considered it a good hit when my drive flew above the woods, hovered for a moment, and then magically careened right to bounce onto the middle of the fairway. It was remarkable how adept I became at routinely making such bizarre shots. No matter that I lost a hundred yards' distance each time—I had gotten my score down into the low 90s by the time I left Okinawa after a year of frequent playing, and I suppose I could have been labeled a fair golfer.

The next twenty years gave me little opportunity to play. It wasn't until I was well over fifty that I began to envision golf as a spiritual discipline—meaning an opportunity to learn all the things involved in doing it well. Mostly the things I had to learn were things about myself: about my temperament, my personality, and the hundreds of roadblocks I put in my own way as I lived life as well as golf. I did eventually learn how to shoot straight. Before that happened, arthritis had taken a sufficient toll that no matter how straight I hit, I could no longer hit the ball very far. Yet my golf score had strangely ceased to be the central focus. By my sixtieth year the real point was that I was learning from golf more rapidly than I ever had learned before, and learning something about how to be a better person. Specifically, I was learning how to use teachers, and how to be grateful for them.

The other theme to this tale can be found in the story of virtually every golfer. One does not simply stroll into the strange world of a golf club, public or private, and start playing. First, one is invited. Then he is shown the ropes. Finally—and usually repeatedly—he is accompanied around the course by people who are not merely patient with his poor play but somehow deeply encouraging. I speak of the theme of mentoring.

Most people think of mentors as teachers. So they are, but they are a rather peculiar and relatively rare species of teacher. First of all, they teach very little—if anything at all—directly. Indeed, a large part of the great art of mentoring is the very difficult exercise of the capacity to not teach. I was already so overwhelmed by the newness of the course and the humiliation of my incompetence that had Norm tried to teach me how to hit the ball as well, it would have been too much for me. I imagine I would have quit right then and there. But he left me alone.

In other words he accepted me as I was. He didn't try to improve me. Good mentoring is often one of the closest things there is to unconditional love.

Ordinary teachers are usually assigned to their pupils; mentors choose theirs. Thus Norm repeatedly invited me to play golf, and even after I'd made it dramatically clear that I was no born golfer, he continued to invite me to play with him. He *wanted* me. There is something extremely empowering about being wanted. Consciously or unconsciously, good mentors know that it is far more their task to empower than it is to teach. Or perhaps they know that the best way to teach is through empowerment.

Usually our mentors are older and wiser than we are. Often we associate them with business and the professions. They are the experienced professors or managers who take us under their wing (as Norm took me under his wing in this business of golf). I have spoken of good mentors, implying there may be bad ones. Indeed, there can be traps in this matter of mentoring. I have, for instance, seen mentors who have taken a student under their wing and then felt they somehow owned that student as a result. All mentoring has much to do with love. The great mentors love so much, they have no trouble letting their students go.

Mentors come and go. Sometimes they outgrow us; sometimes we outgrow them. Another trap may occur when we try to hold on to a mentor we've outgrown because of a misplaced sense of loyalty or even a desire to flee our own growth. There is no proper time for a mentorship to last. It may be decades or years or, perhaps most commonly, just a month or two. I cannot say that either Norm or I outgrew each other; we simply seemed to drift apart, and within a few months it was mainly other foursomes to which we belonged. This was not a cause for sorrow. For me at least, Norm had played his role to the fullest, and he'd played it well. I am very grateful to him.

To a large extent, how well we play the game of life will be determined not merely by the quality of our mentors but also by their sheer quantity. Seek out as many good mentors as you can possibly find! They are the finest of teachers. Just as I envision life as a spiritual journey or pilgrimage rather than as a game (with a clear-cut score at the end), so I envision all my mentors as spiritual teachers, wittingly or unwittingly. I doubt that Norm thought of himself as a spiritual teacher. But the fact of the matter is that he taught me not how to play golf but to take it up in the first place. I couldn't have done it alone. I have come to believe that no one can do much alone.

Furthermore, Norm introduced me to the greatest of all my earthly spiritual teachers. For it so happens that in these last years I have learned far more that matters from golf than I have from any one human being, with the possible exception of Lily. In other words, it was ultimately golf that became the teacher, and golf itself that would be my primary mentor.

If, as I propose, a significant part of the art of living is to seek out just as many mentors as you can find, how do you choose a mentor as opposed to an ordinary teacher? For that matter, how do you choose a psychotherapist? A full answer is too complex for the confines of this book. Yet in relation to Norm I have already offered the most important hints. Look for someone you like and who likes you. Someone who encourages you. And someone who is able to empty herself of any obsessive need to teach. We shall return to these matters on hole 10, where the theme is "Teaching and Learning" and I say a few words about how to search out the right golf teaching professional.

I am reminded of my first truly great mentor in life: Carol Brandt. I was but thirteen years of age. She was in her forties and one of the most prominent figures in the literary world at the time. For some reason I can't explain in the least, she took me under her wing for the next decade. She taught me virtually nothing about writing save a few almost banal practicalities (such as to preserve my typewriter paper boxes for the submission of manuscripts). But she invited me to her parties, where she introduced me to real working authors. Nothing could have been so encouraging to me than that a powerful, famous person simply befriended me at the mere age of thirteen. She actually wanted me around. I have no doubt I eventually became a professional author as a result of her unspoken influence.

Seek out as many mentors as you can find, but remember that it is primarily our mentors who find us. Although I can't explain it, it seems obvious that Carol saw something in me. She picked me out, and I suppose the very best we can do is to be as open and empty as possible to receiving such grace.

I use the word *grace* advisedly. We think the origin of grace to be God, using whatever is within His or Her power to encourage. Carol has not been the only mentor in my life. Nor Norm. But whenever a mentor has come around for me, it has seemed like something of a miracle. Does God work through mentors, among other ways? Although I hesitate to raise the question so early in this golf game we are playing together, I have no doubt that the answer is yes. I said that recently golf has been my primary mentor. Let me amend that. From the beginning until this moment, God has been my primary mentor; golf has been one of Her primary agencies.

We now finally arrive at the second tee of the Exotica golf course to discover what this new hole has to teach us (or to decide, for the most part unconsciously, what we refuse to learn from it).

One thing it might teach us is to enforce the lessons of the previous hole, to mostly put to bed any lingering notions of golf as a linear game—empty ourselves through kenosis of such simplistic thinking. Right from the start we cannot help but note that this fairway does not proceed from the tee to the green in a straight line; it bends. In fact, it bends very sharply at a right angle.

When a fairway bends, it is called a *dogleg*.[2] It may bend right or left, and the person who has played the course before will sagely tell us that the hole "doglegs to the left" or "doglegs to the right." Usually we can see this for ourselves from the tee. If not, we can easily discern it from a simple course map (usually provided by all but the least expensive courses). Only very occasionally, if the green is way on the other side of a hill on a hole we've not played before, may it be most helpful to have a mentor tell us about a "blind" dogleg up ahead.

I don't mean to imply that straight lines are of no consequence in golf. Indeed, this hole, like all others, is measured by them. It is exactly 160 yards from its white tee to the middle of the dogleg, and then 180 yards dead left from there to the center of the green. Add these two sums together, and you get a total yardage of 340, which is why this is a par 4, where even an excellent player is expected to take two shots to reach the green.

The superb player may immediately be attracted to a very different option: namely, to *cut across,* or triangulate, the dogleg. He will realize that in a single straight line it is "only" 241 yards from the white tee to the green.[3] Of course, virtually all of that distance is across a marsh, and the green is not only small but trapped in such a way as to discourage the option. Still, 241 yards is well within the range of a superb golfer. But no matter how superb, the ambitious player would be well advised to read the little booklet he received at the Exotica clubhouse along with the elegant course map when he paid his exorbitant greens fees. Entitled simply *Playing Tips,* it notes about this hole:

> Here is a chance for a birdie [1 under par] or even an eagle [2 under par]. You can bypass the short, sharp dogleg totally by hitting out directly across the marsh and landing on the green of this par 4 with a single stroke. Be forewarned, however, that only three out of ten balls hit in this manner from the white or blue tees do, in fact, land and stay on the green.

As we all know, the shortest distance between two points is a straight line. Yet what this booklet takes pains to point out is that a straight line may well not be the best way to go in golf—even for the expert.

Thus far I have spoken as if there were only two ways to go. But there are other options. Repair to the notes for details if you so desire. There may not be quite as many plots or strategies for a single hole in golf as there are for all the novels put together. But in order to emphasize the nonlinearity of it all, let me simply state that there are actually five different ways to play this hole from the tee alone—and one of them even requires a curveball.[4]

But I must come full circle. While you will miss out on much of golf if you regard it as a purely linear sport, you will also miss badly if you fail to pay attention to its lines. Whatever way you play this hole or any other, to do so decently you must *aim* each and every shot. This, at least, is linear. To aim correctly is primarily a matter of aligning your *stance* before you swing. Your stance is how you stand when you swing your club. The stance of golfers is so individualized that it has been a major subject of many books. But no matter how unique your stance, to succeed you must at least be able to draw some imaginary *line* between the position of your feet and the point at which you are aiming.

On the last hole I mentioned with some disparagement a type of golfer I labeled the "charger"—a man so linear-minded that his sole focus is upon the aiming point ahead of him. I know about him so well because a part of him is in me, all intertwined with my excessive determination. I suggested that the charger usually does not play the game all that well or enjoy it all that much. Only recently have I been learning how to smell the flowers while on the course.

Actually, there are not many flowers on this hole. But it does have an abundance of other features to sniff out—particularly an abundance of my beloved coconut palms, which line its fairway from beginning to end. The charger would regard them solely as an obstacle. But I delight in the gracefulness with which they gently wave in the light offshore breeze. What would it be like to play this hole on the edge of a tropical hurricane, I wonder, as I drink in the soft sounds of their fronds rustling together in today's more ordinary tropical breeze.

I also delight in the two sand traps of the hole. In a sense they are not so much traps as extensions of the beach into the fairway. Truly this is what is meant by a course being "carved into the land." I have played on only one other course where a beach has been so incorporated.

More than anything I delight in the modest Spanish-style mission church behind the dunes, just to the right of the dogleg. Many players of Exotica will pass it by unnoticed. But today I wonder: Does it speak

of a centuries-old Spanish colonization of the island? Is it still used or just a relic? It is not boarded up. It looks used. By whom? By island parishioners on Sunday mornings? By monks or nuns? And what might they do within its confines? Sing? Pray?

And suddenly I am accosted by a most bizarre notion. I imagine that the parishioners of this little church pray for many things, but it strangely occurs to me that they might even pray for us golfers. That they might do so dramatically underscores my original folly in seeing this as a linear and self-reliant pastime.

NOTES

1. Except for big-time tournaments, in North America golfers almost always carry their own clubs around the course, or pull the clubs behind them on a little wagon or else, without any effort at all, on the back of a motorized two-seater cart. It is hard work to carry the typically heavy American bag of clubs for eighteen holes. To hire someone else to do it for you feels to me like hiring slave labor. To hire a woman to do it in the heat of the semitropics seems sadistic. For her to carry double—that is, two heavy American bags at the same time—struck me as akin to atrocity.

   Yet I was being provincial. After Americans conquered Okinawa toward the end of World War II, like me, they were horrified to learn that all the heavy manual labor, such as ditch digging, was performed by the women of Okinawa. Feeling guilty about hiring women for such work, they finally paid a group of men enough to conduct a scientific study. I am told that they found that in a given period of time, the Okinawan women moved three times as much earth as the men. Buoyed by such scientific research, the American authorities finally gave in to the culture. Indeed, as far as I myself was gradually able to observe, caddying double was a job in very high demand by the Okinawan women.

2. As with the word *tee,* the origin of the term *dogleg* for a bend in the fairway is lost in antiquity. Otherwise, it is simple to understand; the bend does look like the bend of a dog's leg. Or a cat's leg or a sheep's leg, for that matter, except now the analogy is so embedded in the history of golf, it would seem strange indeed to call such a turn in the fairway anything else.

3. Figure it out for yourself—if you've got nothing better to do. Remember the famed Pythagorean theorem, that the square of the hypotenuse of a right-angled triangle is equal to the sum of the squares of the other two sides. But there's no need to bother. Even mediocre players soon learn to estimate such distances with quite adequate accuracy, using their eyes alone without having to employ geometry or make complex mathematical calculations.

4. One can frequently triangulate a dogleg in lesser degrees than bypassing it entirely. For instance, if you know what you are doing, you can hit a high shot over the palm trees of the inner corner of the dogleg on this hole so that your ball will land farther into the second part of the "leg," perhaps 150 instead of 180 yards from the green. Or you could aim such a high shot even more to the left so that it would land in the fairway a mere 100 yards from the green. Either way, however, requires sufficient skill to control the height and distance of the shot. Hit too low, and your ball will knock into the palms. Hit too short, and it will land in the marsh. Too far, and it will land on the beach.

The final option is to me more elegant than any of the previously described straight shots. On the last hole I described how players will often hit their ball with a spin so that it hooks to the left or slices to the right. Usually this is done inadvertently with poor or disastrous results. Some experts, however, know how to hit a well-modulated hook or slice *deliberately*. What such an excellent golfer would probably do on this hole is hit a high tee shot over the inner corner of the dogleg, which then hooks to the left so that when the ball lands, it not only does so well into the second part of the leg but will actually keep bouncing down the fairway directly toward the green. What expertise!

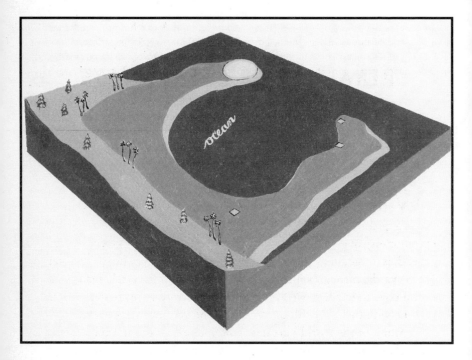

Once there was the best of women who vowed to achieve a state of perfection, but she never quite attained it.

H O L E   3

PENALTIES AND PERFECTION

Walking out onto the third tee, we feel as if we have just stepped into a picture postcard. The red and white tees are on a narrow promontory of coral jutting 40 yards into the ocean. The green, straight ahead, is at the tip of a similar promontory. Separating the two is a gap of 90 yards, through which the waves are rushing to crash against the coral cove to our left. We are thrust out to sea as far as human beings can be with their feet still on dry land. The ocean is everywhere.

Many of the world's greatest golf courses, from the United States to Ireland and Great Britain and on to New Zealand, are strung out along the sea. Most of them will have at least one such hole where the golfer's shot must carry over the ocean. These are eminently photographic. Consequently, we have seen pictures of them as we idly flip through the resort advertisements in airline magazines. Although stunning, they are not necessarily more beautiful than any of the others, only more capturable in picture. While I rejoice in this hole, let us remember that each of the eighteen holes of the Exotica golf course is beautiful in its own right.

In any case, the water dominates this hole. For all intents and purposes, no fairway lies between the tee and the green, only water. It is a mere

117 yards from the white tee to the center of the green on the other promontory, but 90 of those yards are water. As long as your ball lands an inch short of the green, it will be in the water and thereby lost. For the same reasons it is also lost if you overhit the green by an inch. Or even if your ball lands on the green but then bounces across it into the ocean on the other side.

Part of our misplaced obsession with linearity in golf has to do with the idolatry of science in our culture, and in turn, science's idolatry of measurement. Lines have length, and length can be measured with the greatest of accuracy. In recent years, however, recognizing that length alone is not a particularly accurate measurement of a course's difficulty, some golf authorities have developed a different means of assessment, called *slope*. It takes into account things such as the number and placement of hazards—sand traps, for instance—and the fact that the green of this hole is highly unusual and challenging because it has no boundary except water on three of its four sides. Although average in length, Exotica is a particularly "high slope" course.

But this nonlinear concept of slope has not yet caught on much because of its subjectivity. It is not "scientific." Experts can and will disagree violently over the slope of a hole or a course in its entirety. But since no one can disagree over the length of a line, we tend to remain hooked on this business of linearity despite its inadequacy. And nowhere is the inadequacy more obvious than on this particular hole.

Not only are holes divided into pars 3, 4, and 5 on the basis of their length, but they are also ranked from 1 to 18 on the supposed basis of their difficulty. Consequently, you will see that hole 3 is number 18 on the Exotica course scorecard, to indicate that it is the *highest-handicapped,* or easiest-ranked, hole on the course. The sole reason for this ranking is its length; it is not only the shortest hole on the course, but as par-3 holes go, it is about as short as they come.

Now, professionals will have little trouble agreeing with this ranking. Not only do they know within a yard or two where their shot, when it's this short, will land, but they also know just how to hit the ball with a *short iron* so that it takes no bounce. The pro will be displeased if her ball doesn't land within a few feet of the pin[1] and disgusted if she doesn't then tap the ball into the cup, or *sink her putt,* for a score of 2—1 under par, or a *birdie,* on this easy par-3 hole. Virtually never will a pro get a *bogey,* or 1 over par, on hole 3.

The good player will also almost always land on the green, but likely not so close to the pin. So it may take him two putts. Just as the pro will expect to get a birdie on this third hole, so the good player will expect to get a par. Less than one time in ten will his first shot land in the water and afflict him with a penalty.

Now let's take an at-best-fair player such as myself. I'll be able to land on the green about seven times out of ten, meaning that three times out of ten, I'll be afflicted with a penalty or even multiple penalties. The result is paradoxical. I am, in fact, more likely to par or birdie hole 3 than on any other hole on Exotica because it is so short. On the other hand, I am also more likely to get a terrible score—a double or even quadruple bogey—than on any other Exotica short hole because there's so much water.[2] Paradoxically, it is for me both a very easy and a very difficult hole.

Finally, let's consider a poor golfer—either a beginner or a duffer.[3] The length, height, and direction of his shots will border on the random. His chance of landing on this green is probably less than one in ten. He may well accumulate 20 or more penalty strokes on this one hole if he keeps plugging away that long. Because it is all water and no fairway, for the beginner this is unquestionably Exotica's most difficult hole, and its linear ranking as the easiest only serves to make the game of golf seem more absurd.

I've already alluded to the painful matter of penalties. Given the potentially hazardous nature of this hole in particular, now is the time to offer an overview on the matter.

Penalties are analogous to taxes. They are the cause not only of great suffering but also of about half of the complications of the game of golf and most of its arguments. My aim in this book is to keep the subject as simple as possible. Golf purists are likely to take issue with my oversimplification. Golf purists tend to be very argumentative people. They are extremely legalistic.

You see, just as there is a body of law governing taxes, so there is a body of law governing penalties in golf. At times it seems that most

tax law is designed to create loopholes by which penalties may be avoided or at least somewhat modified in one's favor. Not so in golf. The laws of golf are extremely strict—indeed harsh—and are generally designed to demolish any possible loophole or humane allowance.

They are also, like tax law, very complicated. The penalties of golf mostly relate to what are called *hazards,* and as we shall see, there are many different kinds of hazards on a golf course, of which water is just one. Then there are different kinds of water. Here we are talking about ocean water, but one may also encounter on the course lakes, ponds, rivers, streams, rivulets, swamps, and puddles. The laws relating to each have similarities but also occasional exquisite differences. Even the position of the water may make a difference, and purists are likely to be furious with me for saying nothing about the fine distinctions between lateral hazards and other types.

Golf is an international game, and just as tax laws will vary from nation to nation, so may golf law. Indeed, two very slightly different "classical" works govern golf: *The Decisions on the Rule of Golf of the Royal and Ancient Golf Club of St. Andrew's* (R&A) and *The Rules of Golf of the United States Golf Association* (USGA). Each is about as interesting to read as a volume of tax law. Nonetheless, if your golf opponent challenges a loophole you want to take, it can be fun to fib, "But it's considered quite appropriate by *The Decisions on the Rule of Golf of the Royal and Ancient Golf Club of St. Andrew's,"* whether you've read it or not.

Actually, if you have read either or both of these rule booklets, you likely came away confused. This is because the rules are not case-specific. To supposedly combat the confusion and offer clarification, over the past fifty years the USGA and the R&A have developed a con- tinually revised casebook, *Decisions on the Rules of Golf: Official Rulings on Over 1,000 Golf Situations.* It is currently 603 pages long (not including a 93-page table of contents). Do you begin to appreciate some of the similarity between tax law and golf law? I have no reason to recommend that you ever read this volume, save that on occasion it is far more amusing than tax law. Indeed, probably the only reason that it is in print is that each year a sufficient number of people purchase it precisely because of its unwitting humor.[4]

• • •

So I am not going to discuss the esoteric details and circumstances of whether it is a one-stroke or a two-stroke penalty when your ball lands in a body of water; it is a penalty. It doesn't matter so much, as the balls sink to the ocean floor, that you lose them at two dollars apiece. What really matters is that the beginner or mediocre player is likely to accumulate a whole bunch of penalty strokes by hitting a number of balls into the water before he finally lands one on the green. As a result many golfers become hydrophobic. They do not see this as a beautiful hole; they envision it only as a sea of penalties.

Hydrophobia and other phobias are devastating to the golfer. Because she tenses up and hence fails to swing well, the result is that her ball will head straight for the very hazard that she so dreads. It is an example of what psychologists call a self-fulfilling prophecy. Expect trouble, and it is all the more likely to come to pass.

I know of but one cure for such phobias in golf, and no hole could be better designed than this one to teach that cure.

Although only a very short shot is required from the tee, it must be a perfect one. Very much aware of this, the mediocre golfer will likely be thinking only of the huge obstacle to such perfection: all that water. He will be imagining his penalty strokes before he has even incurred them. This is the way I thought about golf for decades.

But then a mere few years ago, a most remarkable thing happened to me. I had just played a hole very similar to Exotica's hole 3 and had dumped two balls into the water before getting one onto the green. That night, waiting for sleep, I lay in bed cursing myself, cursing the hazardous water, and cursing the perfection that the hole required. At that moment a still, small voice, seemingly inside my head, intruded upon my consciousness with a most simple question: *Why do you curse perfection?*

Why indeed? Was it not my fantasy to play great golf? Golf as close to perfection as possible? What on earth was I doing cursing my own dream? Strange behavior! And in that instant it dawned on me that I had managed to lose all perspective of what golf is about.

Golf is about a great many things. And yes, very much among them are obstacles, hazards, and penalties. But above and beyond all these things, it is about perfection.

I wish I could tell you that since my primary focus has switched from imperfection to perfection, I am no longer concerned about obstacles, hazards, and penalties, but I can't. Being a born worrywart, I remain overly concerned about them. But I am no longer exactly phobic about them. And my game has improved as a result.

But how exactly did this occur? How does one change his deep-seated behavior on the golf course or in the rest of life? There is no easy formula. Yet easy or not, there is a formula of sorts. It has three steps:

1. The first step is to realize that something you are doing isn't working; in fact, that it is hurting you. This something is usually a manifestation of a character flaw of some kind, such as my excessive dread not only of hazards on the course but also of all the possible pitfalls ahead of me in the stock market, the roadway, or my relationships. Many people never have such realizations. Others arrive at them on their own. Still others get an assist, as I did in this instance from that "still, small voice" that may actually be identified with the voice of God.

2. We generally cannot heal ourselves of something of which we are unaware. But once we do realize we have created a roadblock for ourselves, then the second step is obvious: Get rid of it. How? Through kenosis. Empty yourself of it. But still, how? How do you empty yourself of something? To that there is no simple answer. Just do it. Work on it—and it is work of a kind.

3. Bear in mind that it is nonlinear work. With something as deep as a character flaw, we do not simply decide to get rid of it one day, and then, poof, it is gone. We empty ourselves of it and proceed, pleased with how we've healed ourselves. But two holes down the course or at the next sharp curve in our lives, we find ourselves afflicted with the same flaw. So we must empty ourselves again. And again and again. After all these years I am still reencountering my unrealistic, excessive dread of hazards, but I go a little deeper each time, and each time I get a bit better at it, which is why I can say I am no longer truly phobic, if not fully healed. This is the way with all psychotherapy, which has often been compared to peeling an onion: You remove a spot of rot from the outer layer, but when you reach the second layer, you find the same spot and must go to work again.

Together we too shall be going deeper into this matter of kenosis as the holes of Exotica proceed. The concept is crucial. Human beings may unconsciously change for the better or "grow" to a limited extent in response to some of life's experiences. But to grow as far as they are capable, they must eventually learn how to *consciously* change themselves. The essence of conscious growth, be it on the golf course or in the rest of life, is this practice of kenosis.

For example, to improve my tennis backhand on Okinawa, I followed the same three-step formula outlined above:

First, I became fully aware how much my poor backhand was getting in my way as a tennis player.

Second, I consciously decided to change—to get rid of that poor backhand, to empty myself of my old pattern—and I went ahead and did it.

Third, I did it over and over again until a better backhand became second nature to me.

I shall be repeating this formula a number of times in the chapters to come. Its core, its essence, and its difficulty are kenosis. But how do you "do" kenosis? A page or two back, in response to this question, I wrote: "There is no simple answer. Just do it. Work on it." This is not the kind of answer that is very satisfying to the average person. Actually, the answer can sometimes be relatively simple and technical. In regard to my backhand, once the will was there, my course was obvious: Stop standing on the left side of the court and start standing on the right. Not easy, but obvious. In most cases, however, such as emptying oneself of a phobia, the mechanics of the kenotic process are not so obvious. Furthermore, such "mechanics" as there are differ from person to person and from situation to situation. As we proceed, you may feel frustrated by my *seeming* evasiveness on the subject. Please try to empty yourself of this frustration, and be alert to the fact that I may drop a little hint now and then—whenever I can.

Perfection is, of course, relative. A purist would argue that the only perfect shot on this par-3 hole must, by definition, be a hole in one. But even the pros consider a hole in one to be a fluke. For them a perfect shot is one where their ball stops within a five-foot radius of the pin so they can then tap it lightly into the cup for a virtually guaranteed birdie. For us average players, however, a ball hit high in the air so that it not only lands anywhere on the green but stays on it constitutes a perfect shot, and we will feel very pleased with ourselves. Yet what about the poor beginner? Is his ball inevitably consigned to the ocean? How can he hit a perfect shot?

We now come to one of the most important principles of golf— perhaps its most sustaining principle: *No golfer is so good that he doesn't occasionally hit a bad shot, and no golfer is so poor that he doesn't occasionally hit a good one.*

The manifestations of this principle are multiple. For this chapter I'll only be addressing two. One is the popularity of golf as a spectator sport. Many people stay glued to their TV to watch the pros play in this tournament or that because the competition at times can be so intense that viewers feel like jumping out of their shoes. Few sports can match—and none can exceed—such moments of high drama. The viewers are also there to gasp in admiration at (or envy of) the sheer excellence of play—the perfection—involved. Finally, they are there to watch the occasional goof with howls of dismay. Were it not for some of the most atrociously poor shots made by some of the very best players, substantially fewer people would be watching golf on TV.

There would also be fewer people out on the course playing golf themselves. The goofs of the pros offer us mere mortals a modicum of solace. Being mediocre, I am often playing with my betters, and while I do not rejoice in their mistakes (unless we have a wager going between us), their mistakes do help me feel less inferior. Besides, it's nice to have the "honors" once in a while.[5]

But the greater reason that so many people are out on the courses is the other side of the principle: No golfer is so bad that he doesn't occasionally hit a good shot. Save for a few born athletes, most beginners at golf are pretty bad. It is largely a learned game. Yes, the beginner on the third tee of Exotica is likely to hit one ball after another into the ocean. Occasionally, however, on her second shot—sometimes even on her first—the ball will go sailing into the sky, and to her amazement, it will fall out of the sky right onto the green just as it should. She has hit the perfect shot.

The feeling that comes from hitting a perfect shot, particularly for a beginner, is hard to describe because it has several components: the amazement of "Golly, did I really do that?"; the pride of "By God, yes, I really did do that." Still another part—the most powerful—has no adequate word. It is akin to hope mixed in with a bit of awe: "Hot dog! You know, maybe I really *can* do that!" Complex though it might be, it is a very good feeling—so good that it can be addicting for certain people. I have played with several beginners who became totally hooked on golf after their very first round solely because they made a single perfect shot out of close to two hundred.

This is good. What is not good is to have a psychology, like my own, that is self-deprecatory to the point of being self-destructive—at least on the golf course. What I did for all too many years, whenever I hit a perfect shot, was to say to myself, "Well, that was certainly an accident" or "That was surely a bit of luck." On the basis of my years of waging the struggle of kenosis—of trying to empty myself of self— let me tell you that such thinking is baloney. A perfect shot is just that: a perfect shot. It is not the result of accident or luck. When you hit a perfect shot, it is because you hit the ball perfectly. Being a beginner, you may not have the slightest idea why or how you hit the ball per- fectly, but that in no way mitigates the fact that you did hit it perfectly. This is important.

I do not mean to imply that there is no such thing as luck in golf. A great deal of both good luck and bad luck are involved, although more good than bad. Bad luck occurs with shots that are only slightly imperfect. Suppose, for instance, that I hit a nice high ball to this green, but I hit it a fraction of a degree more to the left than I want to, and the onshore wind happens to pick up slightly after I've hit it, with the result that my ball lands on the fairway three feet to the left of the green, where there happens to be a slight mound. Landing just on the far side of this little mound, instead of stopping dead, my ball is given some unanticipated topspin that propels it ahead five yards so it just rolls over the edge of the isthmus onto the coral and proceeds to bounce down it into the ocean. Bad luck, yes, and I may curse it, but if

I am honest, I must admit that my shot was slightly—only very slightly—imperfect to begin with.

I believe I can make my point better, however, with an example of good luck of an almost bizarre kind that astonishes me by its frequency. In this case, from the Exotica white tee, I hit the ball with my short iron, but I am tense and anxious to see how it flies. Consequently, I lift both my head and the club head too quickly. The result is that instead of lifting the ball with the face of the club, I hack it with the sharp heel of the club. It feels terrible, and I instantly know that I have sinned. Without any loft, the ball skims in a straight line the whole 90 yards no more than two feet over the waves to hit the coral on the near side of the green. Somehow it manages to hit it at such a lucky angle that, instead of bouncing back into the ocean, as would normally occur, the balls pops 20 feet up into the air and five feet farther on, landing not only on the green but rolling forward another ten feet to stop right next to the pin. That's good luck!

But I don't feel particularly good. I may be glad if I'm concerned with score, but in no way do I feel uplifted by my performance. Although the end result was perfect, there is no way I can conclude that that result evolved from a perfect shot. The undeniable fact is that it was a terrible shot. I feel very lucky, but in no way do I feel proud. If anything, I feel slightly sleazy. We may not know why we have hit the ball well, but we have no trouble discerning in the silence of our hearts between a perfect shot and an extremely lucky one.

Don't hesitate to feel proud of a perfect shot even though it may both seem and be an "act of God." When we are at our best, we are usually "cocreators" with God.

"Be ye therefore perfect, even as your Father which is in heaven is perfect," Jesus said in his Sermon on the Mount.[6] Some people actually take this admonition seriously. Among them are certain monks and nuns. Some of them still wear a robed uniform distinctive to their order that is traditionally called a "habit."[7] The word is occasionally used as a double entendre by a few religious orders, at the ceremony where the novice is "clothed"—first allowed to wear the habit. The novice is spoken of as "donning the habit of perfection." What is meant by this is that the monk or nun will henceforth attempt to make a habit out of being perfect or habitually try to become perfect.

Despite the preconceptions of the secular, nuns and monks tend to be the most realistic of people. Some of them even play golf. They are quite aware that the greatest golfer in the world will occasionally flub a shot. Those who don the habit of perfection—who vow to spend the rest of their lives in the serious, ongoing attempt to become perfect in the game of living—know full well that they will fail again and again and again. Consequently, they live their lives in the midst of paradox. On the one hand, they are completely dedicated to the goal of perfection, and on the other, they are experts in the knowledge that perfection is an impossible goal. It makes for a certain tension, does it not?

When I said that golf was about perfection, I was implying that most golfers are in the midst of the same tension, the same paradox—although not necessarily to the same degree and depth as those who have donned the habit of perfection for all their waking hours. Consequently, a pervasive theme of the remainder of this book will be this paradox of perfection as it gets worked out in the game of golf. In the first chapter I was quick to point out that there is no guarantee that reading this book will improve your game by a single stroke. I can guarantee, however, that reading it will teach you something about how to live in the tension. How? Bear with me. There will be many suggestions on the holes to come, as well as a tiny one in the next paragraph.

The primary place that nuns and monks live the paradox of perfection is within their monasteries. Contrary to popular opinion, monasteries are places not so much of great holy tranquillity and calm as of close quarters, political struggle, and great tension. Life therein is seldom perfect. Yet monasteries are also marvelous learning environments. Those who choose to see golf, among other things, as a spiritual discipline might also want to think of the golf course as a monastery of sorts.

I would like to leave Exotica's third hole by remembering the player for whom the hole is not the easiest but the most difficult on the island, despite its ranking. It matters not whether the player is a woman or a man. She has played enough to have made two or three perfect shots and, thereby, to have had a taste of glory. As the poorest scoring of her foursome, she is, of course, the last to tee off (from the standard red tee). Looking at all that water, although she doesn't show it, she is frankly terrified. She is way out of her league.

Terror, as noted, does not help one's golf swing. She shanks her first ball due right, almost 50 yards out to sea, where the dolphins play. She takes a second ball from her bag, tees it up, and hits again. This time she tops it so that it barely dribbles forward along the few front feet of the tee, just far enough to roll off onto the coral and gently bounce down into the water.[8] What should she do now?

She does the right thing.

The rule books, with all their penalties, govern either formal tournament play or informal competitive play—that is, gambling. But this is not a tournament, and she is not betting with the other members of her foursome. In point of fact, it doesn't matter a hoot what her score is. Or that she keep score. Or that she keep trying to hit onto that stupid little island. Indeed, no rule says that she has to keep playing at all. And certainly she is not compelled to keep playing this particularly ridiculous hole. She takes a third ball out of her bag and tees it up. Then she thinks better of it. She slips her ball and tee into her pocket and announces to her fellow players, "I'm not going to play this hole anymore." No one objects.

This action of quitting play on a particular hole is called *picking up*. The term requires no footnote. *Res ipse loquitur,* lawyers would say, or "the thing [action] speaks for itself." She has simply picked up her ball and walked off with it to the next hole. In a sense, she has taken the law into her own hands, and because the score is of no matter to her, nothing in the rule books prevents her from doing so. Penalties do not apply. She can, if she so desires, begin keeping her score again on the next hole.

Indeed, she has already learned enough about golf to develop some street smarts. In fact, perhaps the first thing one needs to learn about this game of perfection is when to quit temporarily, and the fact that picking up on a hole, if there's no required reason to keep score, may be the very smartest move you can make.

NOTES

1. Marking the cup is a flag atop an approximately seven-foot-high stick that is referred to as the *pin. Being close to the pin* is a synonym in golf for "landing close to the cup." The word *pin* is first found in the literature of golf in 1902, meaning "an iron rod bearing a small flag to mark the position of a hole." However, it would seem to have been adopted by golfers from the much earlier Old English word (traceable to the fifteenth century, presumably prior to the origins of golf) *pynne,* meaning "a cylindrical peg or nail fixed in the center of a target."

2. A *bogey,* as noted, is the term in golf for a score 1 over par. A double bogey means a score 2 over par, a triple bogey 3 over par, a quadruple bogey 4 over par—but let's not go on. Someone is called a *bogey golfer* when he has an average score of 90, or 18 strokes over par, on an eighteen-hole, par-72 course such as Exotica. It is not a disgrace to be a bogey golfer, thank you. I manage to play bogey golf only on my very best days.

   Nonetheless, while totally unclear how the word was assimilated into the language of golf, it was clearly done so with a pejorative intent. The word seems to have been derived from the same seventeenth-century one from which we also now get *bog,* or "swamp." Then it meant "flabby." Shortly it also came to refer to *bogus,* or "false," as well as to *bogies* or *bugaboos*—goblins or terrifying objects that may even have had a sulfurous smell. Both meanings were combined in the scarecrow, which in the eighteenth century was frequently called a *bogie.* By the nineteenth century it had obviously come to be associated with the verb *to boggle,* meaning "to fumble, botch, or bungle."

   I happen to like the Scots a great deal and have witnessed their competence, but I have also witnessed them hit bogeys aplenty on their difficult golf courses. In doing so, I have not assumed that they were fumbling, botching, or bungling. Nor have I ever noted a sulfurous smell about them. I cannot hold the Scots accountable for the entirety of the language of golf, but I believe we golfers collectively do need to begin dignifying the word *bogey* to mean something quite respectable. Otherwise, it seems to me we shall be holding ourselves up to outrageously high expectations and thereby causing serious potential harm to our inner child.

3. The duffer is a most interesting character, a man or woman who plays golf frequently, even incessantly, but never gets any better at the game than the poorest of beginners.

   It is perhaps not an accident that the word *duffer* has its origin in the language of thieves. Among thieves in the seventeenth and eighteenth centuries, a *duff* was a noun used to denote "a false article," and the verb *to duff* meant "to pan off on someone a false article as being the genuine thing for an absurdly high price." During the 1800s a duffer came to be widely understood among the British as "a person without practical ability or capacity; one who is incapable, useless, or inefficient in his occupation—generally stupid, foolish, and the reverse of competent" (Oxford English Dictionary).

   Totally unlike the pejorative nature of the derivation for *bogey,* this derivation is stunningly accurate. The duffer is indeed inefficient in his occupation of golf and incompetent. But why? Why would anyone play golf day after day, month after month, year after year without improving his game one iota? The psychiatrist in me is intrigued.

One might suppose that, despite his poor score, the duffer simply enjoys playing golf. Were this the case, he might even be an object of admiration. To take delight in a game with utter disregard for the score could possibly be a sign of holiness. But I have played with duffers and observed no particular delight nor enjoyment in them. To the contrary, they demonstrate roughly the standard amount of self-hatred, anger, frustration, embarrassment, and excuses (although one might actually expect them to demonstrate a bit more). They generally look grim as they hack away.

It has interested me that duffers don't appear dramatically uncoordinated, and I have come to question that they lack the "capacity" to play golf. I am more struck by the obviousness of the fact that they don't learn anything and don't seem to want to learn anything. Then what are they doing repeatedly out on the course if they don't want to learn anything about golf? Having never to my knowledge had a duffer on my psychiatrist's couch, I really have no idea—but I have a guess. I suppose it may have something to do with either masochism or an unwillingness to learn, or both. Strange as it may seem, I think they like being duffers. And while I cannot personally understand the payoff involved, I am rather certain that they have no desire or intention to be anything else.

So I am brought back to the origin of *duffer* in thieves' language, where a duff was a "false article." I believe there is something false about the duffer. While the perverse psychology behind it is obscure, I think the duffer is a pretend golfer. Perhaps, sort of like some cross-dressing, the pretense is a compulsion that makes his behavior so repetitive. In any case, although he will acknowledge that he doesn't score well, the duffer still announces himself as a golfer; but I myself doubt that he is the genuine article.

4. For example, possibly relevant to hole 3, is Rule 15–1/6, which reads:

    Player Substitutes Another Ball on Putting Green Because Original Ball Thrown to Caddie for Cleaning Came to Rest in Lake

    Q. A player, whose ball was on the putting green, marked the ball's position, lifted it and threw it to his caddie for cleaning. The caddie failed to catch the ball and it went into a lake and could not be retrieved. The player holed out with another ball. Should he be penalized under Rule 15–1?

    A. Yes, Rule 16–1b, under which the ball was lifted, does not permit substitution of another ball. Accordingly, the player incurred a penalty of loss of hole in match play or two strokes in stroke play.

    USGA and R&A, *Decisions on the Rules of Golf,* rev. ed. (Chicago: Triumph Books, 1995), p. 228.

5. Another ancient expression. Park's 1896 book, *Game of Golf,* states, "The privilege of playing first from the tee is called 'the honour.' " Customarily this privilege is afforded to the player with the best (lowest) score on the previous hole. If everyone in the group (usually a foursome) had the same score on the previous hole, then the honor is carried forward from the hole before that and so forth.

Conversely, the player with the poorest score on the previous hole gets to tee off last. Actually, the honor is a somewhat dubious distinction since he who tees off first may show those who follow what not to do. Still, it is an "honor," and I do occasionally enjoy "taking it away" from a better player.

6. Matthew 5:48.

7. The word itself is not unique to the religious. For example, horsepeople will frequently garb themselves in a riding habit.

8. The details of the dreadful subject of shanking will be thankfully deferred to a later chapter. As will topping.

*Once there was a chronically unhappy man who thought
that he could live without limits.*

H O L E   4

_____

FLIGHT, FREEDOM, AND POWER

We come now to Exotica's first par-5 hole, a 510-yard double dog-leg meandering through the salt marsh of the coastal plain all the way back to the clubhouse. In some respects it is rather easy; in others rather difficult. The good news is that hole 4 offers the player the opportunity to make two or three long shots. He can hit all out. Why is this such an opportunity?

On the last hole I spoke of the sublime feeling one experiences from making a perfect shot, and I commented that this feeling can be addicting. There I was actually talking of quite a short shot. *Sublime* is almost a superlative; nonetheless, the intensity of the feeling increases in direct proportion to the distance of the shot. A perfect 250-yard drive from the tee feels practically orgasmic.[1]

Perfection is relative to capacity. With my prematurely aged spine, I simply cannot hit any ball farther than 200 yards these days. Two hundred yards is my capacity, my maximum and ultimate. But one of the nice things about golf is that I will feel just as ecstatic about a perfect 200-yard drive as my younger friend, Wally, will about his perfect 250-yard drive or a pro about his perfect 300-yard drive. For that matter, Lily will feel just as good about her perfect 140-yard drive.

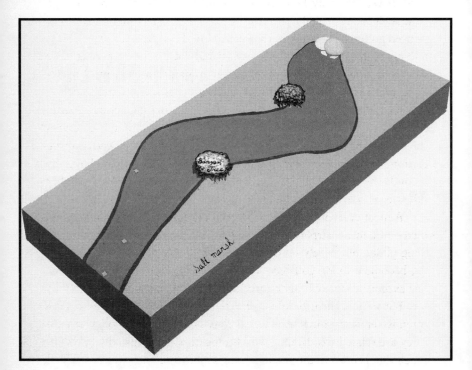

But length alone is not the whole story. One will not feel good about even a 300-yard drive when it is hit deep into the woods. Assuming perfect accuracy, however, the greater part of the ecstasy of a long shot is the flight of the ball.

Here, for nongolfers, my words are doomed to fail. Many non-golfers enjoy watching golf, and when they see a pro hit a perfect 300-yard drive, they may be filled with admiration. But they will not feel ecstasy. It is something that must be experienced for oneself. An experienced golfer may rejoice in the perfection of his partner's drive, but he will not feel ecstasy. He will feel ecstasy only over his *own* perfect drive. I have no doubt that this phenomenon contains an element of narcissism, but it would be a mistake to discount it as solely narcissistic.

Back on hole 3 I described how a player, watching her ball soaring perfectly toward its destination, will feel "Wow, I did that?!" But when she hits a long ball, she will feel something more than objective appreciation for the beauty of the flight she has caused to happen. For a few seconds she will feel she has become the ball. She will feel it is she herself who is soaring over the fairway.

Almost everyone has had the dream, the fantasy, of flying on one's own—not in an airplane, not even in the harness of a parachute or hang glider, but purely on one's own. Of course one does not, in reality, become a flying golf ball. Yet she feels as if she had. Anyone who has experienced it will understand how golf can be addicting.[2]

But *why* is such flight so attractive to us humans? Think of how often we envy the birds. The words *freedom* and *power* come to mind. They are related words. One who has great power is usually free to do much that is beyond the reach of the less powerful. Yet we need to bear in mind that there are two very different types of power and freedom: political and spiritual.[3] Strange though it might seem, our intense attraction to the flight of a golf ball, I suspect, has much less to do with the temporal, political kind of power and freedom than with the spiritual kind. I am reminded that angels in mythology have wings. Could it be that in the flight of a well-hit golf ball, we may receive an indirect and tiny taste of glory—and not the false glory of this world but that true glory that is always and only an attribute of God? I do believe so.

Speaking of sublime feelings, it needs mention that hitting a ball well feels good in and of itself, regardless of issues of flight and perfection. Even a golfer of modest experience such as myself usually knows when he has hit a bad shot before he has seen its outcome. This may be particularly true of long shots, and most particularly those made from the tee with a wood.[4] When the clubhead misconnects with the ball, it feels bad in one's hands. It even sounds bad. Conversely, a well-hit shot feels just right, not only in the hands but the whole body, and it will have the inimitable sound of perfection. In the middle of every club face there is a very small area that golfers refer to as the "sweet spot."[5] All perfectly hit balls are hit there, and will both feel and sound "sweet."

Now I would like to make a minor but most strange correction. In speaking of how, in golf, perfection is relative, I said that everyone has his or her maximum and ultimate capacity. That is true 99.9999 percent of the time. But perhaps one time in a million, on a long shot, a golfer will go beyond that limit, and thereby "exceed perfection." Since it is such a rare happening, it probably never occurs in the lifetime of most golfers. But it did occur to me once, and I can never forget it.

Because I have no idea how it happened, I will describe the context. It was during my early days of golfing on Okinawa, when all but one of the golf courses were owned and managed by Americans. That single exception was a very short nine-hole course that Lily and I played a few times for variety. Okinawan culture centered on ancestor worship, and this worship in turn centered on the construction, use, and maintenance of very large (approximately 12 by 12 feet), stylized, womblike, cement family tombs. These tombs dotted the island in profusion. Some were clearly in active use, but the majority seemed to be archaeological relics from the forgotten past. The reason I tell you this is that the longest and most interesting hole on this tiny Okinawan course was lined on both sides by these tombs, all of which appeared to be of the no-longer-used variety. It was a reasonably lengthy, dead-straight (no pun intended) par 4. In other words, the fairway was basically and entirely an avenue of tombs—or, rather, a relatively narrow avenue between tombs. I wish I could honestly tell you that I felt spiritual vibrations emanating from the tombs, but I can't. Yet such vibrations provide a better explanation than any other that this scientist, with his medical and premedical scientific training, has to offer for what transpired.

Lily and I were playing alone that afternoon as a casual twosome. I stepped onto the tee with my driver, teed up my ball, and seemed to hit it no differently from any other drive in those days. At the conclusion of my swing, I looked up to see my ball moving hard and fast straight down the avenue—but only about eight feet off the ground. My initial reaction was disappointment, since there was no way that such a low-hit ball could be a long ball. Yet no sooner had this thought had time to register than my apparent beeline drive, about 100 yards from the tee, almost lackadaisically ascended into the air and then, like the advertised Energizer battery, kept going and going and going. Eventually the ball landed solidly on the green. I have no recollection of the yardage involved. Anything I would throw out would be a pure guess. All I can tell you is that it is the only time I have ever driven the green of a par-4 hole, and the only time I ever will.

I recount the story because I have very occasionally seen a pro hit such a long shot and because I've talked with course marshals about balls that carry as though supported by magic.[6] Every one of them has witnessed the phenomenon at least once. Not one of them has been able to explain it. In that sense I suppose it could be classified as a miracle.

So the good news is that Exotica's hole 4 offers the player the opportunity to make some great long shots and experience the full glory of flight. The bad news, however, is that it is not easy to make such shots because of the hole's hazards. Among them is a hazard we've already encountered on the first and second holes: the salt marsh of the coastal plain through which these holes meander. No one in his right mind— not always a characteristic of golfers—would plod into a salt marsh to look for his ball, because he almost undoubtedly couldn't find it and certainly couldn't hit it. Moreover, in the case of these salt marshes, the golfer is not allowed to enter them. Exotica is quite conscious of its ecology, and it reserves its marshes for bird nesting. Consequently, club rules forbid walking into them. And to make sure you don't, little white stakes every ten yards along the edge of the marsh indicate it is out of bounds. The penalty for a lost ball or a ball out of bounds is usually the same: two strokes. Yes, I would say that the marsh is a hazard indeed—almost as hazardous as the ocean was on the previous hole.

On many of the world's golf courses, including this one, perhaps the most common hazard is the flora, in the form of woods, forests, trees, and all manner of bushes and shrubbery. Remember the first hole of Exotica, where one had to tee off through a dangerous avenue of Australian pines? Or the second, where the golfer had to decide whether to risk her ball carrying over the crests of certain coconut palms? Most of the beauty, drama, and challenge of this fourth hole is created by the hazard of a mere two trees, one on the right side of the fairway's first dogleg and the other on the left side of its second. But these are no ordinary trees. They are ancient banyans.

By virtue of its sheer gracefulness, my favorite of all tropical trees is the coconut palm. The banyan is my close second. It is not nearly as tall as many tropical rain forest trees, but its trunk can have a redwood's girth. And what it might lack in height, it makes up in breadth. Its dense foliage may extend over as much as an entire acre, and the dark shade it can provide from the heat of the tropical sun has caused it to be an object of veneration. It also has the most complex root system of any tree I know. A few feet above ground level, the roots of the main trunk will extend outward like great ribs as much as a dozen feet. Moreover, its huge lower branches sustain themselves by dropping their own roots into the ground in a curtain of tendrils. One does not easily forget his first sight of a mature banyan.[7]

The male golfer who can routinely drive well over 200 yards will likely drive straight over the first banyan to land in the fairway between the two doglegs. In one respect this is not difficult since, as noted, although the banyan is a very large tree, it is not particularly tall. In another respect, however, the shot requires considerable accuracy. Hit too far or only a little to the left or right, and our long-hitting golfer's ball will be in the marsh.

This raises another major principle of golf: The farther you hit the ball, the more accurate it must be to stay safe. Deviate five degrees from your aiming point on a 150-yard shot, and your ball will land approximately 20 yards to the side of where you wanted it to. Do the same on a 300-yard shot, and it will be 40 yards off target. Twenty yards may well be in the range of safety; 40 yards probably won't. This principle not infrequently allows a mediocre, short-hitting golfer like myself to score better than a long hitter. This occurs most commonly when I am playing with adolescents. Adolescent males, enamored with the glory of flight, love to hit a golf ball just as far as they possibly can, but they have not yet learned great accuracy. Consequently they are often out of bounds and prone to break windows. Such golfers of any age are referred to as "wild." It is no accident, however, that this wildness is a particular affliction of fifteen-to-eighteen-year-old males, with all that surging testosterone.

Of the two banyans, the second is the greater hazard. If one has landed in the fairway between the two doglegs, he or she will need to hit over it also for a straight shot toward the green. One of the challenges for the golfer in this position is that he will not even be able to see the green. The banyan blocks the view with its wide-flung foliage, making it what is called a *blind green*. It is a problem of aiming. It's not easy to aim well when one cannot see the target.

I've just spoken of deviation to the right or left—lateral deviation. Now I must speak of vertical deviation. It is quite possible to hit a golf ball too high—a blooper way into the air that is the equivalent of an infield fly in baseball. It is even more possible to hit a golf ball too low or not even get it off the ground at all. It is also possible to deviate both laterally and vertically on the same shot. Let me use myself as an example.

I did manage to have a short straight 180-yard drive land right where I wanted it to in the fairway, a little to the left and a dozen yards beyond the first banyan—for me, a perfect shot. What should I do now? I wondered. The second banyan I estimated to be 145 yards ahead of me, but I knew its foliage was so wide, I'd have to hit at least 160 yards on the fly to clear it. For me this would require a second perfect shot. I didn't feel secure enough to count on it. It seemed safer to aim for the wide-open fairway of the second dogleg, a bit to the right of the banyan. I pulled out my trusty number-three wood and swung away.

But something went wrong. My swing didn't feel quite right, and when I looked up, I saw that I had hit a very hard line drive of a ball only ten feet off the ground and five degrees to the left of where I was aiming. Actually it would have been a hell of a long shot, with a most desirable outcome, had nothing been there to obstruct it. But something was there. Still on the fly, I watched my low ball sail into the foliage of the banyan and vanish. A second later I heard the crackle of breaking branches. I did not know whether I would ever see the ball again.

When I reached the banyan, I discovered I had been fortunate. My ball had dropped out of the foliage—luckily onto the fairway side of the tree and not the marsh side—and now lay on the dirt near the trunk, amid its formidable root system. While my ball was not lost, I was by no means out of the woods, so to speak.[8]

What to do now? I had two options. One was to hit the ball as it lay. The fact that it lay on dirt was not a large problem. One can often hit off of dirt almost as well as off of the grass of a fairway. The problem was the roots. I could not hit the ball toward the hole because it lay in a cleavage with a two-foot-high root two feet behind it and another two feet in front of it. I had no room to take a backswing, and even if I did, my ball would have just bounced off the root in front. Could I hit out sideways from under the tree? This was more possible. The main trunk of the banyan would be three feet behind me—not enough for a decent backswing but enough for me to give the ball a bit of a push. A push toward where? Although these great roots generally move outward, they do so in a serpentine sort of fashion, undulating this way and that. There was no clear path ahead. Yes, I might be able to push my ball sideways out into the fairway, but far more likely the ball would just hit another root, stop dead, and leave me no better off than I had been before.

My other option was to move my ball by hand to where I would have a halfway decent shot—an option called *taking an unplayable lie*, which incurs a one-stroke penalty.

People *hate* penalties. Particularly men, and especially this particular penalty. It seems to them a weakness to "declare" an unplayable lie. "What do you mean, unplayable? God damn it, I can hit out of anything!" And so they try. And so they fail.

We have come to a sort of spiritual principle. When you are in a situation on a golf course where it seems a toss-up whether to hit the ball or to submit to the humiliating penalty of declaring yourself to have an unplayable lie, you will be better off taking the unplayable lie.

It may seem a cowardly choice, but it is really a very old principle that is summed up by the apostle Paul's words "In weakness, strength."

At age forty I would have taken the bolder option of trying to hit out. Today, well past sixty, I will gracefully submit to the penalty. This is not because I am a lesser golfer. Rather, it is because I am a smarter golfer, having been burned on many occasions by my own stupidity and arrogance.

But how does one take this penalty option of declaring his ball unplayable? The usual way is to move it two club lengths sideways but no closer to the hole. But two club lengths is no more than about eight feet, and the banyan being what it is, it would still leave me within the periphery of its root system. I would also still have to hit forward under the tree's lower branches and through their curtain of vinelike tendrils.

Fortunately my partner was more knowledgeable than I about the rules and informed me of another, less frequently used way of taking an unplayable lie. One can also do it by moving the ball backward however far one chooses, in a straight line away from the hole.[9] This may seem a weak move indeed, but it is what I chose. Counting against myself an extra stroke, I dropped my ball 50 yards behind. Then with a seven-iron I finally hit it over the banyan. I was still well short of the green, lying 4 now on a par-5 hole. But I was better off than I would have been had I stayed under the tree, hacking away among its roots with God knows how many impossible strokes, just to avoid the one-stroke penalty of declaring—and thereby accepting—a minor failure.

Saint Paul's motto "In weakness, strength" sounds practically bizarre in our culture, which almost worships temporal power. Some explication is called for.

Life is ambiguous. Take marriage, for instance. The sad reality is that some marriages are so misbegotten as to be literally killing. The only sane response is to get out. Yet back when I was still in the practice of psychotherapy, I had to vigorously assist many a divorcing woman or man in overcoming unrealistic guilt. Declaring their marriage to be an "unplayable lie" seemed to them not only a failure but an act of moral or spiritual weakness. The major problem wasn't the financial penalty involved but their sense of failure. It was not always easy to convince them that their decision to divorce was, in fact, an act of remarkable moral courage and spiritual strength.

On the other hand, I had to work equally hard to urge more patients to "hang in there" with their marriages, no matter how greener the grass looked on the other side of the fence. It's a bit like the option of trying to get our ball out of the roots of a banyan onto the fairway without a penalty stroke. Respecting the fence may require even greater spiritual courage than trying to leap it. Even the best of marriages are likely to have lengthy periods when the relationship feels more like a prison than anything else. In these cases I found myself pushing patients not only to accept the limitations of marriage but even to rejoice in those limits—to rejoice in submitting to stultifying commitment. Seldom did I get religious about it, but in this kind of work with patients (and within my own marriage), I was consoled again by Saint Paul, who began the last of his epistles (to Philemon) with the words "I, Paul, prisoner of Christ Jesus . . ."

These same sorts of ambiguities about strength and weakness get worked out in parenting and on the job. I've seen many who lacked the strength to assert themselves with their children by exerting moral leadership. I've also seen many who've lacked the strength to be properly led by their children. The decisions involved are neither simple nor easy. Often it is appropriate to boss around your employees, but upon occasion it is even more constructive to let them boss you around.

Willy-nilly, these past few years, I've become something of an expert in teaching people how to lead business meetings. I have yet to see a truly great executive (president, CEO, or chairman of the board) who did not have the capacity to step aside when necessary—often frequently—so as to allow subordinates to temporarily assume the leadership of the meeting. In weakness, strength.

When I decided, on Okinawa, to be the best tennis player I could be—the tennis player God wanted me to be—I decided to stop running around my backhand. Humiliating though it was, I deliberately played to my weak side. Although in the end it paid off, for several months it looked much more like weakness than strength.

What I am saying not only has to do with one's relationship to other human beings but also to God. The spiritual issue involved was never clearer to me than in a brief visit (I've recounted it elsewhere[10]) with a patient I saw many years ago. He was an alcoholic executive who had been attending Alcoholics Anonymous meetings for six months but sought my help because "AA wasn't working." He had memorized the Twelve Steps, he informed me, yet for every night he went to an AA meeting, he spent another night blind drunk. I suggested that the Twelve Steps—simple though they sounded—constituted a body of profound spiritual wisdom that took at least several years to understand. He acknowledged that the steps didn't mean much to him, particularly all the "stuff about putting trust in a Higher Power." But he proclaimed he certainly understood the First Step: "I admit that I am powerless over alcohol." I asked him what he thought it meant.

"It's simple," he replied. "It means that once I take a drink, the alcohol takes over. Once I start, I can't help myself. It means I can't take the first drink."

"Then how is it that you are still drinking?" I asked.

He looked nonplussed for a moment. "I guess I just don't have the willpower."

"Maybe that's what the First Step really means," I suggested. "Maybe it means not only that you are powerless after you've taken a drink, but that you alone are powerless even before you've taken the first drink."

"That's not true," he exclaimed. "It's up to me. I'm a competent person. I can determine whether I'm going to take that first drink."

"That's what you feel, but it's not how you act."

"It's still all up to me," he insisted.

"Have it your way," I said, echoing what another psychotherapist once called the Burger King Philosophy of Life.

Most of us enter adolescence or adulthood like that alcoholic, believing ourselves to be our own person. To some extent this is good. It is good that we should take responsibility for ourselves and have what psychiatrists call a sense of autonomy. It is, in fact, an essential foundation for spiritual growth. But there is a subtle yet crucial point beyond which we cannot "go it alone" successfully—beyond which a sense of self-determination not only becomes prideful and begins to interfere with further spiritual growth but also denies reality.

The plain fact of the matter is that my poor patient in question was too arrogant to admit that he was powerless, and he lacked the humility to submit himself even to the first of the Twelve Steps. He was not yet spiritually ready to begin the more advanced course of his life or to understand that in weakness there may be strength.

In the last chapter I introduced the theme of "living in the tension"—specifically, the tension between our yearning for perfection on the one hand and our tendency toward imperfection on the other. Here I have begun to enlarge upon that theme. We have noted the sublime feeling that comes with hitting a perfect long shot, and related it to the freedom and power of flight. But we've also had to confront the reality of the hazards on this hole. Hazards are not about freedom and power; they are about limitations and powerlessness. I declared an unplayable lie precisely because my ball was *imprisoned* among the roots of the banyan.

So we are speaking of the tension between freedom, power, and perfection on the one hand and imperfection, impotence, and imprisonment on the other. But is this not what life is all about? It seems to me the human condition is most basically that we are willful creatures living in a world that, much of the time, doesn't behave the way we *want* it to. We live in the tension between our will and reality. Sometimes with great effort and expertise, we can change reality or bend it to our will. At other times—also with great effort and expertise—it is we who must change by coming to accept the limitations of the world and of ourselves. How we do this—how we deal with the hazards of life—is quite akin to how we deal with the hazards of a golf course.

Sooner or later golfers who stick with the game long enough will almost always come to see it as a metaphor for life. But the word *metaphor* fails to do justice to all that golf has to teach us. I would go even further and say that, in its own way, golf *is* life and, not only that, "life condensed." If we choose to use it as such, I believe that golf, next to marriage and parenthood, can routinely be the greatest of life's learning opportunities.

When we first take up the game, it is not in our nature to envision the hazards of a golf course as spiritual challenges or learning opportunities. Untrained, it is our nature to get angry at them as mere obstacles to our will, or even angry at God for putting them in our way. "Why are You doing this to me?" we may curse, as our balls fly into marshes or embed themselves among the roots of trees. "God damn it" is probably the most common phrase to be heard on a golf course.

But natural though such anger might be, it doesn't help us play better golf. To the contrary, anger is perhaps the golfer's greatest enemy. Consequently, we shall be talking a great deal about this many-headed monster and how to transcend it. But just one way to begin transcending our natural anger at hazards is to assume full personal responsibility for our imperfection in falling into their clutches. "The fault, dear Brutus, lies not in the stars but in ourselves," Shakespeare had his Caesar say. In other words, blame yourself, not the hazard or God. Now, self-blame is also a trap we shall be discussing, but it is a less deep trap than cursing God or a tree.

For instance, I said "something" went wrong with my second shot on this hole, when I hit it too low and too far to the left so my ball slammed into the banyan. Thirty years ago, by "something" I would have meant I had no idea why the shot went wrong, and for all I knew, the fault might well have been in the stars. Today I would not let myself get away with such subterfuge. Instead, I would immediately ask myself what I did wrong, and the answer would quickly be clear. The reason my ball ended up on the hazard of the banyan tree is that I tried to hit it too hard. And I succeeded. I did hit it too hard.

But wait a minute! Isn't it natural to want to hit a long ball hard? Oh, yes. Indeed, yes. It is as natural as to curse God, the stars, or the tree. Since we keep stumbling over this word natural, it is high time that we began to take a deeper look at human nature.

NOTES

1. A male acquaintance once told me, "When I sink a great putt, it's still just a putt, but when I hit a great drive, I get an erection."

2. The same sort of feeling can be experienced by good skiers or surfboarders, which is why skiing and surfboarding are also such addicting sports.

3. Those who are wealthy or otherwise politically powerful are free to fly the world at a moment's notice, yet their souls may well be in spiritual bondage. Conversely, those who are spiritually free, like Buddha or Jesus, may have the power to influence others far more radically than any king or president. For more discussion of the distinction between political and spiritual power, see my first book, *The Road Less Traveled* (New York: Simon & Schuster, 1978), pp. 284–89.

4. All golf clubs consist of a shaft and a clubhead. At the top of the shaft there is a rubber or leather covering called a grip, because that is where the player holds the club. At the other end of the shaft is the clubhead, which is used to hit the ball.

   Golf clubs can be divided into three types, depending primarily upon the nature of their head: the putter, the irons, and the woods. The head of the putter is at a right angle to its shaft and is so designed for a short shot that rolls along the ground. The heads of irons are like iron or steel blades slanted at different angles in relation to the shaft. The less angled are used for long shots. The greater angled are used for high but shorter shots. The woods are not thin like the blades of irons but are much thicker. This thickness, along with a greater length of shaft, enables one to hit the longest shots. They are called woods because their heads used to be made out of wood. Today, however, they are usually made out of some sort of metal, which can cause nongolfers confusion since they are still called woods.

   For instance, about six years ago I was playing a course in Arizona. A dear visiting friend, Janice, who did not play golf, was accompanying me, riding in my cart, primarily to enjoy the desert scenery. In front of the eighteenth hole was a wide, shallow, but rushing stream, in the middle of which my ball had landed. To reach and extract it, I needed the longest possible club. I yelled at Janice to bring me a wood. Eventually she came running over with a seven-iron (one of the shorter clubs). "Dammit," I cursed her. "I thought I told you to bring me a wood."

   Tears flooded her eyes. "But I looked in your bag," she said, "and I couldn't find any clubs of wood."

   Of course she couldn't since, by that time, like almost everyone else, I had only metal "woods." At least once a year she reminds me of the incident, so at least once a year I get to apologize to her again.

5. That surface of the clubhead that is used to hit the ball is called the club face.

6. Course marshals are employees of a course hired to facilitate its play in a number of ways, including driving around and often telling groups to speed up. In doing so, they get to witness a lot of golf.

7. The banyan, sometimes referred to as the East Indian fig tree, derives its name from both Indian and British sources. In the nineteenth century the common Indian name for a Hindu merchant was a *banian*. During that century many such merchants emigrated to the Persian Gulf, where the sun is really hot.

Because the *banians* tended there to ply their trades under the shade of these magnificent trees, the British in the area began, by association, to call the trees *banyans*. And as such they are most generally known today throughout the English-speaking world.

8. An expression that may well have originally been coined by golfers who have hit into the woods.

9. The rules may occasionally be a bit kind after all; it is as if, long, long ago, they had already taken banyan trees into account.

10. *Gifts for the Journey* (New York: HarperCollins, 1985, 1995), pp. 15–17.

A well-meaning man was so eager to change the world for the better that he left it worse off than before.

H O L E   5

HUMAN NATURE

We are at a point of transition.

In a sense, the eighteen holes of Exotica constitute not one but two golf courses. Until now we have been playing on flat land; at this point we are about to head for the hills. The first four and the last five holes are situated on the island's coastal plain. The next nine holes will wrap themselves up and down both sides of Mount Intrepid. They will be quite different.

The transition is symbolized by the lengthy distance between the fourth green, which is in front of the clubhouse, and the fifth tee, which is behind it. Many will now take a break by going into the clubhouse for a sandwich or a beer, or just to stop at the rest room. We can use this breathing space for a bit of reflection.

Despite its superficial appearance, golf is a strangely nonlinear pastime. Thus far we have constantly been vibrating in the tension between opposites, between perfection and imperfection, between flight, freedom, and power on the one hand and hazards, limits, and impotence on the other. Newcomers to the game are likely to experience all this tension as highly uncomfortable—a major reason that many quit playing. Before you drop out, however, let me point out that tension and

vibration characterize life. Indeed, *vibration* comes from the same root as *vibrant,* meaning "particularly lively." And golf is a particularly lively sport. Dropping out of golf because of the discomfort of its tensions is a bit like dropping out of life.

Whenever we are vibrating between opposites, we are trying to deal with paradox. Like golf, life is full of paradox. For instance, to live well, it is necessary to plan well. At the same time, as John Lennon once put it, "Life is what happens when you're making other plans." Two opposites, both true.

Most people dislike thinking about paradox and will attempt to flee from its inherent tension by running with just one side or another, with just a part of the whole truth. But the spiritual journey is the quest for the *whole* truth, and the path of spiritual progress lies in embracing paradox. Although we defined kenosis as "the process of the self emptying itself of self," the point of being empty is not to have an empty mind; it is to make room for the new, the Other. It is paradoxical; she who desires fullness must seek emptiness. We shall be talking much more about paradox as we ascend and descend Mount Intrepid. Now we are going to explore yet another tension—that between the natural and the unnatural—and thereby immerse ourselves in the paradoxes of human nature.

Human nature is chock full of paradoxes.

Probably the most recognized is the "paradox" of good and evil. Some humans are so good as to be close to angels; some are so bad, they are close to demons; and most of us are somewhere in between, a mixture of both. This is the basic stuff of life.

Why all this variety? Theologians would ascribe its origins to Genesis, in the moment when our progenitors ate of the fruit of the Tree of the Knowledge of Good and Evil. It was at that moment that humans developed free will. Before one can be free to choose between good and evil, one must know the difference between them.

But it's all so paradoxical. Christian theologians further describe that moment of fruit eating as "original sin." Yet if asked what is meant by the saying that God created us in His own image, most of those same theologians would respond: "God gave us free will." Confusing, isn't it?

Psychologists are equally confused. Most would also agree that the essence of human nature is our will and therefore our capacity to make choices. There would be no point to psychotherapy, for instance, if people couldn't be influenced to alter their wills—to make new and different choices. Given the importance of the human will, one might think there would be a vast body of psychiatric literature on the subject. Not so. With but few exceptions, the subject is dramatically ignored by our science of the mind. Why such a glaring lack of appropriate recognition? I suggest that because the subject is so inherently confusing and paradoxical, scientists have simply chosen to stay clear of it. As a consequence, however, we *know* virtually nothing about the human will.

Lay people, for instance, will speak of someone as "strong-willed" or "weak-willed." But there is no scientific foundation for such an assessment. Psychologists have no idea whether one person is more or less strong-willed than another—much less why. We are dealing with mystery here.

Out of my quite subjective experience as a practicing psychiatrist, I actually do believe that some people, like myself and all the members of my nuclear family, are more strong-willed than others. But if my perception is correct, does the cause reside in the genes, in the results of life experience, or in something else? I don't know. Be that as it may, I used to tell some of my patients: "Having a weak will is like having a donkey in your backyard; it can't help you much, but it also can't hurt you beyond chewing on your tulips. Having a strong will, however, is like having a dozen Belgian workhorses—gigantic creatures—in your backyard. Unless they are properly trained, disciplined, and harnessed, they are likely to knock your house down. On the other hand, if they are properly trained, disciplined, and harnessed, then with them you can literally move mountains."

In some cases it was appropriate for me to proceed into the theological ramifications of the matter more deeply by asking: "But what do you harness your will to? You cannot harness it simply to your own will, otherwise it remains still unharnessed. Ultimately, you need to harness it to something higher than yourself, to some kind of 'higher power'!"

Our wills have almost innumerable ramifications—permutations and combinations. For instance, I have already described myself as a strong-willed individual, yet I also remain an inveterate smoker, despite the obvious ravages of smoking upon my body. What's going on? Am I deceiving myself, declaring myself to be strong-willed when the reality is I'm too weak-willed to stop the wicked weed? Or is it that I love smoking, that I don't *want* to stop, and that I'm so strong-willed as to continue at it despite its ravages? The circles for possible debate are endless, as with any subject as mysterious as the human will.

My primary focus in this chapter is going to be the particular manifestation of will that I label "the paradox of eagerness." Remember that in speaking of eagerness, I am talking about just one of the will's many manifestations. And please remember also that when we address a topic as mysterious as the human will, the matter is inevitably debatable.

I feel it necessary to say this because I have a friend who vociferously objects to my categorization of eagerness as a manifestation of the will. He is more inclined to equate it with "impulsiveness" than with any kind of willfulness. I believe he is wrong. I suspect he believes that the will, in its true sense, is always devoted to the good. But then he is not a habitual smoker. I believe we can be as eager to do the wrong thing as the right. I believe we can be eager not only to do something (like emptying ourselves of a bad habit) but also *not* to do the same sort of thing. Eagerness to not do something we tend to label "stubbornness." Yet stubbornness has its place in the world of human affairs, and it may be more saintly than easy compliance. It may take even more will. But until we develop a "science of the will," such definitions will remain debatable. For the moment, however, I hope you will take what I have to say with a generous spirit.

On this hole I have said that my focus is upon the paradox of eagerness. Failure to deal well with this paradox is responsible for far and away the two most common mistakes in golf: hitting the ball too hard and looking up too quickly to see where your ball is going.

When you swing at the ball too hard, you lose your balance to a greater or lesser degree. Indeed, some golfers have swung so hard, they've even been known to topple over at the completion of their swing. While one is usually not aware of this loss of balance until the end of the swing, it is present almost from the start and certainly before the ball is struck. Because of this imbalance, the face of the clubhead will make contact with the ball at an improper angle. The impropriety of the angle may be in any dimension—angled too far upward, downward, or to either side—and often both vertically and laterally. The result therefore may be almost anything horrible: a blooper into the sky, a hit into the ground, a low ball too far left or too far right, a fierce hook or a dreadful slice, or some combination thereof.

When you look up to see where your ball is going before the clubface has even connected with the ball, you unconsciously lift the clubhead. There are two possible results. Instead of hitting the ball solidly, you may strike only the top of the ball. This is appropriately called *topping* and produces a ball that weakly dribbles along the ground. Or you may lift your clubhead so far that it doesn't connect with the ball at all. This totally missed shot is called a *whiff,* and the humiliating process is referred to as *whiffing.*[1]

These two mistakes—hitting the ball too hard and looking up too quickly—tend to go together. For instance, I have never seen a man take an easy swing and then whiff. I have seen whiffs occur only in conjunction with a ferocious swing. While I no longer whiff, I will still top my ball on the average at least once a round, and whenever I do so, it is because I have been trying to hit the hell out of it.

It is not surprising these two mistakes go together, since they arise from the same psychospiritual flaw: an excess of eagerness. I swing too hard because I am so eager to hit it far, and I look up too quickly because I am so eager to see if I have succeeded in doing so. Sadly, of course, I don't see anything until I look down from the sky to the ground a few feet in front of me.

Eagerness is an attribute of human nature. A woman or man without eagerness is significantly ill—either mentally (with the apathy of depression) or physically (with the loss of all appetite). How then can there be an excess of eagerness? It sounds like a contradiction in terms, as if I were talking about an excess of health.

Consider the fact, however, that our eagerness is rooted in our wills. We are eager for something to happen—something as simple as receiving a bicycle for Christmas—because we *want* that something. And wanting is the will's expression. We would will that bicycle into existence, if we could. But our wills are not necessarily devoted toward the right aim or proper goal. For instance, an angry boy might desire a real machine gun for Christmas even more than a bicycle, because he wants to murder his teacher. Furthermore, we may want something so eagerly that we may use the wrong means to obtain it. A childish example would be that of a boy who steals a bicycle without waiting for Christmas. An adult example could be the golfer who wants a long drive so badly that he "kills" the ball, even though he has repeatedly been taught to swing easily.

A strong will is perhaps the greatest blessing that can be bestowed upon a person. A strong will does not guarantee success—it may create a Hitler—but a weak will guarantees failure. Only strong-willed people succeed in life, or at least in certain portions of life such as psychotherapy and golf. No apathetic person ever became a good golfer. But all blessings are potential curses and carry with them their own side effects. Just one of the side effects of a strong will can be a bad temper. It is, for instance, strong-willed people who wrap their golf clubs around trees because that damn little ball didn't go where they *wanted* it to go.

Such fits of temper raise the question of whether we humans can be too strong-willed. The best answer I know was provided by Gerald May in his book *Will and Spirit,*[2] wherein the first chapter is entitled "Willingness and Willfulness." By *willfulness,* May was referring to the unharnessed human will. By *willingness,* he was referring not to a weak will but rather to a strong one that has been submitted to a power higher than itself and is therefore willing to go wherever that higher power directs.

Since it is a manifestation of will, eagerness is a case in point. The point in golf, as in life, is not to get rid of one's eagerness but to harness or discipline it. Look *eagerness* up in the dictionary, and you will find it a highly ambivalent word. It can express all manner of good, such as "keenness, intense focus" and "exuberance." Some of its other synonyms, however, are "impatience, impetuousness, fierceness," and even "violence." This paradoxical definition is a reflection of the fact that disciplined, submitted eagerness can be glorious to behold, while with undisciplined eagerness there will be hell to pay.

Okay, so we need to submit our naturally unrestrained eagerness to a higher power. Does that mean that atheists and agnostics can never play golf well? Heavens, no. On the course one's higher power need not necessarily be God; it can be perfection, beauty, or simply a good game. It can even be merely a low score, although, as we shall eventually see, the idolatry of score may constitute a real trap. I don't mean to imply that God has nothing to do with golf. Indeed, I'll be hinting about Him or Her from time to time, and believe it or not, golf can bring one into a closer relationship with God. Certainly it can bring us to our knees. But the simple desire to play well is sufficient motive for us to modulate our natural eagerness. That's the easy part, however. That's the *why* of it. More problematic is the *how*. How does one modify human nature with its natural eagerness? How do we learn to do the unnatural?

There are no gimmicks.[3]

There are rules and aphorisms. Because trying to hit the ball too hard and looking up too quickly are the most common mistakes in golf, no expressions are more deeply embedded in the language of the game than "Swing easy, and keep your head down," "Keep your eye on the ball," and "Let the clubhead do the work." These admonitions are great truths, but they are so paradoxical that it is difficult to believe in them deeply enough to make one's body conform to them. It is generally very true that the easier you swing at a ball, the farther it will go, but this seems to defy the most basic laws of physics. Keeping your eye on the ball is good advice indeed, but the fact is, you can't actually see the ball at the moment you hit it. And no matter how frequently an elder may tell you, "Look, you'll have plenty of time to see the ball after you've finished your swing," it just doesn't feel that way in your eager bones. What feels natural is to look up to see where the ball is going as quickly as you possibly can.

Hold on to these rules! By themselves they will do nothing for you. But if you *practice* them diligently enough, you will become a fairly good golfer. Guaranteed. Practice, however, is the key.

The point of practice is to make a habit of the unnatural. To me the greatest paradox of human nature is that, in a sense, there is no such thing. I can put it in many ways. The most essential feature of human nature—and what seems to distinguish us most from the other creatures—is the mutability of that nature. For instance, I am fond of telling people, "Human nature is to go to the bathroom in your pants." Isn't that how we all started out, doing what came naturally? But then, although the toilet initially seemed like a most unnatural appliance, for a variety of reasons we decided to do it differently in our society and changed our nature. We have a great capacity for change and transformation—an extraordinary freedom to do the new and different and seemingly unnatural, like going north instead of south in winter to slide down icy hills on slats of fiberglass—or even to learn to love to play a game as strange as golf.

It is human nature to try to hit a golf ball as hard as you can and to look up while doing so. It is also human nature to be jealous, possessive, greedy, selfish, thoughtless, and eager to the point of violence. We do not "naturally" grow out of such things, which is why so many remain selfish, greedy, possessive, and violent—and poor golfers. But we *can* grow out of them, and that is our glory as human beings.

Let us take something as simple as brushing our teeth. When I was a child, my mother used to have to nag me again and again every evening to brush my teeth. Each time I turned it into a thirty-minute ordeal. By adolescence, however, I had made a voluntary habit of it— a practice—that required no more than a minute. Indeed, it now felt *unnatural* if I neglected to brush my teeth upon arising and before going to bed.

So practice swinging easy while keeping your head down. Practice it over and over and over until it becomes a habit—until it becomes second nature—until it feels unnatural to swing hard and look up too soon— and keep on practicing. Golf is so expensive and time-consuming, it would be silly of you to play it repeatedly, like a duffer, without trying to learn how to play it better. So when you put on your plaid shorts and your pretty sweaters, your spiked shoes and your socks with cute pom-poms, think of yourself as donning the habit of perfection.

Do not grow complacent. Golf is infinitely more complex than brushing your teeth. It is possible to make a habit out of a good easy swing, yet as I took pains to point out, even the greatest of golfers will occasionally make a terrible shot. Why? It is because such things as swinging easy and keeping your head down—such perfection—can become at best your *second* nature. Your original nature is still lurking within you, and no matter how good you become, you will still at times lament with Saint Paul that your body will fail to obey what you know is right: "I do that which I would not and seem unable to do that which I would."[4] Such occasions will most likely occur in times of stress. All psychologists know that when when we humans are under stress, we tend to regress—go back to our old ways. Consequently, I shall have much more to say about stress. Certainly you can expect yourself to regress from time to time. But if you look at golf as a continual learning opportunity, such times may not be useless. If nothing else, at such times of regression, you may even get a hint of what some theologians mean by original sin.

Although I believe golf has a great deal to teach about both sin and virtue, this book is still primarily about golf, so in the interest of balance, my discussion of original sin must remain almost sinfully brief.

As noted, the concept arises out of Genesis, chapter 3, the ancient story and brilliant myth of Adam and Eve, supposedly the first humans, living in the Garden of Eden. Despite the fact that God had forbidden them to do so, they ate of the fruit of the Tree of the Knowledge of Good and Evil, which was in the Garden. Their penalty was then to be cast out of the garden. This disobedience in relation to God was the *original* sin.

Theologians have long argued about the psychology underlying this primal act of disobedience. To what extent it was motivated by pride ("Who does God think He is, telling us what to do?") or fear ("We dare not challenge God") or laziness ("Why should we bother to challenge God?"), we do not know. Nor do we really know the reasons for God's prohibition in the first place. Only one thing we do know: Adam and Even ate the forbidden fruit because they were so *eager* to do so that they were *willing* to disobey. Let us, for the purpose of our discussion of golf, simply ascribe the root of Adam and Eve's disobedience to an "excess of eagerness."

The concept of original sin is of import not because of what Adam and Eve did or didn't do thousands or millions of years ago; it is important only because the concept holds that we humans have somehow inherited the problem throughout the generations. In other words, you and I, here today, still must face the same temptations as Adam and Eve. We are somehow still tainted by that "original" sin, even to the point that we cannot not sin. Even to the point of swinging too hard at a golf ball despite the teachings of God and the instructions of our betters, despite even our own knowledge that an excess of eagerness will repeatedly betray us.

So what is the answer to this inherited defect of human nature? The first step is to diagnose the problem: an excess of eagerness. We have now done this, but how do we proceed? The next step is always kenosis. Empty yourself. Don't get rid of all eagerness; that would be to destroy your humanity. But at least empty yourself of a portion of it, a smidgen of your willfulness.

And how do you do so? Through an exercise of the same sort of will that has made you so willful in the first place. Will yourself to be less willful. Consider praying for God's help in the matter. And consider doing it again and again, because your excess of eagerness is a part of the fabric of your very being, of your human nature. No matter how well you do at reducing your willfulness, as most theologians and golf professionals have pointed out, your propensity to sin throughout the course of life will be with you forever, particularly in times of stress. Yet remember that your free will is not only your original curse but also your original blessing.[5]

Enough of theology. Let's get on with it. We arrive at the fifth tee to find that hole 5 is indeed different. It is a rather steep uphill 330-yard, par-4 gentle dogleg to the left. Three hundred and thirty yards is relatively short for a par 4, which is why, on the scorecard, this hole is handicapped or ranked (along with number 3) as one of the easiest holes of the course. Yet even pros agree that it is probably the most difficult hole on Exotica, and some think it the most difficult hole on any course anywhere.

More than five factors conspire to make it so, the least of which is the huge and extraordinarily deep sand trap directly in front of the green.

Another factor is that it runs uphill on the east side of the extinct volcano, Mount Intrepid. Generally speaking, holes that run uphill are more difficult than those that go downhill. On Exotica this has nothing to do with the physical exertion required to walk uphill, since players are required to employ motorized golf carts. It is a matter of simple physics. A well-hit drive will not only go farther through the air on a downhill hole, but when it hits the fairway, it will roll and roll and keep rolling forward. On a steep uphill slope such as this one, however, even the best-hit drive will go plunk into the rising mountainside and stop dead. Don't expect great distance on long uphill shots.

A third factor is the rain forest. When the prevailing moisture-laden wind from the south hits Mount Intrepid, the moisture rises, condenses in the higher, cooler air, and turns to rain. Consequently, this windward side of the mountain is much of the day bathed in passing showers, some of them heavy. The result is the rain forest, out of which this hole has been carved.

A tropical rain forest grows tall. The trunks of its trees are not massive in width, but bare of foliage they rise up and up and up for hundreds of feet until they finally burst into a dense canopy of branches and large leaves at the very top. The pros and other long-hitting golfers love to cut across doglegs with their huge drives, but not on this hole. The height of the forest removes such an option, and they must play the dogleg like anyone else.

Because its high panoply of foliage is so dense, the floor of the tropical rain forest receives almost no light and hence is remarkably bare. One could easily hit a golf ball off of it, but for the golfer whose ball has gone astray, this is not an option. The edges of the forest that border the fairway receive enough sun to grow a six-foot-deep hedge of all manner of exotic tropical plants and vines. It constitutes as effective a rough as a salt marsh. If your ball lands on the forest floor inside this hedge, there is no way you can hit through it. If it lands in the hedge itself, there is no way you can hit out of it. It is extremely doubtful you could ever find the ball anyway. Besides, as the Exotica course marshals will point out to you, these sunlit edges of the rain forest are a favorite habitat for pythons. Declare your ball lost, and take your two-stroke penalty.

A fourth factor that makes this hole so difficult is the deep and fairly wide gulch that runs directly across the dogleg. Given the torrential rains that can fall on this side of Mount Intrepid, such gulches are inevitable, and this is but the first one we shall encounter. The gulch is filled to the brim with impenetrable tropical flora. Should your ball

land in it, I'm afraid it's another two-stroke penalty. The only solace is that a bridge has been built over the left (and narrow) side of the gulch so that you can drive your cart across it without being further penalized by loss of life or limb.

It is 150 yards in a straight line from the white tee to the edge of the gulch, and another 40 yards across it in the direction of the green. Were one to drive 200 yards or more straight across the gulch, the ball would likely bounce into the jungle on the other side. Consequently, there are only two decent ways to play this hole. One is to hit a 200-plus-yard perfectly controlled hook. The other, the only alternative for us mere mortals, is to lay up.[6]

The fifth factor that makes this hole close to impossible is that it is not only uphill but also not flat in another way. Rather than being even, the fairway on both sides of the gulch is filled with mounds, or moguls.[7]

There are two problems with moguls in a fairway. The lesser is that you never know how your ball is going to bounce. Depending upon which slope of the mogul it hits, the ball may leap forward, or it may pop back at you, or it may bounce sharply either to the left or right. The greater problem, however, brings us to a whole new dimension of difficulty in the game of golf: the challenge of the uneven lie.

It is quite possible that your ball will come to rest right on top of one of the moguls or else in one of the little valleys in between them, and do so in such a way that you will have room to plant your feet level with it and hit it with an ordinary swing. In other words, about 40 percent of the time on this hole, you will be fortunate enough to have what some golfers almost consider their right: an even lie. Sixty percent of the time, however, you will have an uneven lie. Although this is a bit of an over-simplification, there are basically four different types of uneven lies.

The easiest for me is an uncomplicated uphill lie. Here the ball lies at the level of your feet but on the uphill side of the mogul—uphill, that is, relative to the direction in which you wish to hit it. Although you may have to change your foot placement slightly, you have all the room in the world for an ordinary backswing, and that's what counts the most.

The most difficult type for me is a downhill lie. If the slope is very gentle, foot placement alone may allow me a more or less ordinary backswing. If it is at all steep, I am not so allowed. Teaching professionals will say the trick is to alter the angling of one's shoulders as well as feet, but it is a trick that I have never been able to learn. Frankly, I do not know how to hit even a moderately steep downhill lie decently.

A third type of uneven lie occurs when the ball is on a downslope in such a way that your feet must be planted on a level above that of the ball. Since this means that the ball will be farther away from you than usual, you would be well advised to lengthen your grip on the club.

The fourth type is its opposite. Here your feet may be at the bottom of the mogul, while your ball lies up on the slope of the mogul above them. This means your ball will be closer to you than usual, so you will probably want to shorten your grip. On a steep mogul the ball may even lie at the level of your shoulders, and in striking it you will feel more like you are swinging a baseball bat than a golf club.

And if that's not enough, your particular uneven lie may be a mixture of any two of the above four types.

Ah, complexity!

I can make two important generalizations about uneven lies. The first is that you cannot totally avoid them except by avoiding all golf everywhere. Even on the flattest and gentlest of courses, an uneven lie can sneak up on you now and then.

My second generalization will sound familiar. We began this hole by discussing the virtues—no matter how unnatural—of swinging easy and keeping your head down. We learned that with practice it can become second nature to do so. But I also pointed out that it is our tendency as humans, in times of stress, to regress to our "original nature." There are many kinds of stress, and on a golf course any difficult shot is just one of them. An uneven lie is a difficult shot, and one's natural response to it is to become anxious, tighten up, and forget all about swinging easy and keeping one's eye on the ball. We want to look up because we're all the more eager to see whether we succeeded in extricating ourselves from the difficulty. So with an uneven lie, remember . . . remember . . . remember to hit easy with your head down.

I shall have more to say, off and on, about the spirituality of remembering.

Meanwhile, simply remember that life itself—with all its joys and vicissitudes—is inevitably an uneven affair. It may be in our original nature to curse an uneven lie, as it is to curse a hazard. But just as we can change the way we swing, so with practice we can also change our attitudes. We can come to look at curses as blessings. Which would you rather live: a life filled with curses or a life filled with blessings? Do you want to damn these moguls for their difficulty or praise them for the variety of uneven lies they provide?

When I first began to play golf on Okinawa, I imagined I would quickly go back to tennis since I was so good at it and since even then it was clear that I would never be more than a mediocre golfer. But I didn't. Oh, I occasionally played tennis again when there wasn't a golf course around, but to my surprise I found that tennis now almost bored me. There are only about thirty or forty different shots in tennis. In golf there are about thirty or forty thousand. In a sense, given not only hazards and uneven lies and doglegs but gauging the distance every time, it would be fair to say that in golf each and every shot is different— unique. This game has extraordinary variety. No other game, save the game of life, can match it. The only ones that come close, perhaps, are chess and bridge, but both run a very poor second. Or as Arnold Palmer once put it, "Golf is deceptively simple and endlessly complicated. It satisfies the soul and frustrates the intellect. It is at the same time rewarding and maddening—it is without a doubt the greatest game that mankind has ever invented."[8]

I meant those last words—of mine and Palmer's—to be uplifting. I have spoken of changing attitudes and changing swings as if such changing were a simple matter of practice, as if donning the habit of perfection were the end rather than the beginning of the journey. In your heart you know better. Awash in nonlinearity, in paradox, difficulty, and complexity, and mired in our own original human nature, the fact is we need all the encouragement we can get.

I know of only two ways to offer such encouragement in this game: the rational and the mystical.

The rational is to urge you and me to keep our sense of perspective (and humor). I use perspective all the time. Whenever Lily and I are having a bad day on the course—which is most days—I remind her or she will remind me that the reasons we are out there, in order of priority, are:

1. It is a most excellent form of *exercise* and a way, at our age, to keep ourselves alive.
2. It is a marvelous avenue of *companionship* that nurtures our marriage.
3. Its natural surroundings have a *beauty* that is necessary for our souls.
4. It provides us with a never-ending opportunity for *learning*, particularly when we remember that . . .
5. The matter of *score* is the least of it.

But often such easy rationality is not enough. We need something deeper, even mystical. Okay, this has been a particularly difficult hole on a difficult course. *Surrender* to that difficulty. Golf is not only like life, but it's like God. It's bigger than you. At this point you can give up. Or you can let it break you. Then you can go on, broken and in awe.

To surrender means to admit defeat. In a minor way it is what we do whenever we declare an unplayable lie. As noted on the last hole, we do not naturally like to surrender, even in such a small way. Yet in the ongoing journey of life, surrender is often the key to success, as we may from time to time need to surrender to our marriages or to the demands of leadership. Still, it is so difficult, we usually need tutoring in the art of surrender. The best tutor for me personally has been the story of Jacob in the Old Testament.

The most critical moment in that story comes when Jacob leaves his family for a little peace and quiet and goes to camp out alone for an evening on the other side of a river. In the middle of the night, however, his peace and quiet are shattered as he is accosted by a stranger for no apparent reason. He wrestles with the stranger hour after hour in the darkness. The stranger seems to have almost superhuman strength. Nonetheless, just as the first faint light of dawn is coming over the horizon, Jacob feels that he is gaining the upper hand. He throws his last bit of energy into the fight. But at that moment when he feels closest to victory, the stranger reaches with a little light touch and yanks Jacob's thigh right out of joint and breaks it.

At this point Jacob clings to the stranger—not to continue the struggle, because by now he knows he is totally defeated, but because he realizes he is in the presence of divinity. "Don't leave!" he pleads. "Don't leave without giving me your blessing!"

The stranger not only obliges but renames Jacob, saying, "Hence-forth you shall be called Israel, meaning 'he who has wrestled with God.'" The stranger then vanishes, and Jacob, wounded and defeated and broken, limps off into the dawn to become the father of a nation.[9]

Not a bad fate for one who has surrendered! So think of the golf course as an angel with which you are wrestling. You will never totally beat the game. What you can do, however, is let it beat you—surrender to it, yet keep on playing.

NOTES

1. The verb *to whiff* is derived from the Middle English noun *weffe,* which, back in the Middle Ages, meant an offensive odor or vapor (something quite common in those days). He who whiffs a golf shot does feel as if he has made an offensive odor, but that is not why or how the word got into the language of golf. Rather, by the eighteenth century *whiff* had generally come to mean "a puff or gust of wind."

   While on the subject, it might be noted that, because it is so humiliating, whiffing often offers the neophyte golfer his first, and perhaps greatest, temptation to cheat. But when he whiffs on the tee directly in front of his fellow onlooking players, there is no possibility of cheating. He must count the whiff for what it is: a missed stroke that, by definition, penalizes him one stroke. But what if he is far off to one side of a wide fairway (or in the rough) and whiffs while no one seems to be watching? It is most tempting to take a few steps forward and backward, casually glance at the sky, as if he had just made a practice swing, and then look as if he is seriously getting down to work. The crucial issue, I suspect, is not whether the beginner fails to count his whiff, but whether he does so with unease or equanimity. If with equanimity, I am afraid he is headed down a bad path, but then I also suspect he was probably headed down that path long before he set foot on a golf course.

2. Gerald May, *Will and Spirit* (San Francisco: Harper and Row, 1982).

3. Actually, I have seen one. Many Christmases ago, knowing of my propensity to top the ball, my family gave me in my stocking a device designed to assist the male

golfer in keeping his head down during his swing. It consisted of a headband to which were attached two long, adjustable but otherwise inflexible suspenders. At the end of each suspender was a metal hook much like that of a coat hanger. The accompanying instructions told the golfer he should fit both hooks under his scrotum, each pointing upward toward the appropriate testicle. I cannot say this gimmick was an ineffective training device since somehow I never seemed to find the occasion to try it.

4. Romans 7:15–24 (paraphrase and condensation).

5. *Original Blessing* by Matthew Fox (Santa Fe: Bear and Company, 1996).

6. It will be remembered that *laying up* is the golf term for deliberately hitting—usually from the tee—well short of the distance one could ordinarily hit, so as to land on the near side of a hazard.

7. The process of constructing a golf hole up or down a mountainside, such as that of Mount Intrepid, is not much different from that of constructing a ski trail. The trees must be cleared, and then the developer is faced with a decision of whether to level the terrain. Here, in golf, there are two traditions. One, which might be called the British tradition, is to build courses into the "lay of the land." The golfer is most likely to encounter fairway moguls on many of the fiendishly difficult courses in Great Britain. The American tradition, on the other hand, is to bulldoze the damn thing so as to make it as easy as possible. In any case, borrowing from the language of skiing, when there are a significant number of mounds in the midst of a fairway, we Americans have come to call them moguls.

    You may wonder why, in constructing (in my imagination) Exotica's golf course, I have largely chosen to go with the British tradition of designing the course into the lay of the land. It is not because I am cheap. To the contrary, building courses into the lay of the land is actually more expensive than simply bulldozing. Nor is it because I am sadistic. It is simply that I think that moguls, like other natural geographic formations, make things more interesting. And beautiful. Most golfers would agree. Besides, it is great fun to design what is sometimes called a "Scottish links course" on a tropical island.

    But one question is left begging, and the etymologist in me cannot overlook it. The most ancient meanings of the word *mogul* stand for a "Mongolian" or a "thirteenth-century follower of Genghis Khan" or "the emperor of Delhi" (until he was deposed in the middle of the nineteenth century) or a "Muslim potentate" or almost any "high and mighty" person. How on earth, then, did American skiers come to adopt the word for mounds of snow on a ski slope? One of the very few English dictionaries that addresses the subject concludes by stating: "derivation . . . uncertain." So I must leave it. Like golf and life, even etymology can be uncertain.

8. Arnold Palmer, *My Game and Yours* (New York: Simon & Schuster, 1963).

9. I am also indebted to Frederich Buechner, who first elucidated this great story for me in his book *The Magnificent Defeat* (Harper San Francisco, 1985).

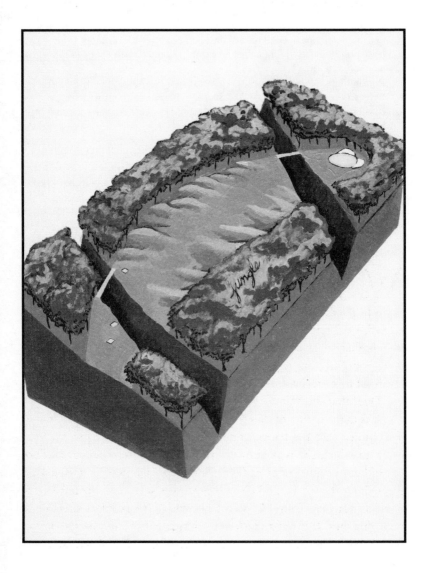

*Once there was a woman who believed she could see
everything with her eyes; actually, she was almost blind.*

H O L E 6

THE INVISIBLE

While I took pains to point out, on the previous hole, that the gulch in the middle of the dogleg constitutes a particularly formidable hazard, I did not mention the fact that it is invisible from the tee. Not only is that snare located exactly where you would naturally tend to drive your ball, but if you don't do your research, you won't even be aware of its existence.

Does that seem unfair? It truly isn't.

It is in the nature of things that not all that exists is visible. On hole 4 we noted that the banyan tree could block the golfer's view of the green to which she was hitting—making it a blind green. Ditches or streambeds or gulches of various widths are common on golf courses throughout the world, and being beneath the surface of the fairway, as often as not they cannot be seen from where the golfer is standing to make his shot. It is not a matter of deliberate deception on the part of the course designer; it is merely a matter of the natural limitations of vision.

All but the least expensive of courses will happily provide you with a course map that designates the position and existence of such unseen hazards as gulches. Believe it or not, however, some golfers suffer from such an excess of eagerness (or laziness) that they do not even bother to look at the map. Any misfortune that befalls them as a result can hardly be construed as bad luck.

Still, maps are but representations of reality and are not the reality itself, and they can never be a substitute for experience. This is why many pros, before playing a high-stakes match, will "walk" a course with which they are not totally familiar. They are checking out the lay of the land. It is hardly an absolute *rule* of golf, but it is a good guideline to "know your course."

It's also a good guideline for the rest of life. Some aspects of life, such as certain illnesses, are truly impossible to foresee (beyond purchasing medical insurance). Although such things may seem like tragedies at the time, when we look back on them, they often appear more like blessings in disguise. We may have much to learn from them. At the very least they teach us that life is bigger than we are and is not totally ours to control; they teach us surrender.

But when I was a practicing psychiatrist, I was even more impressed by the huge number of men and women who customarily failed to foresee the potentially obvious. Like those golfers who are too lazy or eager to bother looking at course maps, they stumbled ahead through life in a chronically self-defeating manner. They didn't stop to think that if they hit their fist against a wall in anger, they might break their knuckles. Or that if they drove too fast, they might get a ticket. Or that if they quit their job without a new and better one nailed down, they might end up long-term unemployed. Or as they began to become old and decrepit, that they might need to hand over the reins to someone else. If you want to drive to a particular destination in Buffalo, a city you've never visited, it would behoove you to get a New York State map or at least a street map of the city—a map of the course, so to speak. It doesn't really cost anything. Yet so many just take off and then get lost.

So *think* about where you're going, in life as well as in golf. This simple principle is so important, let me emphasize it by recounting a very specific golfing example in which I became totally lost because I failed to know my course—or, better, because I failed to adequately think about what lay ahead of me.

• • •

After we returned from Okinawa, where Lily and I first took up golf, my father initiated an annual tradition of taking the twelve of us in the nuclear family (himself, my mother, Lily and I, our three children, my brother, his wife, and their three children) to Bermuda each spring for a vacation. My father loved golf. On many afternoons of those vacations, Lily and I would accompany him and my mother to play Riddles Bay, a lovely and distinctly gentle course. Yet from time to time he would drop mention of Mid-Ocean, also on Bermuda. "Now *there's* a course," he would say. "It's championship," he'd add, hinting at its mystical difficulties and challenges.

Finally I said, "Hey, Dad, how 'bout taking us to Mid-Ocean one of these days?"

"Well, there's an idea," he responded. "It's possible. Why yes, I think we'll just do that."

So a few days later, off we went to Mid-Ocean. I was excited, and determined not to let its challenges overcome me. I'll always remember standing on its first tee. From there the opening hole did not look difficult. It was a sharp but wide dogleg to the left with the bend in a valley so that one would drive downhill and then hit the second shot uphill to the green. I teed up my ball. "Hit it easy," I said to myself as one would a mantra. "Easy. Remember to hit it easy."

And I did. The smooth, straight drive landed right where I wanted it to, in the very middle of the dogleg—a "perfect shot." I pulled out my three-wood. "Hit it easy," I repeated to myself. "Remember to hit it easy." And when my turn came, I did so again. Another sweet high ball went straight uphill toward the green on the horizon. My ball stopped short of the green by ten yards, but it gave me an opportunity for a simple, unobstructed uphill chip shot of 20 yards to the pin, which was still on the horizon.

Such short chips were my forte. I still had a good chance at a par. Ha! Wouldn't that be something if I parred the very first hole of this renownedly difficult course! And when I chipped with a deft and delicate seven-iron, yet another virtually perfect shot bounced well onto the green and rolled—very slowly now—no more than six inches to the left of the pin. I imagined it would stop less than four feet past the pin.

Yes, I would have my par—unless I totally flubbed an easy putt. But two feet past the pin, hardly moving, the ball dropped out of sight. I supposed there was a tiny hollow on the green at that spot.

After enjoying the moment while the others chipped or pitched, I strode onto the green to line up my ball for the putt. But there was no ball. My ball was not on the green at all. Two feet past the pin, the green ended abruptly at the edge of a coral cliff that plunged directly down into a previously invisible ocean. My ball was not on the green. It was in the ocean. Lost in the ocean. My imagined par had been instantly transformed into at least a double bogey.

Those first three good shots I made on the opening hole of Mid-Ocean were the only decent shots I made that day. For the remaining seventeen holes I hacked away at the ball with wild, ineffective fury. Helpless rage is the one absolutely guaranteed cause of depression, and it was one of the grimmest, most depressing afternoons of my life. Back then, although well into my mid-thirties and a psychiatrist to boot, I had no idea how to deal with anger and depression in relation to golf. My sense of outrage at the placement of that cup a mere two feet from the edge of a cliff put me in a funk that lasted for hours. By the middle of the second hole, I gave up keeping score, and I remember nothing more of that beautiful course except my hatred of it. It matters little whether I was angry or depressed; at root they are the same and will ruin you *and* your game as long as they last.

You may think that that was an unfair pin placement—as I thought at the time—but the moral of the story at this point has nothing to do with either fairness or the emotions of anger and depression. It has to do with knowing the course. Had I known the course, I would not have played my chip that way onto the first green of Mid-Ocean. Ordinary course maps cannot capture the fine details of greens. Besides, it is usually customary to change the pin or cup placement every day.[1] But had I walked the course thoroughly before playing it, I would have known that the green ended up in a cliff.

Now, you would be quite correct to assume that I really didn't have the opportunity to walk Mid-Ocean first. Yet in retrospect I still can't let myself off the hook. While I was using my eyes to their limited extent, I was not using my brain. You will remember that I described the pin as being on the horizon of the green. Pins are almost never so situated. I should have wondered why it was in this case. I should have been curious enough about the matter to stroll up to the pin and horizon before making my little chip shot. With that minor bit of effort I could have enlarged my field of vision sufficiently to save the hole.

But probably not the day. Given the immaturity of my psychology and spirituality at the time, it is probable that the "championship" challenges of Mid-Ocean would have defeated me before its third or fourth hole in any case.

At some elegant golf links, you can get or purchase not only simple course maps but extremely elaborate ones that show all manner of distances and angles, with accompanying instructions about what to avoid and advice on how to play each hole. My best male friend, Wally, a dozen years my junior, is a superb golfer. He is a cautious man (which is why he is also our broker). He loves these course books, which he carries around as a Jehovah's Witness does his Bible, and before each shot he will not merely pace around to check out the lay of the land but will scrupulously read the appropriate chapter and verse from his Good Book. Sometimes he drives me nuts as I wait for him to do his research. Mostly, however, I admire his thoroughness.

But such maps are still not a perfect substitute for *knowing* the course. I delight in playing a great new course, even if only once. I delight even more in playing it for a whole week. Yet my greatest delight is in playing the same great course week after week, month after month, year after year. I have played one such course well over two hundred times now, and I am still discovering sand traps and other hazards or quirks that I had never truly *seen* before.

In the case of great golf courses, familiarity does not breed contempt. To the contrary, the better I know a course, the better I am able to play it. The better I can play it with such knowledge, the more I can relax so as to enjoy its beauty. The terrain of a beautiful golf course has sometimes reminded me of a beautiful woman's body: The joy of gradually exploring her every nook and cranny is delicious. Yet even the terrain of a beautiful woman's body will eventually stale.[2] Not so with a great golf course; its topography can continue to intrigue and delight the golfer for a lifetime.

Although 60 yards longer (and thereby ranked as more difficult), this hole is in reality considerably easier than the previous one. It is bounded by the same tall rain forest, but because the dogleg is more gentle, the forest does not prevent a long drive from the tee. While it has not one but two gulches, both are more visible and neither is located exactly where one is most likely to hit a good shot. Of course, if one dribbles his ball off the tee, it will be as lost in the gulch as any other, but in this case the hole is simply penalizing a bad shot and not a good one.

Like hole 5, this sixth hole runs steeply uphill farther around the side of Mount Intrepid. However, it is also a much kinder hole because in constructing it, the bulldozers leveled all the moguls in the middle of the fairway. Moguls still line both edges of the fairway, but they are generally more of a help than a hindrance. A ball that is hit to the edge of the fairway will most likely—but not always—strike one of the moguls at such an angle that it bounces or rolls into the center and offers the golfer an even lie for his second (or third) shot.

What I wish to focus on is not this hole in its entirety but its green. It is time we paid attention to the subject of greens and putting.

In a major sense there are three different games of golf. Until now we have been concerning ourselves almost entirely with but one of them: the *long game*. The long shots traverse 90 percent of a hole's terrain. On the long shots we swing all out with one club or another and get to experience the glory of flight. The long shots are addicting. For the average player, most of the excitement of golf lies in the long shots.

But it is on the little greens that half the game is played out. Once on the green—any green of any golf course—it is "regulation" for the good golfer to be able to sink her ball into the cup with two short strokes. Since the standard course of eighteen holes has a total par score of 72, the par golfer playing in regulation will hit 36 shots from someplace off the green and 36 shots on the green. Yes, in terms of number of strokes, half of golf occurs on the little greens, and we had best indeed pay attention to them and these little strokes called putts.

Greens are obviously called such because their surface is of green grass. Actually, to American golfers accustomed to long wide fairways that are constructed of equally green grass, this may not be so obvious. But golf—and most of the language of golf—originated along the coasts of Scotland, where the grass of the fairways might be more brown than green and where, sometimes, there is precious little fairway at all.[3]

In any case, whether in America or Scotland or anywhere else, the grass of greens is cut much shorter than that of fairways—in fact, very short indeed. Moreover, it is usually a different species of grass entirely and requires elaborately careful maintenance to retain the green's smooth surface under the stress of its heavy human usage. The construction, seeding, sustenance, maintenance, and repair of greens is an entire science unto itself.[4] There is much room for variation in the execution of this science, however. It must be varied according to the climate of the course (including its pest life—insects, worms, moles, and molds, for instance). The variety may be used to create greens that are relatively "fast" or "slow," depending upon their qualities of friction, which may range from that of smooth glass to that of sandpaper. On any one course, however, the science is usually executed in the same manner. A course will usually have all fast greens or all slow ones. Seldom does a course have a mixture.

With that exception, an interesting eighteen-hole course will have eighteen very different greens. Although on the maps they are designated as perfectly round circles of proportionally equal size, some of Exotica's greens are quite tiny, while others are up to three times as large. Their circumferences are as irregular as that of living amoebas: Pseudopods may extend in any direction. Indeed, greens are living creatures. As noted, just to emphasize the point, at dawn each morning or almost every morning, one of the greenskeepers will go around rather drastically changing the position of the cup. Sometimes he will replace it to the back of the green at the edge of a cliff (as on that first green that particular day at Mid-Ocean). Or maybe in the front of the green. Or he may place it way to the side in one of the pseudopods. The nature of the green varies not only from hole to hole but even from day to day![5]

Living creatures never exist in isolation; they exist in relationship to their environment. The nature of a green will depend upon everything that is around it. Such environs are most notoriously sand traps, which egregious subject we will begin to consider on the next hole. But the predominant environmental factor may be virtually anything. For instance, it is common for a small tree to stand just in front of the green at one side. If the cup is at the other side, it's usually no problem. But if the greenskeeper has placed the cup in one of the green's pseudopods right behind that little tree, it can be a major problem. I am reminded, as another example, of an extremely short par 3 I've played half a dozen times on a desert course. In front of its little green is a deep gulch. In back of it is a sheer face of solid rock. Underhit the green, and of course your ball will be in the gulch. Overhit the green ever so slightly, and your ball will hit the rockface, bounce all the way back across the green, and also end up in the gulch.

Until now I have been speaking of greens as if they were all smooth, flat, and even. They are all smooth to a greater or lesser degree. They may or may not be flat and even. On a difficult course, such as Exotica, up to six greens may be relatively flat, but the remaining twelve will be uneven in all manner of possible ways. This unevenness gives the greens their greatest variety and golfers their greatest difficulty.

The entirety of a green may be slanted uphill or downhill. Or just a part of it. Most interesting courses will have at least one "two-tiered" green, where roughly half of the green is as much as three or four feet higher than the other half, with a narrow steep stretch of green between them. One part of a green may undulate this way and another part that way. The variety of undulations in greens is virtually infinite. Unless one's ball has the good fortune to lie within a few inches of the cup, as on the rest of the course, no two putts on a green are exactly alike.[6]

On any putt there are only two decisions to be made: how hard to hit the ball, and in what direction. Sounds simple, right?

On a perfectly flat, even green, putting is rather simple. The direction in which you should hit the ball is already determined for you: You aim straight for the cup or hole. As for how hard you should hit it, you have to consider two variables: the distance your ball lies from the cup, and how fast—or slow—the green is. The second variable can be quite dramatic. Given the same distance, you may need to hit the ball at least twice as hard on a slow green as on a fast one. Still, it is relatively simple. Unless her first putt is extremely long, the experienced golfer has no excuse for not putting in regulation—that is, sinking her second putt in the cup. Otherwise, she has made a significant mistake.

On an uneven green things are not so simple. To illustrate this I will use the most difficult green I know. It is as flat as a pancake, only in this case the pancake is pitched uphill in its entirety at a 15-degree angle from front to back. And let us suppose you have made an almost perfect "approach" shot, so your ball lies a mere eight feet from the cup. But is it eight feet below the cup, above the cup, or to the side of the cup?

The best you can hope for is that it lies directly below the cup. Your aim is once again simply determined by the direction of the cup. As for how hard you hit your putt, you now have three variables to contend with: the distance (eight feet), the speed of the green, and the degree of inclination. Because the latter is dramatically uphill, you will now need to hit your ball twice again as hard for it to reach the cup. Yet in this case there is considerable room for error. If your aim is correct but you hit it too hard, the ball will still be moving sufficiently slowly that it will probably drop into the cup. And if your aim isn't dead center, the ball will likely stop close enough to the cup for you to sink your second putt. Most commonly, the biggest problem with an uphill putt is to underhit it.

When your ball lies eight feet past the cup, you have a steep downhill putt, which is more problematic. You should barely nudge it. If you do so and your aim is correct, it will dribble into the cup. If your aim is off, it will stop near the cup. But if you hit it a mere 10 percent too hard, even with correct aim, the ball will be moving so fast upon reaching the cup that it will likely bounce over it. If your aim is off, it will go way past the cup. Underhitting an uphill putt is a problem. Overhitting a downhill putt is a disaster. On a green such as this, I have seen many—myself included—putt for a cup eight feet downhill, with the result that their ball ends up 20 feet distant on the other side.

The worst-case scenario is when your nearly perfect approach shot comes to rest eight feet to one side or another of the cup. If you aim your putt toward the cup, as soon as the ball gets near it, it will curve downhill, missing the cup by at least a yard. So you must aim well uphill of the cup. How far uphill? Well, that depends upon how steep the slope of the green is and whether your sideways lie is slightly uphill or downhill of the cup. Then you must factor into the equation how hard to stroke this ball, which first must go uphill and then will sometimes gently, sometimes sharply turn to start going slowly or rapidly downhill. Actually, the matter is quite computable with advanced calculus. Even the pros cannot do advanced calculus in their head, but the human brain is so remarkable that the experienced golfer can make a guess that will almost exactly conform to the mathematical calculation. Ultimately, the problem is not one of mathematics but somehow making your body and hands obey those complex laws of mathematics that you already instinctively understand.

I won't go through all the other permutations and combinations (such as long putts across a doubly undulating green). Instead I'll polish off the picture by mentioning three particular situations.

One is rare. The only time I have ever experienced it was on a two-tiered green, when my ball landed on the top tier and the cup had sadistically been placed on the near side of the bottom tier. Separating these tiers, the green might slope as steeply as 30 or 40 degrees. No matter how slowly your putt is moving the moment it reaches the top of this incline, by the time the ball reaches the bottom, it will be moving so fast that it will sail right over the cup. Even the greatest golfer in the world will still face a rare putt that is *impossible*.

A second situation is only slightly less rare. I mentioned that on a given course the speed of the greens is usually a constant. Occasionally, however, for no visible reason a particular green may be faster or slower than all the other greens. Or just one part of a green may be faster or slower than the rest of it. If this situation is the same every day, the problem can be overcome only by a golfer who has played that green over and over again—another instance when it pays to know your course. A guideline among certain golfers says that the grass on a green inexplicably grows toward the water (any nearby lake or ocean) and away from the mountains—or is it toward the mountains and away from the water? I never can remember which, since the principle has never worked for me. Yet a few will swear by it, proclaiming its utility in predicting some of these invisible shifts in the speed, or "grain," of a green. I cannot help but wonder, however, whether these people may not be the kind who need to grasp at any straw to make an often uncertain world *seem* certain and predictable.

Finally—and far more frequently—a green may have a slight yet devastating slope that is invisible. Many golfers have certain tricks or magical gestures they compulsively use to make such invisible "rolls" visible: squatting down to get the surface of the green as close to eye level as possible; holding a club in front of themselves like a plumb line; or both. Sometimes such tricks seem to help. Often they don't. The most common sentences heard on a green are "I could have *sworn* the ball was going to roll to the left (or right)!" and "I could have *sworn* it was a straight line to the cup!" The more often one has played the green, however, the less likely you are to make such exclamations. Practice may not make the invisible visible, but it may make it memorable. Once again it pays to know your course.

Invisible gulches! Invisible fast spots and slow spots! Invisible, subtle slopes!

A hundred years ago in his classic book *The Varieties of Religious Experience,* an extraordinary man, William James, defined *religion* as "the attempt to be in harmony with an unseen order of things." I disagree with his definition. To me religion implies membership in an organization with a specific doctrine or dogma, and I have known many "religious" people who have paid scant attention to the invisible. But James provided us with the simplest definition of what might better be called spirituality. So, borrowing from him, I define *spirituality* as "the attempt to be in harmony with an unseen order of things."

And so I am also back to the notion of golf as a spiritual discipline. As a scientist even more than a religious person, I am an empiricist who believes that the best (not the only) route to knowledge is through experience or experiment. Consequently, I have repeated that there is no substitute for knowing your course, for experimenting with it almost endlessly, until you are familiar with its every hidden gulch and

sand trap and every invisible roll of its greens—as long as you *remember* them.

But I am more than just a scientist or empiricist; I also believe that we can be greatly helped through life by using certain phenomena that transcend experience. I am speaking here of such things as intuition, even revelation, which cannot be explained without resorting to "an unseen order of things." I am a spiritual being. I am *not* a materialist.

I believe ours is a predominantly materialistic culture. Materialism is a basic philosophy or attitude that everything of importance can be perceived, one way or another, through the five senses. Its basic motto is "What you see is what you get, and anything else is not worth considering." In essence, a deep spirituality is the opposite of materialism, holding that what cannot be seen (or touched, or measured, and so on) is more important than what is immediately visible to the untrained eye.

How does one get to be in harmony with an unseen order—or the will of God, if you please? The answer is the same three-step process we've discussed in relation to golf.

The first step is to *want* to be in such harmony. The trick here is that before you can want it, you must believe in it; you must cease being a total materialist. Now, this is not the time or place for me to attempt to convert you to a faith in God. Simply let it be said that I believe, but I probably wouldn't if my experience had not led me to discern that this unseen order of things is smarter than me and has my best interests at heart. In other words, the unseen order is benign, and my faith might therefore be construed as selfish. Furthermore, as a Christian, I happen to believe the unseen order to be active rather than passive; that it is not only helpful for me to attempt to be in harmony with it, but that it wants me to be in such harmony, and that it actively (albeit invisibly and mysteriously) reaches out to me to assist me in being so.

Once you believe in some such invisible order and desire to be in harmony with it, the second step, of course, requires some emptiness on your part. Give God His or Her due. Specifically, set aside or empty yourself of a bit of your earthly, materialistic schedule, so as to make time, make room, for God. Some prefer to do this through regular church, temple, or mosque attendance. My own preference is for solitary prayer. Now, there are many kinds of prayer, most of which involve talking to God with words of praise or petition. For me, the more important kind, akin to some varieties of meditation, is the prayer when I am not talking but listening to God. This requires that I empty myself of the clutter in my mind. Otherwise I cannot hear God when She or He chooses to reveal something to me.

The third step is to do it over and over and over again, to make prayer a daily practice. Actually, my experience is that God is rather unlikely to talk to me or say anything of significance during my specific prayer times. It is also my experience, however, that the more frequently and regularly I empty myself in such ritual prayer, the more likely it is that God will reveal Herself to me at other unpredictable times, such as when I am struggling with a family or business problem—or even when I am struggling on the golf course.

To the immature (not necessarily youthful) player, putting is likely to seem the dullest part of golf. It lacks the glory of flight. One cannot hit all out. But reality is to the contrary: Putting requires the most obsessively gentle precision.[7] And it is most likely to be on the green where competitive golf is won or lost.

Although the photographers try, television simply cannot capture the glory of flight, and I doubt that it ever will. Yet each year more and more millions of people stay glued to their TV sets to watch professional golf tournaments. It is because of the putting. There the elegance and drama of golf are most evident. Indeed, no moment in all of sport is so exciting to watch as a pro making a single putt upon which a hundred thousand dollars may depend.

I have wondered whether the expressions *to putter around* and *putter about*—meaning "to engage in aimless activity"—might have come from golf. There is no evidence they do.[8] But to observe a beginner or a duffer on the green six-putting back and forth past the cup, it is difficult not to conclude that he is puttering around. If his activity is not exactly aimless, certainly his aim is poor.

Even if you watch, on a green a hundred yards in the distance, a foursome of excellent golfers squatting, holding their clubs as plumb lines, marking their balls, striding here and there, and taking tiny practice swings, it will look for all the world as if they are doing nothing more than puttering. But when you are a golfer yourself, you will know this is not the case. Instead, you know that those human beings are utterly purposeful. Aiming with exquisite accuracy can be born only out of the greatest care.

I have played with many very good putters. Once I played with a truly great one. It was on a course with tricky greens that she had never set foot on before. She three-putted once on the eighteen holes. She two-putted ten of the others. She one-putted the remaining seven. She did not use any magical ritual, like holding her putter shaft as a plumb line. In fact, she putted more quickly than the rest of us. One might think that she just happened to have a particularly good day. Yet I had the strange sense that, despite her unfamiliarity with them, she had an inexplicable, mystical *feel* for the greens. I even wondered whether she had actually managed to be in harmony with the unseen order of things.

NOTES

1. There are two reasons that, on most greens of most courses, the cup placement is changed at dawn every day. One is simply to provide more variety for regular players. The other is more practical. Golfers spend much more time standing near or next to the cup than farther away from it. This is in the nature of putting. The result, however, is that the delicate turf encircling the cup very rapidly becomes worn down unless the cup placement is routinely changed.

   The change is easily accomplished. Greenskeepers have a tool that is a cross between a drill and a shovel. With it they not only drill the new hole but capture the dirt and turf, which they then simply replace into the old hole. In this manner you do not end up with a green that is pockmarked with holes. Indeed, the procedure is so precise that the old hole doesn't interfere with putting, and within a day or so you can't even tell where it was.

2. This is not the case, however, with a great woman's psyche or soul. As Shakespeare's Mark Antony said of Cleopatra, "Age cannot wither her, nor custom stale her infinite variety."

3. Some believe golf originated in Holland at the end of the Middle Ages, but most authorities agree the game was first played in Scotland, probably in the sixteenth or seventeenth century. Certainly, as noted, most of the language of golf is derived from the Scottish dialect of the time. Nonetheless, although many have tried to make guesses on the subject, the actual derivation of the very word *golf* remains tantalizingly and mysteriously obscure.

4. Such carefully constructed and maintained greens are not unique to golf. Bowling greens are the most obvious example, but lawn or grass tennis courts are a more common one. To be absolutely precise, one should refer to the green of a golf course as a *putting green.*

5. Variability—or, as it is sometimes called, irritability—is considered by many biologists to be the single most essential characteristic of life—the animate as opposed to the inanimate. Amoebas move away when poked ever so lightly; rocks do not.

6. A shot on the green is called a *putt.* The act of making that shot is called *putting.* And the club with which one makes it is accordingly named a *putter.* The noun *putt* and the verb *to putt* are simply derived from the English verb *to put.* It is an unusually complicated verb, with respect to the number of different adverbs commonly associated with it. Thus, "to put together," "to put over," "to put behind," and so forth have vastly different meanings. But the most basic meaning of put is "to thrust, push, or shove." And what the golfer tries to do with her putter is exactly that: to push or shove her ball into the cup. The extra "t" got added simply because in the Scottish dialect the verb *put* is both pronounced and traditionally written as *putt.*

    Usually the putter is the shortest of golf clubs and the only one whose clubface has virtually no angle. Until forty years ago its clubhead was a simple blade that rested perpendicular to the green. Since then, however, catering to the golfer's desire for almost any kind of magic, manufacturers have developed all manner of clubheads that resemble something out of *Star Trek,* but they generally work no differently—and no better—than the ancient, simple blade.

    In some ways the use of the putter dramatically differs from the customary use of other golf clubs. The length of the swing is a matter of a few inches instead of feet. Generally you are best off if you use no wrist movement in your little swing. One may grip or hold the putter the same way one does another club, or one may do so quite differently. Being such an overly eager and hence nervous man, on the putting green I suffer from a condition golfers have come to call the "yips": The shorter the putt, the more my hands start to shake. This is not good. I have learned to compensate for the yips, however, by a bizarre grip I won't attempt to describe. Let's just say it works for me, and as long as it's legal, anything that works well in golf is okay.

7. Michael Murphy referred to putting as the "anal-retentive" part of golf in his well-known book, *Golf in the Kingdom* (Viking Press, 1972; currently available from Arkana Books, the Penguin Group).

8. There are other possible derivations. For instance, sailors use the expression *to put about* to describe turning a sailboat onto a different tack. Watching a group of sailboats tacking about in a race on an almost windless day, it does appear as if they are merely puttering about.

*There was one man who concluded that the key to success
was humility, and another that the key was self-confidence.
They were both wrong.*

HOLE   7

DEFTNESS

On this third uphill hole in a row, I get yet another opportunity to
extol the variety of golf. Although the tees are still in the midst of the
rain forest, by the beginning of the dogleg the forest and its tall trees
are no more. They have given way to increasingly dry low shrubbery,
and the green is actually situated in desert terrain surrounded by cacti.
What this means for the long hitter is that if he so desires, he can cut
across the dogleg with his drive. What it means for the student of
nature is that this single hole begins in one climatic zone and ends in its
opposite. This is because in our climb up the side of Mount Intrepid,
we have wended around from its windward to its leeward side. The
clouds blowing off the ocean have exhausted themselves of their moisture; indeed, by the green there are no more clouds.

But it is not the variety of the scenery upon which I wish to focus;
it is once more the variety of skills that the golfer must use. I have said
that golf can be divided into three different types of game. We have
considered the long game and the very difficult game of putting. Now
we shall look at the third type, which golfers call the *short game*, and
see that it is every bit as important as the other two.

In a theoretical universe the perfect golfer's ball should land on

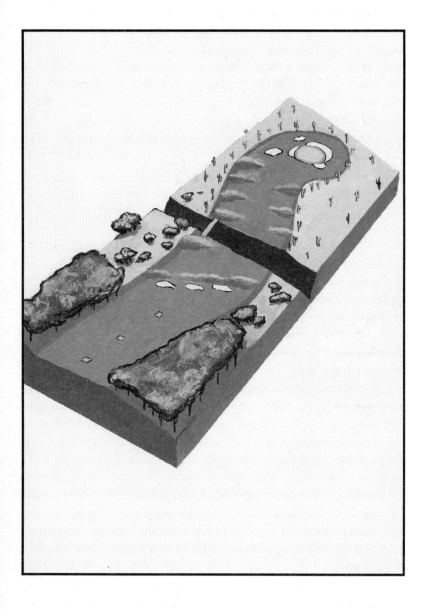

(and stay on) the green with one to three long strokes in accord with regulation. In this theoretical universe there would be no need for a short game; there would be need only for long shots from the fairway and for putts. But that is not the way things work. In the actual universe even the best golfers in the world do not behave according to regulation. At least half the time, they either make a slight mistake, so that their ball just misses the green in one direction or another, or else they hit better than regulation, so that their drive lands quite near the green of a par 4 or their second shot on a par 5. In either case, for their next shot to land on the green—ideally close to the pin—they cannot hit all out; they must hit a *little shot* with less than a full swing. Such a little shot from close to the green is what is meant by the short game.

If the best golfers in the world—the pros—need to employ their short game on approximately half the holes, think about us beginners, duffers, mediocre players, and short hitters. We will be using our short game on most holes—and often more than once on the same hole. I've suggested that putting is half of golf. Now, as we get ever more precise, let me amend that. Putting is roughly 40 percent of golf; the long game is roughly 40 percent; and the short game is at least 20 percent. And one of the things that distinguishes the pros from the rest of us is not that they never have to use their short game, but that when they do use it, they use it better.

The essence of their excellence in the short game is not so much precision (as in putting) or power (as in the long shot) as deftness. Before we can consider the nature of deftness, however, we need first to examine why it is so required. And in doing so, let us start with the subject of sand.

Sand properly belongs on beaches. It does not properly belong on golf courses. Nevertheless, a great many years ago designers began to put it there into hollows or pits called *bunkers*, thereby creating *sand traps*.[1] Although sand traps may be located almost anywhere on a hole, they are particularly relevant to the short game because they are most commonly found adjacent to the green, often encircling it like a moat.[2] Deliberately designed to make golf more difficult, sand traps are appropriately named. They are traps indeed for a variety of reasons:

1. The rules of golf declare sand traps to be hazards, and a rule of hitting out of a formally declared hazard is that your club cannot touch the ground until you hit the ball. This means that you are not allowed a practice swing. Oh, you may see a golfer in a trap wiggling his club about, but since he is not allowed to touch the sand with it, he has no practical way of gauging the depth of the swing he must make. His real stroke must be, to a large degree, a matter of guesswork.

2. Sand is shifty, and it is not easy to get a firm footing in it. For a workable stance, however, the golfer above all else needs a firm footing. Consequently, when you watch most experienced golfers in a trap, you will see them grinding their feet into the sand to get as firm a stance as possible.

3. The sand in a trap is likely to shift less from the wind than from golfers climbing into the trap, establishing their stance, hitting, and climbing out again. For this reason rakes are placed at the edge of sand traps, and after making her shot, the golfer is supposed to use the rake to repair the damage she has done. It doesn't mean she will do so, however, and your ball may well come to rest in the middle of one of her deep footprints. And that is where you must hit it from. Unfair though your extremely uneven lie might seem, the rules of golf are such, in this case, that you have no redress from your predecessor's negligence. Actually, in sand, no matter how well raked, there is no such thing as an even lie. The rake strokes themselves change the microterrain. The lie of your ball in a trap is only more or less uneven, depending upon dozens of factors.

4. Because sand is so shifty, in order to get loft on your shot, you must hit under the ball somewhat more than you would when hitting from the grass of the fairway. Yet sand also has more resistance than grass. This means that from a trap you must hit your short shot harder—with a longer swing. But how much under and how much harder? It all depends upon another dozen or more factors.

5. Several of which are the particular nature of the particular sand in the particular trap. There's white sand and brown sand, fine sand and coarse-grained sand. I've never played a course that didn't have the same kind of sand in all its traps, but each time I play a new course, I've got a new type of sand to deal with. And whatever the type, it will

change when it's raining or has recently rained. Any three-year-old who has built a sand castle knows that there's a vast difference between wet and dry sand.[3]

6. A sand trap may be shallow, or deep, or cavernous. The golfer must adjust his club selection and his swing accordingly. Such adjustments—some of which are subtle—can be made with consistent correctness only out of vast experience.

7. The turf of the fairway almost always overhangs the edge of a sand trap, whether it be a shallow trap or a deep one. This overhang is called a *lip*. If the player fails to loft his ball, it will usually hit the lip and bounce backward, for him to try again.

I've offered seven reasons why sand traps are difficult places. These alone should make it clear that considerable deftness is required to hit out of them with routine success. What I have not yet made clear is that humility may be an element of such deftness.

Some years ago when I was less mature of mind, I hit a nearly perfect fairway wood second shot on a long par 4. I watched my ball soar toward the green with delight. But my delight turned to anguish as the ball fell not only a mere six inches short but into a cavernous sand trap immediately in front of the green. When I reached the trap, I saw that my ball had embedded itself in the sand underneath a gigantic lip. The illustration depicts my predicament. God Himself could not have hit that ball anywhere, even backward. Yet I marched into the trap and proceeded to hack away at the ball five times, succeeding only in embedding it deeper into the sand, before I picked it out and quit the hole in disgust.[4]

What I should have done, of course, was to immediately recognize that I had an unplayable lie, declare it as such, take my one-stroke penalty, and move my ball two club lengths back into the trap, where I would have had a reasonably playable shot. (While one can declare such unplayable lies in a sand trap, the rules forbid removing the ball from the trap entirely.) But I was so furious at just missing the green, I didn't even pause to think.

If one does pause to think, the problem is not deciding what to do about such an obviously impossible lie; it is deciding what to do about

the nearly impossible ones. And here I have no advice to offer except to be sufficiently humble as to have a reasonably accurate sense of your own limitations.

Not all the environs of a green are sand traps. Mostly it will be from the fairway or a low grass rough that the good golfer will be hitting her short shots to the green.

The short game might also be called the "in-between game." In playing the short game, the golfer generally uses strokes that are in between hitting all out and putting. Such strokes can be divided into two types: pitching and chipping.

For *pitching* the golfer employs one of his highest-numbered (most highly angled) irons, usually one specifically designed for the purpose, called a *wedge*. He uses a stroke exactly the same as if he were hitting all out, save that he takes less of a backswing and otherwise hits the ball more softly. The result will be a high arcing ball that travels anywhere between five and 75 yards, depending solely upon the gentleness of his stroke. Because the loft of a pitch is so great, when the ball lands on the green, it will generally stop dead.

To make a *chip* shot, a golfer will use a lower, less angled iron, and his stroke will more resemble a long putt. Generally he will neither cock nor break his wrists; he will "straight-arm" his short stroke. This will produce a shot that lofts much lower than a pitch and rolls forward once it lands on the green.[5]

When to pitch and when to chip? If any obstacle lies between you and the green—most commonly, a sand trap—you need loft, so you will want to pitch over it. But if your line to the pin is unobstructed—as it is on this seventh hole, where the ball lies slightly to the right side of the fairway and in front of the green—then you could either chip or pitch. The matter is purely optional. The point is to get your ball as close to the pin as possible with a single shot. Some players, like myself, feel they can do so more accurately with a chip shot. Others feel more comfortable pitching. Indeed, some golfers virtually never chip.[6]

Most greens are surrounded by a narrow band of grass that is slightly longer than that of the green but much shorter than that of the fairway. This is called the *skirt* (or *apron* or *fringe*—the language of golf is rich!). It is illegal to use any club other than a putter on the green.[7] One may, however, chip or pitch from the skirt if she so chooses. Or she may putt. Indeed, she may even putt from the fairway itself. When used for such a long shot from the fairway, the putter has been facetiously referred to as a "Texas wedge."

The problems and temptations of the short game are essentially identical to those of the long game—with one exception: hitting the hell out of the ball. Save out of a deep sand trap, not even a duffer is stupid enough to strike a pitch or chip with all his might.

But we can be so excessively eager to see the results of our short shot that we jerk our heads up before we hit the ball. The consequences are usually even more disastrous than with a long shot. Imagine your ball lying ten feet in front of the green and 25 from an unobstructed pin. All you want to do is to make a sweet little pitch—but as you do, you lift your head up to see just how sweet it is. With your head, up come your hands. The result is that the face of your pitching wedge does not scoop gently under the ball; rather, the bottom edge of that face hits the ball dead center. Instead of lofting delicately into the air, as you intended, your ball careens like a ricocheting bullet all the way across the green, straight into a deep sand trap at the far end. This has cost you at least one, probably two, and very possibly three or more strokes. It has also been plain ugly.

By virtue of the steep grassy slopes of either the moguls or the borders of the sand trap adjacent to a green, one is more likely to encounter difficult lies in the short than the long game. Hence one is all the more likely to tense up and sin by forgetting the great principles of golf: "Relax, hit it easily, smoothly; keep your head down and your eye on the ball; follow through toward the pin." I say "one" is more likely to sin in the short game. True though it might be, it sounds abstract. The less abstract reality is that *I* am more likely to sin in my short game. And among the whole gamut of my sins in this regard, the most foul is my proclivity to shank the ball.

Shanking is so foul a sin that some golfers have begged me never to mention the verb *to shank* again in their presence, as if the word itself might even be contaminating. Its etymological derivation requires no explication. It means to hit the ball with the shank of the club—that is, not with the face of the clubhead but with its shank, the crooked place where the shaft of the club is joined to the clubhead.[8] What makes the word so terrifying is not the mechanics it describes but the result of those mechanics: a ball that goes low, fast, and somewhere between 60 and 80 degrees to the right of where one is aiming.[9]

Since *shanking* is a word in the vocabulary of all serious golfers, one might assume that most of them have done it at some point in their lives. I have, in the form of broken windows at almost right angles to the tee of a par 3, seen evidence that others do it. Yet I have never seen anyone else shank in a foursome I've been playing with. It often seems to me that only I am capable of such a monstrosity.

Once after I shanked while playing with a true golf guru with whom I'd been accidentally paired up, I desperately asked him what I was doing wrong. "I dunno," he responded. "It's complicated, but I suspect it's mostly your nerves."

By which he meant he had already observed me to be a particularly nervous person. For nervousness, translate "an excess of eagerness." I do not mean to imply that I always shank my short shots.[10] In fact, I do it less and less these days. When it does happen, I now stop to examine the state of my nerves, and I think I have figured out what I mechanically do wrong when I shank.[11] Not only do I hurry to look up, but I stop short my swing while doing it. Indeed, I start to pull back even before I hit the ball, and in the process I turn my wrists outward. Even though my stance is proper for aiming at the hole, at the moment of impact my clubface is almost at a right angle to my stance. I have learned to correct this absurdity by remembering on my next short shot to follow through—not only to keep my eye on the ball but to swing through toward the pin while doing so—to let my swing complete itself as nature or God intended and as if I were not a nervous Nellie inclined to render himself almost spastic. Relax, Peck, relax.

Following through is a principle not just of the short game but of every single shot. Your swing should end up toward whatever point at which you are aiming. On a long shot straight to the green, teachers will instruct you to "follow through toward the hole." In the short game this instruction becomes: "Follow through toward the pin." And on a straight putt it will be: "Follow through toward the cup." (By rule, the pin is removed from the cup as soon as the players are ready to putt on the green.)

Whenever I even slightly check my swing on a long shot—when at the completion of my swing, as a right-handed player, my clubhead is pointing to the right of where I am aiming—the result is virtually guaranteed to be a slice. Occasionally, trying to hit the ball too hard, I will overswing (with my clubhead ending up to the left of my aiming point). The result will be a vicious hook.

One seldom slices or hooks putts, but the same principle holds. For years and years my tendency was not to swing through when putting but to tap the ball, stopping my little swing dead the instant I connected with it. The results were seldom good. Lily pointed out to me what I was doing wrong. She had watched good putters and noted that, while their backswing might only be an inch, their follow-through would be as much as four inches. When I tried following through toward the cup, the improvement was dramatic, but it took me the better part of a year before following through with my putting swing even began to be second nature for me.

Still, it is in my short game that my failure to follow through has been the most devastating. Oddly enough, a person's "natural swing" follows through toward the hole, the pin, or the cup. Then why do I do the unnatural? I've already discussed this in terms of an excess of eagerness that leads me to look up too quickly. I also look up because I'm afraid I'm not going to do well. I literally choke up.

All I need is confidence.

I particularly need more confidence in sand traps.

If you look at sand traps with a sense of perspective—which is hard to do—you will realize that not only are they designed to be difficult, but also that they have deliberately been designed to tense you up. To "beat" them and their enemy designers, you must remember once again to do the unnatural: relax. Relax in a sand trap? Relax when you're not allowed a practice swing, when you have no firm footing, no surety of how deep or hard to hit? Yes. As noted, because of the resistance of sand, you need to use a longer stroke to pitch out of a trap than you would use in other shots of similar distance in your short game. But it is all the more important that such a stroke be *smoooth*. Don't tense up. Remember to stroke it easily and smoothly and to follow through toward the pin.

The pros you watch on TV make getting out of a sand trap look simple and easy. The rest of us seldom make it look so pretty, and sometimes we make it look downright ugly. Beginners and mediocre players, for instance, are prone to play what may be called sand trap Ping-Pong. This is when the player hits too low and hard from one trap, causing his ball to skim across the green into a trap on the other side. Then he does the same thing again, so he ends up in the original trap. And so on. Only one thing is sadder than watching someone playing Ping-Pong golf five or six shots in a row; that is doing it yourself.

The reason the pros make getting out of a sand trap look easy is because they have practiced doing it infinitely.

Well, I hate to practice. Part of it may go back to my childhood, when I was forced to take piano lessons and, in between them, to practice. "Have you practiced your scales today, dear?" my mother would lovingly nag, nag, nag. I think it is generally in our nature to detest practice, and I believe we can thoroughly overcome this natural disinclination only when God has clearly called us to excellence in some particular endeavor. Let me make it clear right here and now that God is not calling me to be a pro golfer, and I doubt She is calling you that way either. I play golf primarily for fun. Nonetheless, we are more likely to enjoy golf—or to have fun in any other field of human endeavor—when we know what we are about. And like it or not, that takes practice.

To endlessly practice hitting a golf ball out of sand is not exciting.[12] I've suggested that the pros spend an enormous amount of time on such a boring activity because of their calling to excellence. The flip side of this calling, however, is humility. I may think about sand trap practice: "This is boring. I want to have fun." But they think: "I'm not good enough yet. I need to practice my follow-through. I need to learn how to get more loft. I need to figure out how to put backspin on the ball. I need to add a touch of distance." Need, need, need. Is there any way we can better exemplify humility than through the expression of need—and through a willingness to follow up on that need with practice?

• • •

Finally I am prepared to define deftness. As I noted early on, what amazes me most about the pros is not their huge long game nor their delicate putting but their extraordinary short game, particularly in the sand. When I hit out of a sand trap, I feel plain lucky if my ball lands and stays on the green somewhere. Yet they routinely hit trap shots that end up right next to the pin with exquisite accuracy. The word that comes to my mind over and over again, when I watch the pros at their short game, is *deftness.*

It is an unusual word. *Deft* is derived from two Old English words: *Gedefte,* meaning "mild, gentle, meek, or humble," and *Gedaefen,* meaning "becoming, fit, or suitable."

The latter derivation is not surprising. The short game of the pros is indeed "becoming"—even pretty. But what is this about meekness and humility?

In his mystical classic *The Cloud of Unknowing,* an anonymous thirteenth-century British monk and spiritual teacher wrote: "Meekness in itself is nothing else than a true knowing and feeling of a man's self as he is. Any man who truly sees and feels himself as he is must surely be meek indeed."[13] *Meekness* is such an old-fashioned word, I have simply borrowed this as my definition for up-to-date humility: "Humility is a true knowledge of oneself as one is. Anyone who truly knows himself or herself will be humble indeed."

The key word here is *true.* Genuine humility is always *realistic.* Were I to tell you, for instance, that I am a lousy writer, that would not be humility. It would be what I have come to call pseudohumility. For the fact of the matter is that, as writers go, I am not all that bad. To label myself "lousy" would not only be an unnecessary self-putdown; it would be a pretense. Were I to tell you that I am a good golfer, however, that would be the height of arrogance, for the reality is that I am not a good golfer; I am a mediocre one.[14]

Humility, which has always been considered a spiritual virtue, keeps popping up in this book. I've repeatedly envisioned the game of golf as a spiritual discipline that could teach me humility, among other things. The pros are humble people, at least as far as golf is concerned. They have to be. They have to be realists about the course they are playing. And they have to be realists about themselves as they play it—

about their limitations and particularly about the potential pitfalls of their own personalities. Yet with genuine humility they must also be realists about their own extraordinary virtues and capacities that they have developed through practice. They must accept and count upon these virtues in themselves.

This brings me to the other thing that most awes me about the pros in their short game: their confidence. It is so awesome to me because I so lack it in my own. On any given chip or pitch, particularly out of a sand trap, I am thinking more about all the ways I could screw up the shot than how I might succeed at it. Given the poverty of my short game, this is realistic of me; I am likely to screw it up. But this creates a kind of sand trap in my own psychology: It makes me tense when I most need to be relaxed. I am just starting to work on this problem. It is my hope that I will have enough time left to sufficiently practice my short game to gain just a touch of the self-confidence that the pros have.

What a pair: humility and self-confidence! It is a prescription for deftness. Like me, you may not be called to be a pro golfer. Yet if playing golf can teach you to develop this combination of humility and self-confidence, it is a learning you can take with you elsewhere, so you can be a pro at whatever you are called to do. Think of a stockbroker who is simultaneously humble and self-confident, and you will be thinking not only of a deft broker but probably of a great one. Show me a similarly deft cook, and I will likely be looking at a great chef. Or a politician. Or an executive. Or a computer programmer. Or a lover.

Or a writer. It takes an extraordinary amount of confidence to be an author, to put oneself out to the public, to not only believe one has something worth saying but to dare to believe that others will find it worth reading. It borders upon arrogance. How I came by such confidence is a long story: weekly themes I had to write in a British grammar school; praise I received from teachers that spurred me to enjoy writing; mentors who took me under their wing, and more. I had a lot of practice as a child and youth.

But I have also needed humility in many guises. The most obvious one in adulthood has been my willingness to work with editors. Editors suggest changes in my first—or second or third—drafts, improvements in manuscripts that I tend to believe are already beautiful. Making these changes feels like killing myself off. Yet with a bit of kenosis, I am usually able to empty myself of my pride and realize that the suggested changes will make for a better book. And so I set about the business of rewriting, which is at least as dull and tedious as endlessly practicing hitting out of a sand trap. Yet every one of my books has vastly benefited from editorial criticism of various kinds—including my own self-criticism. I can say with confidence that half the art of writing is the humble art of rewriting.

Whenever opposites are paired to create a whole, as they are in deftness, that whole is called a *paradox*. People have trouble with paradox. Indeed, its derivation from the Greek implies that paradox is "beyond logic" or "aside from common sense" or "outside of doctrine." Yet paradox is the foundation of all essential truth, and the capacity to embrace paradox is the most essential key to psychospiritual growth, whether it be on the golf course, in the boardroom, over the stove, or even in the bedroom. It is time we looked more deeply at the subject, and so we shall on the hole to come.

NOTES

1. There is much confusion between these two terms. Many golfers use them synonymously. Others see sand traps and bunkers as very different phenomena. I will not be able to end this confusion, only to clarify it.

   The original golf courses in Scotland three hundred years ago probably did not have true sand traps. But being built into the lay of the land, often near dunes on the edge of the sea, they did have deep hollows in between the moguls. For no clear reason the Scots came to call these hollows *bunkers*. The Oxford English Dictionary suggests that over time the turf at the bottom of certain bunkers became worn away, exposing the sand or sandy soil underneath. This made the bunkers even more difficult to hit out of. Now comes a misanthropic moment lost in the flow of time. Observing that the eroded bunker was more challenging, some hateful person decided to actually *add* sand to its bottom. And at that hateful moment the sand trap was born—along with the distinction between "true" bunkers (with grass at their bottom) and "true" sand traps (that are filled with lots of sand).

   I suspect that the confusion over this distinction will continue because the word *bunker* sounds so much like three other words of uncertain origin; *bunk, bunko,* and *bungle.*

Bunk most commonly refers to a bed on a ship, and the expression *to bunk down* means "to go to sleep." A player caught in a deep trap may feel as if she will never get out—as if she had bunked down in the sand trap for the night. *Bunk* also refers to something outrageously false, as when we say, "That's bunk," or when we "debunk" something by exposing its fallaciousness. This meaning of *bunk* is obviously related to *bunko,* the term for "a swindling game."

Certainly golfers who land in sand traps—even shallow ones—are prone to feel that they have been swindled somehow. Or else that they have bungled, which, in a sense, they have.

2. Sand traps that are not adjacent to the green are referred to as *fairway traps*. When they are shallow, a good golfer can hit a long shot out of them and thereby not be significantly penalized. This is not the case if the trap is deep. From the map of this hole, you can perceive that a line of moguls has been preserved in the middle of the fairway 100 yards ahead of the white tee, with deep sand traps built into them. The poor golfer who has blundered into one of them will have to hit a tiny blooper to get out—if he can get out at all.

3. It fascinates me that scientists have not yet been able to fully explain the adhesive quality of wet as compared to dry sand. All they can do is lump it in the category of "surface phenomena" or "surface tensions."

4. In studying the behavior of neurotics, Freud discerned a "repetition compulsion," by which he meant our profound tendency as humans to do the same stupid thing over and over and over again. Indeed, he eventually concluded that human beings have within themselves not only a life wish but also a death wish. Certainly my behavior in that sand trap, marked by its refusal to bow to reality, would have struck an objective observer as close to suicidal.

5. How the words *pitching* and *chipping* got into the language of golf is unknown (although we may assume the Scots did it). But their use is not unreasonable. One can move a ball in many ways. One is to pitch it, as a player does in baseball or cricket. The other is to chip it, the way one chips at a tree with an ax. Chipping may sound the more brutal, but then one may want to consider the delicacy of chips that can be made from wood or plastic, as they are so used in electronic circuitry—for example, microchips.

6. In one circumstance, usually not close to the green, a player must chip: when his ball has landed in the woods in such a position that low branches obstruct a full backswing behind him and a lofted shot in front of him. His only route back to the fairway will be by a chip shot low enough to sail out underneath the branches.

7. There is one rare exception to this rule. Should it so happen that a golfer has broken his putter—usually in a fit of anger—then he must putt with one of his irons, but only by stroking the ball with the heel of the blade. It is not easy to putt in such a manner.

8. The joint between the shaft and the clubhead of a wood is vastly different from that of an iron. Shanking is therefore a problem mostly associated with the use of irons. It can occur with long iron shots. But since irons are used exclusively in the short game, for me, at least, shanking becomes ever more common the closer I get to the green.

9. When a left-handed player shanks, his shot will veer off at an equally absurd angle, only to the left of where he was aiming.

10. Were that the case, I would long ago have given up golf, committed suicide, or submitted myself to the daily ministrations of a teaching professional.

11. What follows is not intended as a prescription for anyone else but merely as a possibly accurate self-diagnosis of my own personal pathology.

12. For practice, many golf clubs have a driving range, a putting green specially designed for the purpose, and similarly another green (with or without a sand trap) where one can exercise her short game. I have been intrigued that there may be as many as two dozen golfers out on the range hitting long balls; perhaps half a dozen on the putting green; and at most a single player practicing short shots. Make of this what you will.

   How do you practice hitting out of sand when there is no practice trap? One way is to go to an empty hole on the back nine at dawn or on the front nine at dusk. What if you are not a member of a club or the club rules forbid such practice? The problem is hardly insurmountable: Go to where sand naturally occurs. Simply take a trip to the nearest beach.

13. Translated by Ira Progoff (New York: Julian Press, 1969), p. 92.

14. This same elaboration is contained in my book of edited lectures, *Further Along the Road Less Traveled* (New York: Simon & Schuster, 1993), p. 87.

There was a woman who learned while driving her car to always look both to the left and the right as well as both ahead and behind. She never had an accident.

H O L E   8

PARADOX

To think paradoxically, we must hold two opposites in our minds simultaneously. I'm not sure we humans are capable of thinking about two things at once and certainly not about opposites. What we can do, however, is bounce back and forth—vibrate—between opposing concepts so rapidly as to make our consideration of them virtually simultaneous. When we learn how to do so, the two will become One and the opposites a Whole.

Most great golf holes are paradoxical. Consider this par-3 desert hole, carved out of the leeward side of Mount Intrepid. One might say that beauty and difficulty are not true opposites, but she would do so, I suspect, because she is already a paradoxical thinker. Most of us humans have great trouble reconciling difficulty with beauty, and many golfers have been heard to comment about a particularly tricky hole: "It's an ugly one." Beauty and ugliness are both in the eye of the beholder, and to the trained eye, both can be there simultaneously.

Some would say the design of hole 8 is notably beautiful. Even from the map one can appreciate its sweeping curves, and from the sky it might look like a tender young fetus or a tantalizing question mark.

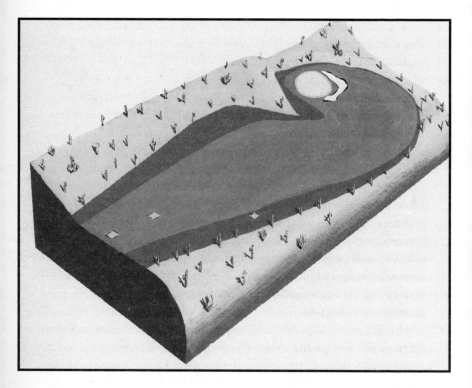

Yet others would say it must have been designed by a sadist, without a shred of human kindness in his heart.

It is simultaneously hard and easy. An average-length par 3, 160 yards from the whites and 130 from the reds, it's a snap for either the male or female pro. For the beginner or mediocre player, however, it is one of the more challenging holes on the course.

The pro would immediately rejoice at finally having a flat hole once again. He would also note that the green is unusually large and hence inviting. What the mediocre player would instantly notice with trepidation is the nasty outcropping of desert blocking the front of that green and the gigantic sand trap obstructing its other open side.

The desert is harsh. Its predominant color ranges from ugly brown to gray, dreariness that only enhances the bright green of the rich grass. In fact, the hole itself is a man-made oasis and, like all oases, a thing of softness and beauty.

This oasis is not cheaply bought. It is watered extensively every evening by water that must be pumped most of the way up and around Mount Intrepid. It is one of the most difficult holes on the course to maintain and hence one of the reasons Exotica is so expensive to play.

But the view from this hole alone is worth the price. To the right of the tee and fairway is a panoramic vista revealing that Exotica is by no means a small island or Mount Intrepid its only extinct volcano. We are, in fact, overlooking several volcanic mountain ranges—steep, weather-carved mountains now brown, now dark green. There is a focal point in this vast landscape. Right on top of the mountain nearest to us sits a magnificent—almost gaudy—Buddhist temple glittering in the midday sun.[1] If we stop for a moment not only to look but to listen, we notice the silence and are struck by the peace of this mountainside desert oasis hole.

But we must hurry quickly on. One of the things that makes this hole so oasislike is the unusual width of its sward of green grass. Not all of that width is fairway. In fact, the fairway is relatively narrow, because half of the grass constitutes a phenomenon we've not discussed before: cultivated rough.[2] It doesn't faze good players in the least. Along with the outcropping of desert and the gigantic sand trap that guard the green, however, it worries me a great deal.

Its grass is longer than that of the fairway, and a more precise shot is required to hit out of it. The natural temptation under these "rough" circumstances, of course, will be to tense up, try to hit the ball harder than you ordinarily would, to lift your head too early, and to fail to follow through. So as in other tense situations, it will be all the more important for you to remember to relax, swing easy, keep your head down, and follow through.

Relax, relax, relax; the refrain is becoming repetitive. To keep ourselves from being bored, Lily and I love to play with words. So we have developed a strange sentence to remind us of the importance of this refrain: "An excess of nisus has been the nidus of many a golfer." *Nisus* is simply an unusual synonym for *striving* (or *eagerness*). *Nidus* is a word most commonly used in medicine to denote the center of an infection. So this possibly amusing sentence translates as "An excess of striving or eagerness is at the center of many a golfer's serious problem."

It is only one side of the truth, however, one side of a paradox. For the fact of the matter is that for many other golfers a *lack* of striving has been the central problem. The pros have become so good precisely because they've striven—and striven hard—for excellence. And even I, with my excess of eagerness, have done more poorly than I should on the course because I have failed to pay attention—to the placement of a pin on the horizon, to the location of a hidden sand trap, to an obviously unplayable lie. In some ways I have not cared enough, not given the game the attention it deserves.

It would be easy for me to say, "Strive, but not too much. Relax, but not too much." It is recommending a middle path without offering the slightest suggestion about how to find it.

The central doctrine of Buddhism is the "Middle Path." When I first ran across it in my teens, it smacked to me of averaging and compromise. Gradually, however, I began to suspect that the doctrine had suffered in translation, and I wondered if the Buddha hadn't meant, not averaging, but an embrace of opposites. I suspected, for instance, that in all his talk of moderation, he was not actually urging us toward some unending and impossible state halfway between sobriety and

intoxication. I began to imagine he might have urged us, "You must have the capacity for sobriety *and* the capacity for intoxication."

So I do not wish to say in relation to golf, "Strive, but not too much." Instead I want to say something perhaps even more demanding but at least more precise: "Strive and don't strive—simultaneously."

But how on earth does one do that? It may be helpful to look at this matter of paradox more broadly than just from a golfer's point of view.

As far back as I can remember, the world has seemed to be filled to the brim with paradox. Perhaps it is because I am a Gemini, and my sign is that of Siamese twins facing in opposite directions.[3]

At the age of seventeen, I took an elective course in world religions. Possibly the fault of the textbook used, I was not excited at the time by any of the so-called Western religions: Judaism, Christianity, or Islam. Nor by Confucianism. But I was held almost in thrall by certain aspects of the other Eastern religions: by the mystical writings of the Hindu Upanishads, by Lao-tse (the legendary founder of Taoism), and by the branch of Buddhism called Zen. None of these were popular in America back in the early 1950s, but it so happened that an extremely lucid English writer, Alan Watts, was just starting to popularize Zen Buddhism. Over the next few years I devoured his books. By the age of twenty, I firmly labeled myself a Zen Buddhist.

Zen, in essence, preaches paradox. When I discovered Zen, I felt I had intellectually come home. Zen masters customarily taught their students by the use of riddles that have come to be called "koans." "Strive and don't strive" represents such a koan. The goal of the masters was that their students achieve a state of "enlightenment." When a student finally cracked the code of a koan—not only in his mind but also in his heart—then he would be enlightened.

Some years ago a hobby of mine was collecting lightbulb jokes. My favorite, naturally, was "How many Zen Buddhists does it take to change a lightbulb?" Answer: "Two—one to change the lightbulb and one not to change the lightbulb."

Laugh we may, but this business of paradox is *true*. I write these sentences on a January morning when Lily is out shopping for our combined needs. The reality is that I am able to be writing only because Lily is not writing.

I am very much like the philosopher who was asked by a student, "Professor, it is said you believe that paradox is at the core of all truth. Is that correct?"

"Well," the professor answered, "yes and no."

If you think you have discovered a great truth, and it is not a paradox, then I suspect you may be deceiving yourself.

Shortly after it began in India, Buddhism migrated to China. In the late Middle Ages it migrated again, this time to Japan. While the Chinese had developed the sect of Zen and perfected the use of the koan, it was Japanese masters who linked the teaching of Zen to activity. Centuries before golf was imported to Japan, a deep relationship developed in Japanese culture between Zen and a variety of arts and sports: *sumi-e* painting, haiku poetry, flower arranging, tea ceremony, archery, and the martial arts. "Strive and don't strive," along with "discipline and freedom" and "humility and confidence," became teaching mottos for all of them.

Approximately thirty years ago I read an American newspaper account of a Zen sect that apparently owned four golf courses in Japan. Its followers believed that the paradoxical skills necessary to play a fine game of golf were the same as those needed to achieve enlightenment. They considered the clubhouses to be their temples. The newspaper picked up on the story because there was a question—probably in regard to the taxes—about the "church status" of these golf courses. If I remember correctly, the Japanese court upheld the sect's claim. The American newspaper professed horror at this verdict, but knowing what I know about Zen, it made perfect sense to me.[4]

Anyway, my notion of golf as a spiritual discipline is hardly original.

The actual practice of Zen seems to have become a lesser part of Japanese culture today than in previous centuries. Perhaps it is in the process of migrating once again, now to the United States. When I first labeled myself a Zen Buddhist back in the 1950s, I kept pretty quiet about it since almost everyone would have thought me weird. Now it is fashionable. As is Taoism. So we are practically awash with books on the Zen of this and the Tao of that, the Inner Game of this and the Inner Game of that. And in a real sense, this is another such book, although to my knowledge no one has written about Exotica before.

While Zen may be migrating, I wonder whether its pervasive past in Japan might not account for some of the passion of modern Japanese for golf, a passion hardly restricted to Zen Buddhists. I have watched them playing our American courses, and for the most part, they play like everyone else. They even seem to have their own duffers. But I still think they have something to teach us.

An interesting piece of behavior is seen often among Japanese golfers, but also in golfers of all nationalities. When a golfer hits a pitiful shot, and he is not holding anyone up by doing so, he is prone to drop a second ball onto the fairway. This is not because he doesn't intend to play his first ball as the rules require. It is simply because he wants to get rid of the terrible feeling that the first shot has left him with, by hitting the second ball "just for fun." Often this practice succeeds. With remarkable frequency (since we are unaware of any change in our swing) that second shot will be perfect, sailing straight ahead with grace and beauty. How to account for this phenomenon? The answer is simple. The golfer is not excessively striving when he hits that second shot precisely, because it doesn't *count*. His resulting imperceptible relaxation has made all the difference.

This phenomenon has recently given rise to a not-uncommon aphorism among American golfers: "As the Japanese say, 'Hit second ball first.' " Some might see it as a "Confucius say" type of joke—even one with possible racist overtones. To me, however, it is a lovely teaching koan. Think about it.

I alluded to the "mystical" writings of Hinduism, Taoism, and Buddhism. What did I mean by mysticism? Aldous Huxley, who wrote the simplest and most succinct book I know about mysticism, entitled it (both mysticism and his book) *The Perennial Philosophy*.[5] By *perennial* he meant something that not only blooms repeatedly over the years but also blooms ubiquitously. Mystics have made their mark, placed their stamp, on every major religion in every culture throughout the past three thousand years—and, I suspect, even before, but that's unrecorded.

Mystics and *mysticism* are much maligned and misused words, at least in the United States over the past century. On the one hand, many have proclaimed themselves mystics who weren't. On the other, many have criticized their enemies as being "mystical," i.e., "fuzzy-headed," when those enemies were guilty only of clear thinking. It is therefore crucial that we give them a precise definition. It seems to me that genuine mystics can be defined by three specific yet interrelated characteristics (all of which must be present to meet the definition):

1. *A vision of underlying Unity.* Most people see the world as a place filled with distinct entities. To them, golf is a game and therefore separate from "real life"; human beings are totally distinct from hippopotami and cherry blossoms; God is up there and we are down here. Mystics, however, see invisible connections underneath the surface of things—connections between males and females, between us and the other creatures, between us and people out of sight (including those who are not changing the lightbulb along with us, but may be praying for us nonetheless). As I write these words, I am thinking very hard about my brothers and sisters who will read them—relatives whom I will never meet but whose blood comingles with mine and that of the salt sea from which we all came. Perhaps we can become so much in harmony with the "unseen order of things" that we can actually become One with God.

2. *A core language of Paradox.* It is not surprising that most people perceive a world of separateness since that is what our language (and hence our thinking) is all about. Words divide things into categories. For instance, the noun *cat* stands for a category of furry land animals with whiskers, and the noun *fish,* for a category of scaled creatures who live underwater. A fish cannot fall into the cat category (even if it's a catfish). But mystics, with their love of making connections, are primarily in the business of transcending categories. Where most people see cats or fish, they see "abundant life." While mystics can speak everyday language, they are most at home with the language of paradox. Yet as they go about the business of reconciling opposites into unities, mystics would prefer not to have to use the language of words at all—certainly not that of prose. Poetry can, upon occasion, come closer

to the heart of things. In any case, as a professional writer, I am not entirely alone in bemoaning the inadequacy of words. Many theologians are in the same camp. They take pains to point out that the name of "God" is, in truth, inexpressible.

3. *The taste for Mystery. Mystic* and *mysticism* are obviously derived from the same root word as *mystery.* On the one hand, mystics are people who love to solve mysteries. On the other, they are quite comfortable living with the unknown and the unknowable. If you meet someone who thinks she has all the answers, who has God all sewn up in her back pocket, then you have not met a mystic. Indeed, genuine mystics delight in the knowledge that it is not within our human purview to know everything, and they will make no secret of both what they know and what they don't know.[6]

Although the originators of the great religions have generally been mystics (certainly Buddha, Lao-tse, and Jesus; probably Abraham and Muhammad), the vast majority of their followers have not. Were you to wander into the Buddhist temple on the mountaintop beyond Exotica's eighth hole, it is unlikely that you would hear any talk of paradox. Probably you would find the worshippers therein as intellectually and emotionally distant from the Buddha as Muslim fundamentalists are from Muhammad and Christian fundamentalists from Jesus. Perennial though mysticism may be, mystics have always been in the minority. The Zen Buddhists, the Hasidim of Judaism, and the Sufis of Islam, for instance, are all tiny "sects." Most worshippers of popular religion are looking for answers and for the sense of certainty they may provide. They shy away from the more mysterious parts of their chosen faith.

While Zen was my first spiritual home, after fifteen years I became restless. Stumbling along, to my amazement I gradually discovered in Christianity a world of paradox that had been lying quietly in wait for me. Take the doctrine that Jesus is both human and divine—not 50 percent one and 50 percent the other, but "fully human and fully divine." What could be more paradoxical than that? Or that God resides both inside of us in Her still, small voice and simultaneously outside of us in all of His transcendent otherness? Or that salvation is the result of a mysterious mixture of both grace and works for which we will never have a mathematical formula? Then there were the words of Jesus himself: "Whoever will find his life shall lose it, and whoever loses his life for my sake will find it." Or: "You must be as wise as serpents and innocent as doves."

So it happened, at the age of forty-three, that I was nondenominationally baptized, entering "the church" through the back—or at least, the narrow—door of Christian mysticism. Indeed, we Christian mystics are not even well enough organized to have a sect or denomination of our own. We just kind of hang around.[7]

I may have made it sound as if mysticism is the most mature form of religious expression, and so I believe it to be—intellectually. My cerebral cortex comprehends perfectly well what is meant by "Strive and don't strive," but my guts don't get it at all; they seem to know only how to strive. And one of the many reasons you may find me out on the golf course is that I am still trying to comprehend paradox and mysticism within the very fiber of my being. I came to golf intellectually mature, but at the age of sixty-three, I am still using it to gain greater emotional maturity in the potentially unending journey of spiritual growth.

If you are a very good golfer, it is probable that you are emotionally mature—at least on the golf course. Probable but not inevitable, for, as I shall recount, I have seen even a few excellent players behave immaturely while playing golf. And I have also known a few excellent players who were atrocious spouses, parents, or business people, and a couple who were even crooks. But they are exceptions. The fact is that for those who are ready, golf is a powerful teacher of emotional maturity, and most of the good players I know have been able to take its emotional lessons home with them.

Let me ask you this, however: Have you also been able to take golf's intellectual lessons home with you? And let me ask that question in the context of yet another paradox.

Unquestionably the ultimate reason to play golf is to play—that is, for fun and relaxation. Once I had the pleasure of playing an eighteen-hole round with a great mystic. At its conclusion, as we were packing our bags into the car, he exclaimed, "God, this has been wonderful.

You know, for the past four hours I haven't even had to think!" Actually he had been doing a lot of thinking: about the location of sand traps and other hazards, about which club to use, about the shape of the greens and whether to play it safe or "go all out." What he meant was he hadn't been giving a thought, as he was usually compelled to do as a healer and teacher, to all the truly big problems of the world.

On the other hand, the truly big problems of the world do exist. How are we to solve them? It is, if we think about it, up to the people most affected to solve their own problems. Yet the mass of people want quick and easy, black or white solutions, which will not work. They need to learn paradox. But how? They are not likely to ever get near a golf course. While we cannot solve their problems for them, it does seem to me incumbent upon us golfers to take the paradoxical, problem-solving skills we have been fortunate enough to learn on the course and somehow teach them more widely. But once again, how? How do you extend the lessons of the golf course to the world? It seems to me a question of the first magnitude.

Finding the answer has great relevance to our daily lives. When do I sell stocks, for instance? Because of my excess of eagerness (or greed), my tendency is to hold on to them too long or dump them too quickly. Of more import is my questionable ability to properly deal with our own now-adult children. When do I offer them unsolicited advice if I see them headed in an apparently wrong direction—advice they will only resent? And when is it proper for me to withhold such advice, not only fearing their resentment but also knowing full well that I cannot—and should not—live their lives for them? This latter course sometimes feels the more caring. At other times it feels downright uncaring. In relation to my very flesh and blood, I must ask, "How do I care and not care, simultaneously?" I don't have it down pat, but I can say that I'd be much less deft at it were it not for my intellectual understanding of paradox.

I also don't have it down pat in my public life. Fifteen years ago I was quoted by a reporter (correctly) in the *Los Angeles Times*: "And if that isn't arrogant enough, Peck says, 'Perhaps the greatest political problem we have is how the 5 percent of us who comprehend paradox can communicate with the 95 percent who don't.'" It isn't that I haven't tried to bridge the gap in my own small way. An equal number of years ago, I had the opportunity to address the combined school superintendents of the United States, and one of the recommendations I made was that Zen Buddhism should be taught in the fifth grade, when children are first and most open to learning to think paradoxically. The recommendation was not favorably received. A few years later I conducted two separate daylong seminars for a well-educated public on the subject of "Thinking." A substantial portion of these seminars centered upon the matter of paradoxical thinking. At the end of each, I solicited feedback from the audience. In both cases it was the same. People said, "I came here wondering how you could possibly spend an entire day speaking about this. Now I leave concluding that the subject is too large." On an intellectual level, I was not disappointed by this feedback; some part of my message had gotten through. On an emotional level, however, I was not uplifted. From the emotional tone of these events and the written feedback, it was clear that they were among my least pleasing and popular seminars.

Yet it seems to me that we may glean the germ of an answer from these sorts of experiences. Perhaps we should begin to teach paradoxical thinking by focusing upon the most essential of all paradoxes: the paradox of emptiness and fullness.

When my audiences complained that the subject of thinking was "too large," what they meant was that, by the end of the seminars, their minds were "too full." On one level I don't blame them. Paradoxical thinking is thinking where we take all possible factors into account, requiring our minds to vibrate back and forth between opposites with great rapidity. Even though we may be sitting in our armchairs, we are very busy when we are thinking well. Our brains are racing. I think we need to be taught to rejoice in this busyness, this mental fullness.

But bear in mind we can think clearly only when we have had a good night's sleep. As far as researchers can determine, most of the brain activity during sleep (including most dreaming) is devoted to emptying our minds of preoccupations and concerns so that we can begin the new day with a more or less clean slate. With freshness. Up to now I've spoken of kenosis as a conscious process. Now we learn that we also practice it unconsciously, through the gift of sleep. And what a gift it is! Without enough sleep, people go crazy.

Paradoxically, these matters can be complex and they can be simple. For the moment let me simply say that we humans have things we need to gain and things we need to lose, things we need to give up and things we need to add on. Our whole lives are a process of vibration between fullness and emptiness. We need to teach our children to rejoice in this vibration and to joyfully see it as their task to learn how to make it ever more efficient. Remember that *vibration* and *vibrant* are virtual synonyms. I am certain that when God first looked upon all this vibration—this vibrancy—He concluded, "It is good!" And I am certain He stills feels the same.

NOTES

1. Remember the Christian Spanish-style mission church near the beach adjacent to the dogleg of the second hole? Now we have a Buddhist temple. On this elegant, brief golf "package," we will not give the natives of Exotica the attention they deserve. But now at least we realize they are a multicultural people who seem to live together with remarkable harmony.

2. One of the many meanings of *rough* is "uncultivated land." Another is "difficult." In golf these two meanings come together. Thus far we've primarily encountered two types of uncultivated land bordering Exotica's fairways: salt marsh and rain forest. As noted, they are difficult indeed for the golfer. For *difficult*, read "impossible." It is unlikely you can ever find your ball in such a rough, and if you do, it will almost inevitably be unplayable.

    On this hole the uncultivated rough is the desert—and it is not quite impossible. If you enter it to look for your ball, there will be no pythons—not even rattlesnakes, as reputedly appear on Arizona courses—only zillions of cactus spines, mostly invisible, that will easily pierce you through the thickest of clothing. Braving that, you have a half-chance of finding your ball, probably embedded within or lying at the foot of one of the two hundred varieties of cacti on the finely chipped, rock desert floor. If you do find it—and it's a vaguely playable lie—there's a half-chance you will make your shot, although you'll undoubtedly damage the bottom of your expensive clubhead in the process. But what the hell. For a golfer that little chance is worth it.

    But what's this about "cultivated rough"? The grass of greens, which is usually grown from a seed different from fairway grass, is mowed and rolled daily. It is maintained at less than a quarter of an inch in height. The grass of fairways is generally mown every two to three days and is kept at a height between half an inch and one inch. It is perfect for its purpose, which is to support your ball just enough to enable you to hit ever so slightly under it without any obstruction. The grass of cultivated rough, however, is mown no more than weekly and is kept between two and four inches in height.

The nice thing about cultivated rough is that you can almost always find your ball in it and, once you find it, you can hit it out. But you cannot hit out of it easily the way you can off the fairway. Your ball will be embedded within this longer grass to a somewhat variable depth so that you're never quite sure how deep to hit. That's one problem. The other is the resistance of the grass. Before it connects with the ball, your clubhead will have to cut through several inches of this grass. It will therefore be and feel impeded. Although hardly the worst of problems, it is unlikely that your shot out of a cultivated rough will be quite as long or accurate as you might like.

3. I was born on May 22, 1936. I do not know the time of day or night. As a psychiatrist, I have been both intrigued and repelled by astrology. On the one hand, it seems to me mostly employed simplistically, and I have every reason in the world to gravely distrust any "system" that can be used to explain everything. On the other hand, I have been struck in a number of cases by a certain correspondence between people's astrological sign and their psychology or personality. In any case, I am not yet ready to schedule my golf dates in accordance with my daily horoscope in the newspaper.

4. Thirty years is a long time ago. I did not keep that newspaper article, and today I cannot even remember the paper, so I cannot attest to the accuracy of my story.

5. Aldous Huxley, *The Perennial Philosophy* (New York: Harper & Row, 1945).

6. Earlier I said that "mystics and mysticism are much maligned and misused words." In part this is because groups of people throughout history (and most often on the fringe of one of the great world religions) have claimed that they were privy to a certain body of knowledge that the common folk were "not yet ready for." They established themselves as "mystery cults," whereby their supposed special knowledge was kept secret—except from those who went through initiation rites in order to be enlightened. These were cults indeed—as are the CIA and certain capitalist businesses today—with all the vices inherent in cults. They are properly maligned. However, they have never had anything to do with genuine mysticism.

Genuine mystics, in turn, have also been maligned throughout history, long before and long since Jeanne d'Arc was burned at the stake. This has not been because they kept secrets. Rather it is because, in attempting to explain themselves, they have inevitably spoken the language of paradox. Comprehending the core of truth, they've seen their efforts at communication often succeed only in enraging the majority.

7. The deepest, most thorough, and scholarly book I know on the subject of mysticism has a definite Christian slant. Written by Evelyn Underhill almost a century ago, it is appropriately entitled *Mysticism* (New York: Meridian Books, 1955).

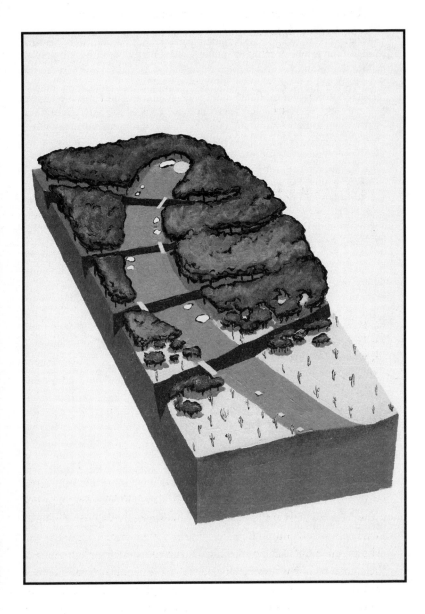

A man whose perspective does not include the invisible connections between himself and the rest of the world is not just lonely but lost.

HOLE 9

CLIMATE AND PERSPECTIVE

The map makes this ninth hole, unlike the eighth, look like an ugly worm. But that's just because maps are inevitably two or three dimensional, whereas reality is at least nine-dimensional.[1] In fact, it is a pretty hole. It happens, however, to be 599 yards long—well more than a third of a mile—and in order to map it on a single page, we have to make it appear narrower than it actually is. The map also fails to capture the extraordinary beauty of its green, nestling at the feet of the towering trees of the rain forest. Ah, the distortions of limited perspective!

Although it is unusually long, this is our first downhill hole—all the way, as it winds from the back of Mount Intrepid down its side to the base. Downhill holes are not only easier on the lungs than uphill ones, they are also generally easier on your score. A well-hit ball will both carry farther through the air and roll farther once it lands.

The greatest difficulty of the hole is the four gulches that transect it—the same four that we encountered as we climbed up Mount Intrepid on holes 5, 6, and 7. Imperfect though it might be, the map does show you how to deal with them. But don't focus solely on your play. Pause for a moment during the middle of the hole to enjoy the glorious view over the top of the rain forest to the ocean in the distance.

And appreciate how this hole once again traverses two opposite climates. Exotica is the only course I know, the world over, that has such dramatic climatic transitions. Yet wherever it is played, there is a deep relationship between climate and golf, and we should talk about it.

For starters, this ninth hole presents us with a common challenge in golf not mentioned before: the wind. It hasn't been a challenge until now. Down on the coastal plain, the prevailing wind off the sea is a breeze, figuratively as well as literally. Unless there is a storm, it is more of a gentle breeze than a wind, and it need not be taken much into account.

As we climbed Mount Intrepid, the breeze became much more of a wind the higher we got. But on holes 5, 6, and 7, that wind was at our back, which is usually considered to be an advantage rather than a challenge, since such a wind will carry your ball a bit farther. Only minor adjustments are required. The biggest problem with the wind behind you is the temptation to eagerly hit the ball harder so you will get your longest drive ever. By now you've hopefully learned to avoid such temptation.

The previous hole, being on the leeward side of Mount Intrepid, was protected from the wind. On the middle half of this one, however, we are hitting dead against it. In this case the natural temptation again is to hit too hard, not to take advantage of the wind but to "overcome" it. What a strange fantasy underlies this temptation! Trying to overcome the wind is the equivalent of attempting to hold back the tide.

Hitting too hard against the wind is particularly devastating because the harder one hits, the more likely he is to slice or hook the ball. Slices and hooks are bad enough on a windless day. Against a strong wind their evil is dramatically magnified. A sliced drive under this circumstance, for instance, will not only curve to the right but will do so earlier and more viciously. Indeed, it can even start to come back at you like a boomerang. Hit low and, by all means, straight against the wind.

Although we golfers cannot overcome the wind, we can adjust to it in various ways. The commonest way is club selection: choosing a lower club so as to shoot lower and farther than usual. If you would normally hit a seven-iron to the green on a windless day, but you're hit-

ting dead against an eight-mile-per-hour wind, you'll best use your six-iron. This one club adjustment downward is why golfers customarily refer to such an antagonistic breeze as a *one-club wind*. If it's blowing straight against your face at 16 miles per hour, then you've got more than a breeze to contend with; it's a significant wind, and you'd best use your five-iron. This two-club adjustment downward leads us to call it a *two-club wind*. A *three-club wind* of 24 miles per hour feels more like a minor gale and requires a further adjustment down to your four-iron. I could go on to *four-* and *five-club winds,* but one seldom plays in the midst of such real gales.

Golfers tend to be ritualistic people. One of their frequent rituals, usually when they're on the tee, is to pick a small tuft of grass and toss it into the air to assess the strength and direction of the wind. Sometimes this tickles me. The fact is, if there's enough wind to worry about, you can feel it on your face, and even the moderately experienced golfer can thereby assess the wind's strength with quite adequate accuracy.

Not that the matter is totally simple. Toss a tuft of grass up in the air on this ninth tee, and the blades will fall flat on your feet. The tee is still on the leeward side of Mount Intrepid and therefore windless on most days. But 200 or more yards ahead, where you want your drive to fall to earth, there is usually a two-club wind to push it back. If you thought about matters, you might realize this and hit accordingly. But probably you won't realize it until you've played Exotica at least once or twice. It's another example of the benefits of knowing your course.

The course I know best is strung out along the bluffs of the northern California coast. Just one of its many virtues is that sixteen of its eighteen holes have a view over the Pacific Ocean when the fog's not too thick. One of its few vices is the wind. Half the time it's relatively calm. The other half there's a steady two-, three-, or even four-club wind. At its extreme this wind can cause two problems I've not encountered on any other course I've played. The worst is that it can be hard to hold your stance. The wind can literally blow you off your feet—particularly when your windbreaker's the slightest bit loose and starts to act like a sail. There's no way to adjust to this, other than to purchase the tightest windbreaker you can find. The other problem is that the wind will frequently affect your putts, slowing them down when you're putting against the wind and speeding them up when you're putting with the wind. But this you can compensate for.

I once played that windy course on a windy day with a middle-aged visiting pro (not a tournament pro but a teaching one). From the moment we were introduced on the first tee, I sensed him to be a somewhat grim man, almost sour. But he was a very good golfer indeed. Despite the wind he shot 6 over par for the eighteen holes, qualifying him as truly excellent and way beyond my league. He spoke hardly at all, and I doubt he was too happy playing with the likes of me. When we were finished, I asked him what he thought of the course. "It'll never be dull" was his laconic assessment. I had the feeling he was being gracious, knowing it was my home course, so I pressed him further, inquiring whether he would ever want to play it again. "No," he replied. "There's too much goddamn wind."

To me there's nothing reprehensible about swearing, including *goddamn*. Good parent that He is, I know that God is quite capable of absorbing such anger and would much rather we be in an angry relationship with Him than none at all. But it's also like water off a duck's back for Him, and cursing the wind strikes me as so much wasted breath. I wouldn't even have remembered the event had the man been a mediocre golfer like myself. But for someone to play so well in the wind and then curse it seemed strangely sad. It seemed a loss of perspective.

Next to wind, the greatest climatic challenge to golfers is precipitation, past or present, primarily rain. I have never played in snow, sleet, or hail, although I don't doubt that many others have. Some will play golf in the midst of anything, and they refer to those of us who cancel our tee times when it is pouring outside—and obviously is going to continue to pour—as "fair-weather golfers." I accept their disapprobation. I *am* a fair-weather golfer.[2]

The first problem with playing in the rain is that you are likely to get soaking wet. This can mostly be prevented by layering yourself in oilskins or Gore-Tex, but it's not comfortable. There are always cracks in such attire, particularly around your ankles. In a downpour one's golf shoes can ship water faster than the *Titanic*.[3] Besides, you're not likely to be carrying your oilskins around on a hot summer day just in case a torrential thunderstorm happens to come by.

An even greater problem with playing golf in the rain, for those of us who wear glasses, is that we can't see. I have long been legally blind without my glasses. I could, I suppose, wear contact lenses, but the notion of getting contacts (with all the problems inherent in them) just so I can golf in the rain as an amateur strikes me as absurd. I suspect most of those who would label me a fair-weather golfer have 20/20 vision.

A third problem with rain is that it will get not only you wet but also your clubs. Grips are remarkably effective—when they are dry. When they get wet, however, they become so slippery that they fail to serve as grips at all. Several times while playing in the rain I've had my club go flying right out of my hands at the conclusion of a swing. Once again, adjustments can be made. Some golfers purchase fancy hoods to protect their clubs from the rain, although I have found that a plastic garbage or grocery bag can do just as well.

Yes, adjustments can be made to make golfing in the rain possible. But the sum total of these adjustments is such that when I see golfers out on the course in the midst of a serious, prolonged rainstorm, my reaction is far more one of pity than admiration. And in this respect I belong to the majority.

Precipitation recently past can have other effects that challenge the golfer. Wet sand congeals as much in sand traps as it does on the beach, and wet or soggy greens are dramatically slower than dry ones. These are not huge problems, however, and they can be overcome with relatively minor adjustments. The only exception is actual puddles. I advise you against trying to hit your ball out of a puddle. Go scuba diving instead, if you like water that much. I also advise you not to try to putt through a puddle on a green; your ball will stop dead. Golf balls and undiluted water were not meant for each other.

Major precipitation, like three feet of recently melted snow or 15 inches of rain during the past month, makes the average fairway mostly a swamp for a matter of days or weeks. It can't even be mowed. In such circumstances a club declares "winter rules." What are winter rules?

Well, nobody's quite sure.

When you hit even a slightly lofted shot into a fairway swamp, for instance, your ball is likely to "plug." This means it will bury itself one to two inches deep into the ground, like a plug into a drain. You simply cannot hit a ball that is plugged. According to winter rules, you can claw it out of the mud and move it to drier land (although no closer to the hole without incurring a penalty).[4]

But what happens if your ball has plugged itself so deeply into the mud that you can't find it at all? Must you take a two-stroke penalty for a lost ball after you've hit a perfectly good shot down the middle of the fairway? The winter rules may be unclear about the matter. I, for one, do not think you should be so penalized—particularly when your fellow players agree they witnessed your ball land in the fairway.

Such witnessing is important, I believe, because some golfers will use winter rules as a license for anything. Like explaining away any lost ball. Technically, when you move your ball out of a fairway swamp, you should just drop it on a drier area, but commonly players will gently tee it up on a very particular tuft of grass. Indeed, they may so tee it up in the rough. In fact, I've even seen some kick their ball entirely out of the rough, cultivated or uncultivated, excusing their action on the basis of "winter rules." When you're playing with others and keeping score at all, such behavior should at least be subject to consensual decision making. If you're playing by yourself, of course, you can do anything your conscience allows.

There are still other problems with playing in such conditions, which I won't enumerate.[5] The fact is that, despite the benefit of winter rules, it is simply not quite as enjoyable to play golf on a soggy course as it is on one in top condition.

There is one climatic phenomenon slightly akin to precipitation present, however, that I do often find enjoyable: dense fog. It is a situation most golfers will probably never encounter, whether it be winter or summer. But since the course I know best is on the coast of northern California, it is one I run into quite frequently. In dense fog you cannot see the green from the tee, even on a relatively short par 3. Most of your best shots will go sailing into the air only to vanish totally in the mists. It is exciting for me to look for my ball when I can only surmise where it might have come to earth. I feel like a child on an Easter egg hunt. But remember, I am a short hitter talking about a course I know well. Were I a long hitter on a course with which I was not intimately familiar, I imagine I would find dense fog to be even more of an anathema than pouring rain. Almost everything is relative.

Then there is the factor of temperature. For several reasons one does not play golf when it is below freezing.[6] The hottest day on which I've ever played was 102 degrees Fahrenheit in the shade. It almost killed me. Between those extremes, however, temperature is no problem on the course—as long as you dress accordingly. If it's cold, bundle up. If it's hot, be sure to take a towel to mop your brow. Since Exotica is so close to the equator, it has relatively little variation in temperature. Courses in the temperate zone, however, may be quite cool in the early morning or toward evening in comparison to midday. Most experienced golfers go forth prepared for pretty much anything anytime.

Climate and ecology are close relatives. One of the angriest letters I ever received was from a woman who had learned that I encourage golf. "Don't you know, Dr. Peck, that golf courses are ecological disasters?" she chastised me, going on for pages about the evils of fertilizer, the misuse of land, the abuse of water, and so on. Already condemned, I made no reply.

Like other mystics, enamored with interconnections, I am actually a born ecologist. I am also a lover of beauty and fun. It seems to me that what this lady was saying could also be said about lawns, flower gardens, swimming pools—both public and private—and most farms, as well as a huge number of other artifices that nurture us humans. To be as strident as she is is the equivalent of arguing on behalf of slums. Many quite lovely housing areas would, in fact, look like ecological disasters were it not for the fairways that amble between their homes and that serve as commons—communal lawns—for the homeowners.

The majority of golf course designers and managers are remarkably ecologically minded. My critic listed the abuse of water as one of the sins I was encouraging. It is true that golf courses use an enormous amount of water to spray their fairways and greens to keep them all verdant. However, I have yet to play on a course in an area where water is potentially scarce that did not use effluent water for the purpose.[7]

I have a need to talk about golf carts, and this section on ecology seems a more proper spot than any—particularly since my letter-writing critic listed them as one of the ecological sins I was encouraging. By golf carts, please understand that I mean small four-wheel motorized vehicles that seat two people and carry their clubs on a space in back. The matter of golf carts and their management is a tangible symbol of the extraordinary variety of golf courses.[8]

In the interest of generating revenue and speeding up play, and as Exotica is an elegant venue high in tourist demand, the use of carts there is mandatory. Periodically the resort considers offering caddies to help the local economy, but what with many hundreds of workers in the hotel and at the course, it is already far and away the largest employer on the island. It does, however, license a dozen boys and girls to discreetly hawk on the cart paths the lost balls they've found and washed to look like new. Given the exceptional drainage, carts are allowed on all fairways, and the gravel cart paths extend only from the front of the green to the end of the next tee. Narrow concrete bridges span the gulches.

Just as some look down on others as fair-weather golfers, so those who like to walk the length of the course carrying their clubs may look down on cart riders as weaklings. In my case they are right. I am weak, although perhaps not spiritually so. Due to a severe degenerative disease of my spine and, more recently, arthritis in my hips, I cannot walk the entirety of nine holes, much less eighteen, even with a caddie carrying my bag for me. On a course such as Exotica, where one can ride the fairway, I can make eighteen.[9] What I am saying is that without carts, despite their possible ecological vices, I would have had to stop playing golf over five years ago. Thank God for golf carts. And thank God for golf. It is, given certain mechanical aids, the only outdoor sport I know that can still be played—and even played well—by those of us who are both ancient and decrepit (but not yet bedridden or wheelchair bound). It's a blessing.

We work and play not only in a geographical climate but also in an economic one. Throughout the world today the most glaring feature of that economic climate is the rapidly widening gulf between the rich and the poor. I have no specific suggestion here to alter that reality. I do believe it terribly important, however, that we don't become oblivious to it. The fact is that the vast majority of human beings in all nations do not have the money or the leisure to play golf. As we ride our carts along Exotica's fairways, it would be wise for us to remember that we are privileged. That playing golf is a privilege. When you are trying to hit out of a cavernous sand trap, it may be quite difficult to remember that it is a privilege. Nonetheless, if you can remember it—if you can think of yourself as fortunate at that moment—your attitude may be such that you will hit out of it more easily.

The climate of our times is even vaster than its economics and meteorology. Whether we appreciate it or not, we are all of us agents of history. When we die, each and every one of us will leave this world a bit better or a bit worse as a result of our presence in it. How are we to live with this awesome responsibility? The answer, of course, is a paradox.

Tom Langford, who was dean of the Duke Divinity School at the time, wrote a book entitled *Christian Wholeness*.[10] (He might as well have called it *Jewish Wholeness* or *Buddhist Wholeness* or, better yet, *Human Wholeness*.) In it he described thirteen pairs of opposites or paradoxes that we humans must come to embrace if we are to lead lives that are truly whole. One of those pairs he labeled "liberation and celebration."

By *liberation* (as in liberation theology) he meant the responsibility we all have to liberate ourselves and others from poverty, oppression, racism, and all the other sins and evils of the world. When we celebrate, on the other hand, not only are we enjoying ourselves, but we are praising God (or the universe) for all the beauty and goodness in the world. We are called to both celebration and liberation. If we lose sight of either, we become unbalanced. We lose our perspective. As Langford so cogently pointed out, those whose primary focus is liberation tend to become "fanatic and glum," while those whose primary focus is celebration tend to be "frothy and glib."

In keeping our balance, I do not mean to imply that we should devote each of our days exactly 50 percent to liberation and 50 percent to celebration. As Ecclesiastes might have put it, "There's a time to work and a time to play." Golf—and hence this book—is fundamentally a matter of play and celebration. Consequently, I will not again focus upon our gigantic large-scale societal obligations. Although golf has its moral lessons, we need to keep our perspective about the fact that it can be—indeed, *should* be—fun. Nonetheless, as I celebrate golf, I shall from time to time be reminding golfers of their everyday paradoxical obligations to one another and, above all, to themselves.

NOTES

1. I won't bother you by listing dimensions other than length, breadth, and height, except to note that mystics consider God or "the unseen order of things" to be an additional one, along with some others, to be eventually discussed.

2. Okinawa sits square in the middle of what the inhabitants of the western Pacific call "Typhoon Alley," so I have played golf several times on the close periphery of typhoons. The experience was one of hilarity more than golf.

3. When playing, all serious golfers wear special shoes that usually have spikes or cleats in their soles. Although helpful, it is not essential to do so on a flat, dry course on a dry day. But wet grass is slippery, and I once broke my ankle because I was too careless to put on my golf shoes when I went out on an empty course to hit a few practice balls in between rain squalls. On another occasion, when I didn't even own a pair of golf shoes, I almost drowned on a course in Arizona. Arizona, of all places! I had scooted down the steep bank of a pond to try to retrieve my ball. I not only failed to retrieve the ball, but I couldn't get back up the bank and kept slipping farther down. My partner, a stranger until then, finally had to pull me out of this predicament by my armpits. "My God, man, don't you have spikes on?" he asked with astonishment. I am red-faced until this day. Golf is a potentially dangerous sport. You can, for instance, get hit by lightning, another player's club, or a hard-hit drive. But its most common dangers can be avoided by not being too cheap to buy a pair of golf shoes or too careless to wear them.

4. Some golf clubs will mark the particularly swampy areas of its fairways with a boundary of chalk, thereby designating them as spots from which you may remove your ball unpenalized. Such markings also serve to warn the groundskeepers where not to mow, since attempting to mow them will grind up the turf.

5. The most common is divots. Divots are slices of turf that even the pros routinely create as they hit under the ball with their iron shots on a dry course. When the turf is damp, the divots are likely to be gigantic (and impeding), and in making them the player will often spatter himself with mud. It has been suggested that the bizarre drinking toast "Here's mud in your eye" originated out of the trenches of

World War I. To my knowledge, its origin had nothing to do with golf, although if it did, it might be more explainable. Incidentally, this is the one advantage that a sight-impaired golfer may have in wet conditions: Only his spectacles will get muddied, and not his corneas.

6. This is not because golfers won't play in subzero temperatures; it is because they are not allowed to. It is not because you cannot stick a tee into frozen ground; it is that walking on a frozen green will destroy it. This is why during the winter, on certain otherwise playable courses, you should be prepared for your scheduled tee time to be postponed for up to two hours on account of what is called a "frost delay." The authorities won't let you out to play until the greens are thawed.

7. For *effluent,* read "untreated, recycled sewage water." This may be a reason for you to rinse thoroughly after you get home from the course, particularly after you've gotten "mud in your eye."

8. I can think of at least five different categories of courses in this regard, along with subcategories:

   i. Courses that have neither carts nor caddies. Often these are the plainest and least expensive courses. The golfer must carry his own clubs or else pull or push them on a cheap, simple two-wheeled contraption.

   i. Courses where the golfer must walk throughout but is required to hire a caddie to carry his or her clubs. In "underdeveloped" countries this practice serves to provide desperately needed local employment.

   iii. Courses where the player must ride a golf cart. On some courses these carts are gas operated; on others, electric. There may be three reasons to make carts mandatory:

      a. It may increase course income through cart rental fees.

      b. It may speed up play, which means that more golfers can be accommodated.

      c. Occasional courses are extremely spread out, with journeys of half a mile or more between tees. They would be impossible without carts.

   iv. Wherever carts are used, mandatory or not, there will be cart paths. These run not only in between tees but generally alongside the length of the hole. They may be constructed of dirt, gravel, macadam, or some other substance.

   v. Carts are never allowed on the tees, or on or near the greens. Otherwise the rules are variable:

      a. On some courses a cart must stay on a cart path at all times. The player must always walk from the path to make her midfairway shots.

      b. On other courses the 90-degree rule prevails, meaning she can drive her cart onto the fairway to make her shot, but only at a right angle in relation to the location of her ball, and after hitting she must immediately drive directly back to the path.

      c. On still other courses the player may drive her cart along the middle of the length of the fairway.

      d. On yet others carts are allowed onto the fairways of the majority of holes but not on a minority, which are ecologically delicate.

e. The rules can change at the reasonable discretion of the course manager. After a heavy rain, for instance, a course that normally allows carts on its fairways may restrict them to the path for several days or more.

f. There can be any permutation or combination of the above. Many courses, for example, have both carts to rent and an unpredictable supply of caddies on hand, but they will also allow you to carry your own clubs, if that is what turns you on.

9. On a course where carts are restricted to their paths, play is actually no faster than on a course without carts. By the time one has walked to his ball, hit it, and walked back to his cart, no time has been saved. That bit of walking, constantly relieved by sitting in my cart, I can handle for nine holes. It is good exercise for me. I must admit, however, that on such courses I occasionally play what is called "cart golf." This is when one doesn't play the hole as best as it can be played but rather hits as close as he can to the cart path so he won't have to walk so far.

10. Thomas A. Langford, *Christian Wholeness* (Nashville, TN: Upper Room Books, 1979).

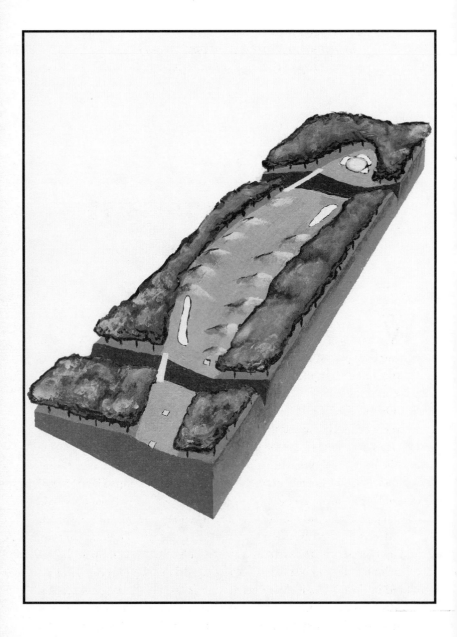

*To be a good teacher, exercise your compassion and
imagination; to be a good pupil, exercise your
capacity to learn independently.*

H O L E   1 0

TEACHING AND LEARNING

We have arrived at "the turn": the point of transition between the
first nine holes and the last nine of the customary eighteen-hole round,
the transition from the front nine to the back nine. My blood begins to
pulse a bit faster.

On the surface of things, there is usually no dramatic difference
between the front nine and the back nine. Even on this very special course.
Exotica's back nine is, for the most part, a mirror image of its front nine.
For the next two holes we shall climb back up the other side of Mount
Intrepid. Then we'll play another par 3 at its leeward top. Then we shall
descend again on another long par 5 and play the last five holes out on the
coastal plain. Still, this moment usually engenders a feeling of excitement.

Most superficially, it is a simple matter of score. Golfers don't just
add up their score at the end of eighteen holes; they add it up at the end
of each nine. Indeed, scorecards are designed for this purpose. If I have
scored in the 50s, as is my wont, on the front nine, I may still score in
the 40s on the back nine and end up with a total score under 100 (making it an excellent day for me). And if by some fluke I've scored in the
40s on the front nine, it then becomes conceivable that I might continue
doing so on the back nine—even to the point of breaking 90 for the
whole eighteen. (Oh, glory!)

More deeply, underneath this enamorment with the score and fascination with magical numbers lies something more mystical. The turn is a moment of hope. Although seldom fulfilled in my case, it may offer hope for glory. In all other circumstances it is, at the very least, a moment of hope for redemption. No matter how badly I've played until now, on the back nine I may redeem myself. I just might.

So the back nine offers the opportunity for a fresh start. And this book will take advantage of that opportunity. Its flavor will shift somewhat. The illustrations will change from those of the Exotica course to ones that are more "abstract," illustrating principles rather than geography. No longer will I be giving detailed descriptions of the holes and how to play them. Indeed, just for fun and variety, I won't even describe this hole at all. Or the next one. And I will turn from the primarily physical stresses of golf to its more psychological stresses. Thus far I haven't even mentioned half the stress—and the virtue—of golf: other people. So I shall be speaking much more about people, of how they can help us or hinder us on the golf course (and in the course of life). And more about how we can hinder ourselves, particularly through anger—sometimes in response to other people and sometimes only in response to our own fallibility.

But in the one most important respect the focus will be the same. Throughout I have been suggesting that golf can be—indeed, should be—looked upon as a spiritual discipline, which means it represents an extraordinary learning opportunity. We are free to use it as such or not. The plain fact of the matter, however, is that whenever we learn something of significance, our spirit or soul makes a growth leap. Conversely, when we fail to learn, our soul fails to grow. If we cease learning entirely, it rapidly begins to shrivel.

Since golf is so much about learning, it would seem smart to find yourself a teacher immediately—not a mentor, but a golf teaching professional. Well—maybe yes, maybe no. The matters of teaching and learning are not that simple.

I've recounted how I *chose* to take up golf at the age of thirty-two. In my late childhood and early adolescence, however, golf was something foisted upon me.

My father loved golf and was very good at it. He wanted me to be like him in all respects. Among other things that meant he wanted me to love golf and play as well as he did. He was also a great believer in lessons. Consequently, starting at the age of ten, I received a number of lessons from the local teaching pro. Additionally, my father was a compulsive teacher himself. "You lifted your head on that one. Remember to keep your eye on the ball next time," he would say. And before I began the next shot, he'd instruct me, "Now keep your head down. And remember to keep your left arm straight." So it would go, shot after shot, every shot. It was not fun.

In many ways my father was a wonderful man. He taught me some extremely important lessons about how to live well, and he taught them just by being himself. But he left me with an aversion to golf lessons. I have forgiven him for this, but the aversion continues to plague me to this day.

Nine years ago, when I was at the supposedly mature age of fifty-four and my father was already deceased, Lily and I took a lengthy vacation at an elegant golf resort on the island of Kauai. Lily was not then as hooked on golf as she is today, so half the time I would play without her. What happens on a busy, elegant course, such as Exotica or the one on Kauai, when you make a tee time as a single, is that you will be matched up with one, two, or three other golfers. On a particular day that will long live in my memory, I was matched up with a handsome blond visiting teaching professional in his thirties, his beautiful new bride, who was in her late twenties, and another single, a gray-haired psychiatrist, who was probably sixty. I was quick to give the teaching pro very strong nonverbal messages that I didn't want to receive any pointers from him. The other psychiatrist didn't need to do this, since he was at least as good a player as the pro.

So that left the pro with only his young bride to prey upon. And prey he did, starting on the first tee. "Hit all out," he told her. "Don't worry about a thing. Just use your natural swing, and don't hesitate to make it a big one." She was just getting settled to do so when he then would say, "Hon, I'm afraid your feet are all wrong. You're aiming way off to the left. Here, let me show you how to place your feet." And he did. And he did it again. In fact, he did it every shot she made, including each of her putts, for every one of the eighteen holes.

His wife's game naturally did not improve as we went along. Mine got worse and worse. I couldn't concentrate on my own ball. I seemed only able to concentrate upon the travesty to which I was a witness. When the young woman happened to hit well, I congratulated her. "Nice shot!" I'd exclaim. "Now you don't need any more lessons." But her husband didn't seem to get the message. Nor did she. Eventually I began to think she was as pathological as he. I kept hoping she would say, "Hey, won't you just shut up and let me play the way I want to?" But she didn't, and he didn't shut up. And with an unwavering smile on her face, she just took it and took it and took it.

It was one of the most unpleasant afternoons of my life and certainly one of the poorest rounds of golf I'd ever played. I knew what my problem was from the start. All of my own hot buttons were being pushed, yet I seemed helpless to stop my emotional disintegration. The other psychiatrist, however, looked utterly unfazed. His calm, considered game was consistently close to perfect throughout.

When it was finally all over, I asked the psychiatrist if I could talk with him for a few minutes. "I need your help," I said. He agreed. I told him about my father. I explained how I couldn't concentrate on my game because I was so caught up empathizing with the pro's wife and the abuse she was receiving, and how it all made me feel as if I were an eleven-year-old back trying to play golf with my father. "But it didn't seem to upset you," I concluded. "Didn't it bother you?"

"No," my colleague responded monosyllabically.

"It didn't bother you in the least?" I asked with amazement.

"No."

I began to wonder if I was crazy. "My God," I pleaded, "didn't you think there was anything wrong with the man?"

"Well," my colleague acknowledged, "I did imagine that some morning they'll find him in bed with a five-iron stuck in the middle of his forehead."

That fellow psychiatrist taught me something about detachment, and although I'm better at it now in many ways, I'm still trying to learn the lesson almost every time I'm on the course.

Detachment is the opposite of attachment. Psychiatrists often use a professional synonym for attachment: *cathexis*. The relevant verb is *to cathect.* We cathect something whenever we invest emotional energy in it, whether that something be another person, a rose garden, playing golf, or hating lessons.

To most lay people *attachment* implies a positive relationship of loving or liking. The reason psychiatrists use the special synonym *cathexis,* however, is our experience that human attachments are almost as likely to be negative as positive, hateful as loving.

For example, I once saw a late-middle-aged man for an hour-long psychiatric evaluation. He spent the entirety of the hour angrily talking over and over again about his hatred for the corporation that had, supposedly unfairly, fired him some eighteen years previously. I couldn't get him to speak about anything else. It was obvious that the primary emotional investment of his life was in that corporation, which he hated, and in that hateful event of his distant past. He was still cathected to the corporation. I referred him on to a psychiatric social worker for psychotherapy, but he quickly dropped out, unwilling to practice detachment or "de-cathexis," preferring to hold on to his attachment no matter how strange, angry, and self-defeating.

The only way I am different from that man is that I realize that my hot buttons about lessons are a sign of a negative cathexis—a ridiculous attachment to events of fifty years ago; that it is all self-defeating; and that I do need to practice de-cathexis or detachment.

How do you learn detachment? The only answer is our three-step process, by now hopefully familiar:

1. *Self-diagnosis.* You don't want to detach yourself from everything, only from those cathexes, positive and negative, that are causing you a problem, such as ruining your golf game or some other aspect of your life. Realize you have a problem, and name it. Usually you will be able to do this by yourself. Upon occasion you may need to seek the services of a professional (golf pro or psychotherapist) to assist you in finding the right name for your disorder.

2. *Kenosis.* Having named your problem, get rid of it. *Empty* yourself of your cathexis, your emotional investment in your old pattern. You have to want to do it so badly that you are willing to surrender those old attachments. It is primarily a matter of will and . . .

3. *Practice.* Empty yourself of the destructive attachment, and reempty yourself of it, and do it again and again and again. We don't speak of "*doing* detachment"; we speak of *practicing* it. A neurosis is not like a little pebble you just kick off to the side of the path; usually it is more like a huge boulder obstructing the road ahead of you—a boulder you must chisel away at day after day, month after month, year after year.

I cannot blame my teaching neurosis entirely on my father. I also blame the pro he hired to give me lessons. He might have been a very good pro for some people, but not for an eleven-year-old. Actually, from talking to others who have taken lessons, either as children or adults, I get the impression that many teaching pros are not very good teachers. This is not surprising. The problem is inherent in their role. Their role is to teach golf, and being well-motivated professionals, they want to make damn sure that their pupils (or their pupils' parents) get their money's worth. Consequently, they overteach.

A typical lesson with a beginner is not a dialogue. Out on the driving range, the beginner will hit a ball. The pro will make a proclamation. The beginner will hit another ball. The pro will make a second proclamation. And so on . . . and on and on. In between the beginner's attempts to hit the ball, the pro's proclamations will go something like this:

"You're trying to hit it too hard. Hit it easier this time."

"That's better, but you lifted your head up. That's why you topped the ball. Keep your head down. I'll watch out for the ball for you."

"Very good. But you need to remember to keep your left arm straight. Don't worry about your right elbow, but bend your left one as little as possible."

"You're hitting flat-footed. You want to raise your left heel off the ground as you're making your backswing. Here, like this."

"Now do it again, only this time really lift your left heel."

"That was fine. But you're still flat-footed on your follow-through. Remember, left heel off the ground on your backswing, and *right* heel off the ground on your follow-through."

"Well, you'll get the hang of it. Now I want you to cock your wrists on your backswing and then uncock them as you hit the ball. That will give you more power. Here, watch me, watch my wrists."

"Much better with the wrists, but you forgot to keep your left arm straight."

"Where are you aiming? I want you to aim for that pin over there. What you want to do is draw an imaginary straight line from the tips of your toes to the pin. Like this."

"Your feet were pointed right, but you lifted your head up again. I guess you wanted to see if you really were aiming correctly, ha ha. That's natural. But keep your head down until you've finished your follow-through. You'll still have plenty of time to watch your ball."

"Well, you sliced it. That's because you didn't follow through."

"Well, you sure corrected it. You hooked. That's because you followed through too much. You want to follow through toward the pin."

"Good. But you're still a bit flat-footed."

"I know I told you to cock your wrists, but not that much. You're overcocking them. Cock them gently."

"Watch your left arm. You've really got a problem with that arm."

"Bend more at the knees. Not too much, just a little."

"Now let's take a look at your hips. Golfers tend to forget about their hips. Now what you want to do is . . ."

I won't go on. When the pro says at the conclusion of your lesson, "See you same time next Thursday, right?" how do you answer him? The problem with such overkill is that it can create not only an aversion to golf lessons but an aversion to golf itself. Please don't let that happen to you.

It might help you to pity the poor golf pro. He is in a bind. Among other things, chances are he received no training in the subject of teaching and learning. Psychotherapy is mostly about teaching and learning, yet when I was in training as a psychiatrist, I received no instruction about it, either. I mostly received instruction in analyzing what was wrong with people, and I imagine golf professionals mostly receive instruction in how to analyze what's wrong with a person's swing.[1]

Yet the greater problem, I still believe, is our roles. It is the role of a teacher to teach; the role of a psychiatrist to supposedly "make" her sick patients healthy; and the role of a golf professional to "make" his pupils into good golfers. As quickly as possible. And we receive strong messages from our professors, from our pupils and patients, and from our own egos that we damn well better do it. But it's all wrong.

What good psychotherapists learn—often only after many, many years of practice—is that their real role is to build a good relationship with their patients, a relationship that is mostly fun or so enriching that they actually come to enjoy psychotherapy. If this can be accomplished, then the patient will probably get well by himself. Sometimes we speak of this as the therapist "being in community" with her patient. Such relationships are naturally healing, and the therapist doesn't need to do much of anything else. I believe the same principle holds for the teaching of golf.

How might I today, as an elderly psychotherapist, give an eleven-year-old beginner his first golf lesson? Let's call the lad Tommy. We'd meet at the clubhouse. Taking an estimate of his height, I'd pick out from the collection a child's 7-iron of the right length. "Come on," I'd say, "I want to take you to a favorite spot of mine."

Wordlessly, I'd walk Tommy out to a knoll overlooking a short par 3, and we'd sit down there in the rough. Then I'd begin the way any psychiatrist would, asking, "What brings you to see me?"

"I'm here for a golf lesson."

"Have you ever had a golf lesson before?"

"No."

Good, I'd think. *That's one piece of baggage we won't have to carry.* Out loud I'd ask, "Have you ever played golf before?"

"Just a couple of holes with my parents."

"Did you like it?"

"No. I wasn't any good at it. I guess that's why they want me to have lessons."

"How about you? Do you want to have golf lessons?"

At this point Tommy looks flustered. "I suppose so," he stammers. "I haven't thought about it."

"Let me tell you something, Tommy. Golf is a sport. It's not like something you have to do. No one should have to play a sport he doesn't enjoy. If you decide you don't want golf lessons anymore, just say so, and I'll tell your parents it's not the right time for you. Okay?"

Now Tommy looks embarrassed. "You mean it's my choice?"

"Yup. Entirely. I want you to remember that. Will you?"

"Okay."

After a moment of silence, I ask, "Since you don't know yet whether you're going to like to play golf, what do you like to do? What do you really like?"

"I like to read."

"Oh? What do you read?"

"All kinds of stuff. Comics. The Hardy Boys and Nancy Drew. Dickens."

"Dickens? What have you read by Dickens?"

"*David Copperfield. Tale of Two Cities. Oliver Twist.* Now I'm starting on *Great Expectations.*"

"No kidding? Which did you like best so far?"

"Tale of Two Cities."

"That's my favorite too. You know, Tommy, you're a lucky man."

"Why?"

"Because people who like to read a lot tend to do better in life than those who don't. And the younger they start liking to read, the better. Particularly when they read things like Dickens. You're very smart to be able to read Dickens at your age."

I allow a silence to fall between us. After a minute Tommy can't bear it anymore. "When are we going to start the golf lesson?" he asks.

"You're in a hurry, are you? Okay. Stand up and hold this club as if you were going to hit with it."

Tommy does so.

"Are you right-handed?" I ask.

"Mostly."

"Do you write with your right hand?"[2]

"Yes."

"If you want to, you can hold the club just the way you're doing now," I say. "People hold their clubs in all kinds of ways. But it's not the most common way. Would you like me to teach you what I think is the best way?"

"Yeah."

"Okay. Place the top part of the grip in the palm of your left hand and close your hand around it. Excellent. That's what golfers call 'shak-

ing hands with the club.' Hold on to it in that shake-hands position. Now bring your right hand up just below your left. That's right. Here comes the tricky part. I want you to take the little finger of your right hand and wrap it over the index finger—the bottom finger—of your left hand. Perfect. You've got it. I didn't even have to touch your hands to show you. How does it feel?"

"Okay, I guess."

"All right. Keep on holding the club that way, firmly but not tight. No need to get white knuckles. Now start to swing the club. Swing it any old way you want. Little wiggles. Big swings. Great. How does it feel?"

"Okay."

"Does it feel as good as when you were holding it before?"

"Yeah. Better maybe."

"Great. Keep swinging it."

I let him swing the club for another minute. "Still feel okay?"

"Yeah."

"Do you think you can remember to grip it that way?"

"Yes."

"Let's see. Drop the club on the ground. Okay, now pick it up the way you did before. Perfect. Swing it a little more. Good. Are you sure you can remember that grip?"

"I'm sure."

"Wonderful," I say. "It's been a very good lesson."

Tommy drops the club, aghast. "You mean that's all?"

"Yup."

"Aren't we going to hit any balls?"

"Nope. Not today. That's the next lesson. Next lesson you can hit all the balls you want. Hundreds of them."

Tommy's face is a mixture of eagerness and disappointment. "So this is it?"

"Yes, except for your homework assignment."

Tommy's face now totally falls. "Oh no, not homework."

"Remember I told you that golf is a sport," I remind him. "You don't have to play golf if you don't want to. You don't have to take lessons if you don't want to. And you don't have to do golf homework if you don't want to. But you might want to do *this* homework. Shall I tell you about it?"

"Sure."

"Well, I brought you to this knoll for a reason. Right from this spot where we're sitting, you can see the men's tee, the women's tee, and the green. You can watch how every player swings, and you can see exactly how well their shot works. You can even keep score on them. My homework assignment is for you to come to this very same spot for a whole day—let's say nine to two—and watch how the players swing and then see how they do. Even two days if you're up to it. What do you think?"

"It might be fun."

"Let me tell you what would be even more fun. That would be to be scientific about it. Bring a pad of paper and some pencils, and write down the grade you'd give every player. Two grades. A grade for their swing and a grade for their shot."

"I'd be like a teacher."

"Partly. But there'll be some surprises. You'll see some players with graceful swings who make lousy shots. And you'll see some players with awkward swings who make great shots. Still, if you keep close score, like a scientist, I'll bet you that the players with graceful swings will make more good shots than the ones with strange swings. Just keep a scientific record of your grades."

"Neat."

"You'll see some players take graceful practice swings, but then when they actually hit the ball, they'll be awkward," I continue. "I'll explain to you why that is some other day. Anyway, just grade their swing when they're hitting, not when they're practicing."

"Okay."

"And I want you to watch the women just as closely as the men. Good golfers are all beautiful to watch, and some women have the greatest swings I know."

"Okay."

"Now, if it's raining or you can't come out here for some other reason, what I'd like you to do instead is to watch one or two pro tournaments on TV. You don't have to grade the pros—they're all good—but I want you to look at their swings very closely."

"Wow," Tommy says, "this is the first time I've ever been told to watch TV for homework!"

"There's a reason for this homework," I go on, chuckling. "About ten minutes twice a day, I'd like you to swing this seven-iron. You can take it home with you and bring it back next time. Just swing it in the air. Outdoors. I don't want you to hit anything with it. But I want you to swing it the way you've seen the good players or the pros do it. In fact, when you're swinging, I want you to imagine that you already are a pro. Imagine that you're one of the best golfers in the whole world. Any questions?"

"No—yes. Are you sure next time we can hit some balls?"

"I'm sure. So you do want to see me for another lesson?"

"Yeah."

"Well, when we get back to the clubhouse, I'd better buy you a glove, then. I don't want you to get blisters with all that swinging."

Ambling back, I suggest, "If your parents ask you what we did today, tell them that we worked on your grip. Nothing's more important than your grip. By the way, what did you like best about *Tale of Two Cities*?"

"The ending. Maybe it's gruesome, but I liked it when Sydney Carton went to the guillotine. I mean it was sad, but I liked it at the same time, you know what I mean?"

"I sure do," I responded. "You don't happen to remember what Carton said at the end, do you?"

"Yeah. 'It is a far, far better thing that I do, than I have ever done; it is a far, far better rest that I go to, than I have ever known.'"

"You are good," I comment. "You are really good."

Naturally I made a few adjustments to Tommy because of his age and unusual intelligence. Nonetheless, if I ever had the opportunity to give a fifty-year-old beginner his first golf lesson—and if I could get away with it—I'd do it pretty much the same way.

I do not want to imply that the majority of golf teaching professionals aren't good teachers. Nor that you shouldn't avail yourself of their services. It is likely I'd be a better player were it not for my aversion to lessons.[3] Remember that virtually all tournament-playing professionals have their own teaching pros.[4] They can't afford not to.

I receive a huge number of inquiries about how to find the "right" psychotherapist. My suggestions are almost identical as to how to find the "right" golf teacher. Don't hesitate to shop around, even if it means going far afield—within reason. If your first lesson is with a pro you don't like, don't continue; immediately seek another. You want—and need—a pro with whom you feel a certain emotional connection, a woman or man whose style and rhythm of teaching will match your style and rhythm of learning. You deserve a pro with whom you can be in relationship, "in community."

On the other hand, I don't mean to imply that my personal aversion to lessons has all been to the bad. I suspect it is one of the factors that has made me a self-learner in golf, as well as in theology and other spheres of activity. I never go out on the course these days without first thinking, *I wonder what the next two hours will have to teach me?* I vow to learn at least one thing from each nine holes, and usually I succeed. Usually it is something prosaic, like the invisible roll to the left or right on a certain green from a certain point while putting. Often it is a relearning, like, *Relax, Peck, relax. Remember to relax before you hit.* Occasionally, however, it is something relatively new and practically earthshaking.

I write this after returning from a nine-hole round. On the eighth tee, facing a three-club wind, I hit a horrible drive dead into a ball-eating uncultivated rough a mere 40 yards ahead. The lost ball was not the problem. The problem was that my backswing felt wrong well before I hit the ball. The moral: "If your backswing feels wrong, *stop.* Don't try to complete your swing. Stop and start over again. Readjust your stance. Take a practice swing. If it feels good, then try it for real. But don't hesitate to stop in midswing if your backswing doesn't feel just right." I've watched some of the best playing pros do this in nationally televised tournaments. Why shouldn't I do it too? It may seem prosaic, but it was like a profound and veritable revelation to me that I could halt an impending atrocity merely by acting rapidly on my feeling—even if it means looking like a fool. Better to look like a fool before you've hit the ball than after.

I have known many middle-aged or elderly golfers who do not seem to be self-learners. They are constantly checking in with their pros, looking for some new tip from on high. It is as if they are unable to give themselves tips. Since their game usually never gets any better, I have wondered if they don't have an authority problem of sorts.[5] It is not that they are antagonistic to authority (as I myself used to be until my psychoanalysis at age thirty). It is the other way around. They seem to need an external authority to tell them what to do. Conversely, they seem unable to assume the authority to figure out things for themselves.

I also don't mean to imply that I can never ask for help. If I happen to be playing with a particularly good golfer, I will on occasion ask him or her toward the end of the round, "If you had *one* thing to suggest I might do to improve my game, what would it be?" I have received a few good free tips that way from pros and amateurs alike. In golf as in the rest of life, we need our fellow human beings to give us a helping hand from time to time. The art is in the timing—knowing when to ask for help and when to help yourself.

I have often been asked, "Dr. Peck, since we're all neurotic, how do you know when to get into psychotherapy?"

"When you're stuck" is my standard reply. If you are clearly maturing psychospiritually, and one by one getting rid of the roadblocks you've placed in your own way without external assistance, there's usually no reason to invest a lot of money and time in professional psychotherapy. But at least once—and often several times—in the course of a lifetime for most people, that's not the case. If you find yourself butting your head up against the same stone wall over and over again without knowing why, without even knowing what the wall *is*, then it's time to get yourself off to a psychotherapist. Still, doing so requires great smarts. Most of us are not so smart. Sadly, most people will spend their entire lives butting their heads against the same stone wall without ever awakening to the fact.

The same principle holds true for golf. As noted, even the greatest tournament-playing pros will make an occasional shot that is truly dreadful—even a shank. The pro will then immediately analyze what he did wrong, making sure not to make the same mistake on his next shot. We amateurs, not so well trained in stringent self-examination, have a tendency to hit two or more shots in a row in an identically mistaken fashion, duplicating the atrocious outcome precisely. Unless we are beginners or duffers, we do then recognize the handwriting on the wall at this point and attempt the necessary change.

But the attempt may not succeed. If the handwriting on the wall is a slice, for instance, and we persist in slicing one long shot after another despite our sincere effort to change something about our swing, then we are stuck. We might ask one of our fellow players what we are doing wrong. Should no good answer be forthcoming, *that* is the time to get yourself off to a teaching professional. You don't understand the nature of the roadblock you have created for yourself, and you need the pro for what he is trained to do best: analyzing the disorders of grips, stances, swings, and, not infrequently, states of mind.

NOTES

1. It might seem strange that teachers receive so little instruction about how to teach and how students learn, but the fact is that good literature on the subject is remarkably scarce. There is an egregious body of research that psychologists must study called "learning theory," but it has much more relevance to Pavlov's dogs than to human beings. Consequently, the training of teachers is far more content-oriented than process-oriented. I'm not sure what the problem is, but I suspect that good teaching and good learning are inherently mysterious processes and hence a somewhat "mystical" subject. It is no accident, then, that the best hints I know about the matter are provided in relatively esoteric religious writings, such as those about Zen Buddhist masters and their koans. For someone who wants to delve more deeply into this important topic, I would particularly recommend the several edited collections of Sufi stories by Idries Shah (published by Penguin). Sufism, as you will remember, is a mystical offshoot of Islam and, as interpreted by Shah, seems to have its central focus on matters of teaching and learning. I would not necessarily push these stories off on golf professionals, but I do urge them on all who aspire to be psychotherapists. Then again, maybe the best golf professionals are, most basically, born psychotherapists.

2. There are more elaborate tests to discern true handedness, but this is usually all that's called for.

3. During my childhood I had a piano teacher who didn't help either.

4. Teaching pros need not be great or even good players themselves. Often they are not. There is a long tradition in many sports of "nonplaying coaches." But they do need to love the game, whatever it may be.

5. Often their game will actually get worse after a visit to the pro. Many a man I've met on the course who is not doing well tells me, "I went to see my pro last week, and he taught me a new grip. I'm still trying to get used to it. Of course I'll get the hang of it pretty soon. He's really a marvelous pro. Does wonders for my game. I don't know what I'd do without him." Sometimes I'll meet the same man a month or two later when he's slipped back into his old grip and is clearly doing a bit better.

Among the great arts of living, some need to learn how to speed up; others to slow down. Many of us need to learn both, each in its appropriate time.

H O L E   1 1

TIME

I wish to speak of golf and time.

Many nongolfers consider the game itself to be nothing but a waste of time. They're entitled to their opinion, of course, but they're wrong.

Still, there are ways to squander time while at golf. The greatest— and most common—is looking for lost balls in the deep rough. The rules place a limit of five minutes on this activity (if one knows the rules). The reason the rule is so liberal is because of the penalty if you can't find your ball. Usually you can't, and often when you do, it is unplayable. Moreover, while waiting, I have watched many a player finally find his ball and hack away at it, only to hit it a mere ten yards ahead into the same rough and then have to begin looking for it all over again. Unless it is high-stakes tournament play, after a minute of searching, a decent player, not wanting to delay his fellow players as well as those behind, will shrug his shoulders, exclaim, "Well, it's just a ball," drop another one, and get on with it.

The rational reason to search for your ball, as stated, is the score penalty if you can't find it. But people are not always rational. For many golfers a ball is not "just a ball." They will develop a mystical attachment to their ball that compels them to look for it regardless of

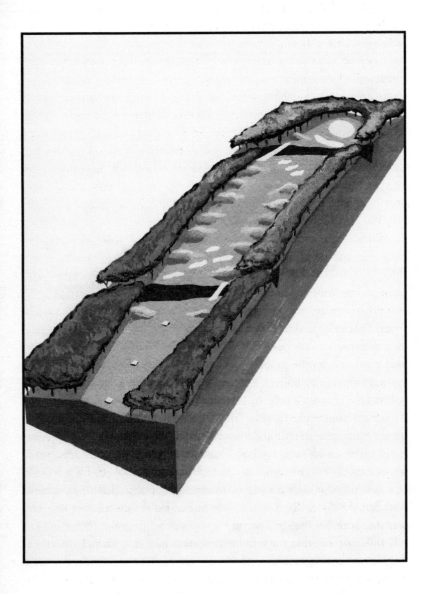

matters of score. They have lost a "friend." Even when they cannot find it, if while searching they happen to discover someone else's long-lost ball, they will feel strangely better. It is as if God had somehow replaced their old friend with a new one.

They will feel better particularly if the found ball is all white and unscarred. Once I managed a two-day tournament for a small group of highly rational and richly compensated top business executives. As we convened on the second morning, I mentioned that we had a box containing several dozen extra balls that they could have if they so cared. The words were hardly out of my mouth before these usually dignified men dived into the box, thrusting one another aside like a pride of starving lions at their prey. Yet had our roles been reversed, I might have done likewise. A brand-new golf ball is very beautiful. It is perhaps the cleanest thing in the whole world.

Nonetheless, on some occasions we need to remember that a ball is just a ball, and searching for it isn't worth either our own or others' time.

I dropped mention that golf is at least a nine-dimensional game. Length, breadth, and height are the dimensions we are most accustomed to think about. Space and time are two more.[1] For me, other people constitute a sixth dimension, and myself a seventh.[2] If we cannot factor both others and ourselves into the equation, the mathematics will be limited at best, and our thinking as imperfect as a flat soufflé.

My focus on this hole will be upon the dimension of time. Time is as shifty as the sand in a trap. To a five-year-old, next Christmas feels like an eternity away; for a sixty-year-old, it seems more like tomorrow. Time passes slowly when we are bored and rapidly when we are enjoying ourselves. Psychoactive drugs may dramatically alter a person's time sense.[3] Although there are mystical reasons to believe that time itself can shift, usually it is not time but our consciousness in relation to it that is doing the shifting.

Toward sunset, in the rain, or on a day when the constellations are in a bizarre configuration, one may get to play on an almost deserted course. On such rare occasions time need not be a factor. But given the popularity of the game and the law of supply and demand, the playing of golf is usually governed by the clock. Intensely so. One needs to make reservations for tee times; some busy courses do not even grant tee times to couples or twosomes, much less singles; carts may be mandated to speed up play. But stress is involved in being governed by the clock. Many golfers, for better or worse, seem to be immune to this stress. As a particularly anxious person, however, I often find the stress of time on a course to be every bit as much of a personal hazard for me as its sand traps and marshes.

For me the stress of time in golf is inextricably interwoven with my feelings about other people and, in particular, my feelings of obligation (healthy or neurotic) to them and my expectations (healthy or neurotic) of their obligation to me. The feelings of obligation that so bedevil me have two primary foci when I am playing golf: the people playing immediately ahead of me on the course and those playing immediately behind me. I shall now address each of these sources of tension in turn.

I hate waiting. I'll do almost anything to avoid standing in a queue. Delayed plane flights agitate me to a point where I can no longer think clearly or concentrate. I could go on and on.

To a certain extent, my aversion to waiting is the flip side of a virtue. One of my identities is that of an efficiency expert of sorts. As a psychotherapist, I used to try to help my patients stop spinning their wheels. Later, as an author and lecturer, one of my goals was to urge my audience to live their lives more efficiently. I hate waste of any kind. Wasted time is anathema to me, particularly when it adds up to a wasted life.

Ambiguities—even paradoxes—are involved in this matter of efficiency. One of them is succinctly summed up in the old proverb "Haste makes waste." Once when proofreading the transcription of a letter I'd dictated, I saw I'd written, "I hate to make hasty decisions." I made a handwritten footnote to the sentence: "P.S. I just lied to you. I love to make hasty decisions, but gradually I've learned usually not to." This is particularly true in my role as an author. Writers continually bump up against problems about how best to say what they want to say— knotty problems for which there are no quick solutions. The ideal solution will invariably come to me if I just wait . . . thoughtfully. But such waiting is not wasted time; it is thinking time. I write more slowly these

days in my old age, but I usually have less rewriting to do, and by wait-ing, on balance, I have become a bit more efficient at the business.

So I have learned something about how to wait properly. But not enough. And recently it is golf that has been teaching me how to do it better.

Golf is full of waiting.

The greatest kind of waiting in golf is one that I deeply enjoy. Much of the enormous etiquette to the game, which I shall address in depth on the next hole, has to do with the sequence in which the oth-ers with whom you are playing make their shots. A good deal of the time, you are waiting for your fellow players to hit. With but few exceptions, however, I do not find this kind of waiting the least bit onerous. We golfers like to watch one another shoot, and generally we feel that the waiting involved is a kind of dance, like an elegant minuet, in which we are as much participants as onlookers or mere bystanders.

But the waiting for golfers with whom you are not so engaged, who are playing one to 300 yards ahead of you—a foursome with which you have no relationship—is not enjoyable. It is boring, and when I am bored, I become irritated. For *irritated*, read "angry." My anger in this regard falls into two categories: reasonable and unreasonable.

Most of the time when players ahead are slowing you down, it is because the players ahead of them are slowing them down, and so forth. One can see enough of the course ahead to realize when this is the case. On a busy day play tends to move a bit slowly. That's just the way it is on a packed course. There's no point in getting annoyed at the golfers on the green ahead for taking their time with their putting when a four-some is standing around waiting on the very next tee. Yet I used to. This amazes me. It amazes me that I used to get angry at golfers for playing too slowly when, in fact, they were moving along as fast as they could under the circumstances. This is what I mean by unreasonable anger.

I put this anger in the past tense as if once upon a time, long, long ago on a bright sunny day, I was suddenly, magically healed of such ridiculousness. That's not the way it was. As noted, neuroses are not like little pebbles you simply kick off the path. I had to work at emp-tying myself of unnecessary impatience, long and hard. Even today when waiting on the course, I will feel twinges of the old irrational anger and must still remind myself that the golfers in front are taking their time through no fault of their own. But with such reminders I am now generally able to sit in the cart sniffing the flowers and enjoying the scenery.[4]

Why did I bother to work toward this current state of relative spiritual exaltation? I wish I could tell you that it was for the good of my soul (which it proved to be), but it was merely in order to play halfway decent golf. One cannot play decent golf when irritated. It is as simple as that. And I was damned if I was going to let my utterly unreasonable anger prevent me from playing well and enjoying it.

What about reasonable anger, however? Perhaps 25 percent of the time when the players ahead are holding you up, it is not because they too are being held up; it is because they are playing slowly—more slowly than they *should,* than they are supposed to. There are one or more totally empty holes ahead of them. They are not keeping up the proper pace. They are guilty of a moral infraction of sorts—a serious breach of golfing etiquette—and I get furious. Am I not right to do so? This anger I have not yet learned how to deal with. It is righteous anger, anger with cause, reasonable anger. But it screws up my game just as much as any other kind of anger, and while I have begun to work on it, I still have a very long way to go.

Why do some people play golf more slowly than they should? I mentioned the most common reason, endlessly searching for balls lost in the rough, but other reasons occur with damnable frequency:

• One or more of the players ahead is a beginner (or severe duffer—it is difficult to tell which from a distance). It's impossible to take twelve or more strokes to play out a hole without delaying the better players behind you. A busy course at a busy time of day is not a good place for beginners. Yet at some point, I remind myself, beginners must get themselves off of a driving range and onto a real course. On the other hand, those in the beginning stage may need to remind themselves that they are not required to play every hole out and that they can "pick up."

• It may also be difficult to discern between beginners and those who are plain thoughtless. For instance, on a course where carts are restricted to the path, it is not uncommon to see a man pick a club, amble 30 yards out to the middle of the fairway where his ball lies, decide it's not the right club, amble back to his cart, select a different club, and stroll back out onto the fairway again, before even preparing to make his shot. All experienced, efficient golfers, on the other hand, will take with them as many clubs as they might need whenever they depart from their cart. Is the one-club-at-a-time man a beginner who doesn't yet have the experience to know better, or is he an experienced golfer who's just not thinking? In either case he infuriates me.

• I have watched players a mere hundred yards ahead on the fairway take as many as seven practice swings before finally hitting for real. On such occasions I am willing to give you two-to-one odds that their real shot will be poor. Seldom is there any need to take more than two practice swings; usually no more than one; and, as I shall eventually discuss, there are times when one might be well advised to take no practice swing at all.

• Some players can do equally well at holding you up by an excessive waggle.[5] The waggle is a ritual of many possible components: touching the ground with the clubhead, lifting the clubhead above the ball, planting your feet into the ground, bending your knees up and down, wiggling your hips, resetting your feet, flexing your wrists with a foot-long pass over the ball, ad infinitum. It is usually performed in a magical sequence and is often repeated several times. Like so many things, in moderation the waggle can be regarded as normal behavior. Even a pro may do a ten-second waggle before hitting. That moment just before swinging is a dramatic one. After twenty seconds, however, the waggle loses its drama. After a full minute it becomes embarrassing to your fellow players and enraging to those playing behind you. While squirming, I have even watched golfers with a routine two-minute waggle. Women seem to be as prone to this obsessive-compulsive behavior as men. Anyone with a waggle more than forty seconds long is in need of counseling—if not deep psychoanalysis.

• Golfers not inclined to excessive practice swings or waggles on the tee or fairway may suddenly become fiends upon reaching the green. I've already mentioned some possibly useless time-consuming rituals to assess invisible slopes. Add on to these seven minuscule practice swipes, and you have a very slow putter indeed. Golfers learn that putting well is a most deliberate matter. Overlearning it, however, and making your putt into an interminable affair is a blatant sin.

- Etiquette is civil. Etiquette to excess becomes uncivil. If the balls of three players land on a green and the ball of a fourth goes way wide into deep rough, full etiquette calls for all four golfers to look for the lost ball and not to putt until it is found, or until the aberrant player drops a second ball and hits it onto the green. But this holds up play. Unless it is a tournament, experienced players on a busy day will putt out while allowing their partner to search for his own ball and hit it to the green when they're finished. Etiquette also properly includes the foursome behind you, and proper golfers will learn to know instinctively when to waive one type of etiquette for another.

It is this issue of etiquette that makes me so angry when I am being unnecessarily held up on a golf course. I have listed some of the most common reasons golfers may play with excessive slowness, but usually they all add up to the same thing: golfers who unnecessarily and consistently, hole after hole, delay players behind them by being inconsiderate. I think I am right to be angry at it. Yet when I allow this anger to so distract me that I play poorly as a result, I also think I am doing something wrong. Clearly I need to learn how to be angry and not angry simultaneously. It is another paradox that I understand perfectly well in my mind but that has yet to seep into my guts. My learning goes on. As does the de-cathexis and the detachment—the kenosis, the continual process of emptying myself of that anger which is destructive while still retaining that which is constructive.

What one despises in others, he tends to despise in himself. It is natural, therefore, that I am as anxious about unnecessarily delaying players behind me as I am angry at those who do so ahead of me. The problem is that my anxiety in this regard is just as deadly to my game as my anger.

I have improved. In years past I used to be anxious whenever anyone was playing behind me, even if I wasn't the least responsible for holding them up. But just as I have mostly gotten over my anger at golfers ahead of me when they're playing as fast as a crowded course allows, so now I am usually calm about golfers waiting behind me when I'm playing as fast as I can on a busy day.

Being so scrupulous about all this, I personally, as an individual, never cause anyone unnecessary delay at golf. My problem these days comes when I am part of a foursome where one or more of the others is atrociously slow. Where does my responsibility lie in the matter?

In one instance the answer seems clear. Whenever we are slow because I am introducing one or two beginners to the course, it is appropriate for me to take charge.[6] Or Lily. "We're holding up a group behind us," we'll say. "We need to let them play through." So we will stand aside, wave at them vigorously, and literally let them play through us.[7] On a busy course, playing with beginners, we've waved through as many as six parties on six holes, taking three hours to play those few holes. It's tedious, but that's a price one may need to pay for the privilege of mentorship.[8]

But what if the beginner is someone else's guest and his host seems oblivious to the fact that we are delaying the foursome behind us? Is it my responsibility to say, "We're holding people up. Why don't we let them play through?" Or what if a stranger I've been paired up with has a two-minute waggle and seems equally oblivious? Should I tell him, "You've got the longest waggle in the state of Texas. How about we try to speed it up?" Of course, being a compulsively nice guy, I am as terrified of seeming rude to my fellow players as I am of seeming inconsiderate of those behind.

I hate these kinds of decisions. I am so busy trying to make them, I lose my concentration on my game. It is guaranteed that I will hit poorly under such circumstances. Good golf requires a calm mind. I know some golfers who manage to keep their calm at all times. I am unclear as to what degree they may have been born less sensitive than I or how much it is a learned skill. I am not willing to sacrifice my capacity for sensitivity on the altar of playing better golf, but insofar as I can learn the skill of setting aside or bracketing my sensitivities just for the fifteen seconds required to make a shot, I can think of no harm in doing so. There is a vast difference between the absence of emotion and disciplined emotion. It is the latter I need to learn.

For instance, when I am a member of an obstructing foursome, I will rush my shots—as if by doing so, I could somehow speed us up. It is bizarre behavior when I think about it. Rationally I know that the five seconds I save by rushing is not going to diminish significantly the delay we are causing those behind. Rationally I know that I am not so totally responsible for my coplayers' ill manners. "Haste makes waste," as I quoted. Rationally I know that a rushed shot will almost invariably be a poor one. Yet I do it anyway. Lord, please help teach me balance.

Because golf is such a good teacher, I have suggested, good golfers are usually good people. But there are exceptions.

One winter afternoon on an almost-deserted course, Lily and I, as a twosome, were preparing to make our third shots against a three-club wind on a par-5 hole—when a golf ball came bouncing in between us on the middle of the fairway. Someone had obviously "hit into us." Hitting a ball into the players ahead of you is one of the greatest no-no's of golf. Not only is it disconcerting; if the ball happens to land on your head, it might kill you.

We waited for the culprit to appear. Very shortly, racing ahead on his cart, he did: a six-foot-two, strongly built, thirty-year-old single. He apologized profusely, saying that he hadn't seen us from the tee. It seemed a valid excuse—indeed, the only valid one possible. The geography of this particular hole was such that he probably hadn't seen us. We acknowledged as much and exclaimed over the extraordinary nature of his drive: 270 yards dead against a strong wind and right into the middle of a narrow part of the fairway.

He asked if he could join us. We explained we were only playing nine holes and preferred to play by ourselves. We suggested that he play through. "Thanks," he said. "I'm only playing nine also, but I'm in a rush. I've got to be back in San Francisco by six." It was three P.M. San Francisco was about a two-hour drive away.

He then hit what was presumably his second shot: a lovely low-iron 180 yards over a grassy canyon to an elevated green. His ball landed just wide of the pin, scooted across the green, and came to rest in a steep, cultivated rough behind and above the green. He would have a delicate, potentially difficult tiny chip shot. If he played it well, he should be able to putt in for a birdie.[9]

He rushed ahead in his cart down into a hidden part of the canyon, where there was a bathroom next to the cart path and a fairway approach up to the green. Both Lily and I knew we couldn't reach the green against the wind, so we took our third shots, landing as expected in the canyon, from which we would hopefully make good pitch shots after the young man had finished the hole. We went back to our cart and drove into the canyon to find not only the young man's cart but also one of the course marshals in his own cart. We were surprised not to see the young man on the green.

Lily and I chatted with the marshal. As we did so, the young man came out of the bathroom, took his putter and chipping wedge, and walked up to the green. After a couple of minutes, we and the marshal ran out of things to say to each other. I looked to see how the young man was doing. He had only just finished examining the lay of the green. I watched him then climb up the bank, and I counted as he slowly took seven practice swipes with his wedge.

Suddenly, without thinking, I exploded. "For God's sake," I yelled at him, "first you hit into us, then we let you play through, then you go to the bathroom, and now you seem to be doing your damnedest to further hold us up. I thought you said you were in a hurry."

After glowering at me and taking one more practice swing, the young man did make a good chip shot and then proceeded to sink a five-foot putt for a birdie. But he was not happy. When he got to the pro shop, he complained about me, stating I had ruined his chance for an eagle.[10] As recompense he demanded that he be allowed to play an additional nine holes that afternoon for free. Having received by radio a report from the marshal about the incident, the pro shop staff politely refused his demand.

The staff of a good golf course is substantial. Approximately half perform the great multitude of complex tasks required to keep the greens, tees, fairways, sand traps, and cart paths in top condition.[11] The other half are administrative personnel; while their duties are varied, the largest one, by far, is that of time management.[12]

Among these administrative professionals, for instance, there are one or two *starters*. With a list of reservations in hand, they stand at the first tee and make sure that players tee off in an orderly fashion. If players are late for their tee time, the starter may put an early foursome in front of them. He will tell eager players, "You can't hit quite yet," when there are golfers just around the dogleg ahead. Or he may rush conversational ones gently, saying, "Please tee off right away." And he makes sure that the players know the rules of the course. Starters are trained to be as polite as humanly possible within the confines of their role.

But my favorite professionals are the *marshals*. They cruise the course in their own carts. Their primary job is to maintain the rate and flow of play. For this they have a standard, which in the United States is four hours and fifteen minutes for an eighteen-hole round—an average of fourteen minutes a hole.[13]

Marshals can relieve one considerably of the frustration of being caught behind an excessively slow foursome. Many of the times when I've been angry at such a foursome, a portion of my anger should have been directed at the marshal for not doing his job. Or at the overall administration. Once at an elegant, extremely expensive course on Hawaii, my partners and I were interminably delayed by an extraordinarily perfectionistic and ritualistic foursome ahead of us. I kept looking for a marshal, but none came. When we finally finished, it was a six-hour round. Not a pleasant day. When we complained at the pro shop, the attendants said they didn't know where the marshals were. It was inexcusable. It is the job of the pro shop to be in contact with the marshals and know where they are, almost to the hole. My suspicion is that the course didn't have any marshals—that the administration considered them to be an unnecessary expense. It is valid, I believe, for inexpensive, uncrowded courses to dispense with marshals. It was not valid for this one.

Marshals are properly named. They are policemen. Among other responsibilities, it is their role to spot players who have sneaked onto the course without paying greens fees or are violating other rules—such as hitting their ball from an out-of-bounds position in someone's front yard. They ultimately have the authority to remove golfers from the course for these obvious infractions as well as for more subtle ones. A good marshal, for instance, will not only ask an excessively slow foursome to speed up, but will then keep close watch on them. If they fail to speed up or if they slow down again, he will likely instruct them, "This is the second time I've had to talk to you. Three strikes and you're out. I mean that literally. If I see you playing slowly again, I'll escort you off the course. And there will be no refunds."[14]

Not all marshals are good. Their most common problem is failing to exercise their authority adequately. It is not comfortable to confront a foursome, much less to order one off the course. Nonetheless, it may need to be done. The less common failure is to overexercise their authority. Once while playing in Arizona we were being slightly held up by a foursome in front. A marshal came by and said, "The course is wide open in front of the people ahead of you, so speed it up."

"That's not our responsibility," we tried to tell him, but he raced off in his cart, leaving us behind in a cloud of dust with a bad taste in our mouths. It is not pleasant to be chastised for doing nothing wrong. What the man should have said was "I wanted to let you know I've asked the foursome ahead of you to speed up, and I'd appreciate it if you'd keep pace with them as best you can. Thanks. Have a nice afternoon." One's choice of words can make all the difference.

It is said that "a good man is hard to find." That's not my experience with marshals. The vast majority of them are fine men, able to be firm when required but otherwise polite, even downright friendly. Initially it surprised me how many of them are retired business executives. The more I thought about it, however, the more sense it made. There is a huge pool of retired talent out there. As the timekeepers of golf, marshals need all the political skills of a well-trained executive. The job may not be highly paid, but if you love golf—and all good marshals do—what better way might you spend your late middle years than cruising a beautiful course helping people out?

So a significant part of golf is time management. Since a few highly skilled golfers remain grossly inconsiderate of others in relation to the matter of time, it is clear that playing the game is not guaranteed to teach one time management. But I persist in stating that golf is potentially a spiritual discipline, and if you regard it as such, you will learn many of life's most important lessons. None of these lessons or learnings is more important than time management. Ask any good parent or manager, and she will tell you that there is nothing she wants more for her children or employees than that they should learn this art.

It is an art because it is a balancing act. And it is so important because much of life is a balancing act—at least a life well lived. A generation ago in my first published book, I wrote at some length about balancing as a discipline. Yet but a few pages back in this, my thirteenth book, in relation to my tendency to rush some of my golf shots out of neurotic anxiety about time, I prayed, "Lord, please help teach me balance." Am I just another writer teaching what I myself most need to learn? Yes, but there is more to it than that. You see, the balancing act of life goes on, and as we age, the balances we have struck must be restruck and restruck again.

Not surprisingly, the essence of the art of balancing is the spiritual practice of kenosis. We must continually give up, renounce, empty ourselves of certain things if we are to keep our balance. Because it is such a tangible example, let me recount a story I told in that first book so many years ago:

> I remember first being taught this one summer morning in my ninth year. I had recently learned to ride a bike and was joyously exploring the dimensions of my new skill. About a mile from our house the road went down a steep hill and turned sharply at the bottom. Coasting down the hill on my bike that morning I felt my gathering speed to be ecstatic. To give up this ecstasy by the application of brakes seemed an absurd self-punishment. So I resolved to simultaneously retain my speed and negotiate the corner at the bottom. My ecstasy ended seconds later when I was propelled a dozen feet off the road into the woods. I was badly scratched and bleeding and the front wheel of my new bike was twisted beyond use from its impact against a tree. I had lost my balance.

> Balancing is a discipline precisely because the act of giving something up is painful. In this instance I had been unwilling to suffer the pain of giving up my ecstatic speed in the interest of maintaining my balance around the corner. I learned, however, that the loss of balance is ultimately more painful than the giving up required to maintain balance. In one way or another it is a lesson I have continually had to relearn throughout my life. As must everyone, for as we negotiate the curves and corners of our lives, we must continually give up parts of ourselves. The only alternative to this giving up is not to travel at all on the journey of life.[15]

But as noted, the practice of balancing and its necessary kenosis goes on and on. Let me return to the immediate present. I write this very page on a Friday afternoon in an Edinburgh hotel. The reason Lily and I are in Edinburgh is that it is the final day of a three-week revisit to Scotland. The reason for our revisit has not been to play golf; it is because much of Scotland is the most beautiful land we have ever known.

Since we are in our old age now and our health is declining, major travel is becoming ever more difficult for us. Consequently, as I write this my heart is somewhat heavy. The fact is that this is probably the last time we shall ever see Scotland again. Frankly, I am grieving.

The process of grieving is one of relinquishing our cathexes, our attachments and passions. It is naturally a time of sadness. Sometimes minor sadness, as in this instance. Sometimes enormous sadness, as would be the case were Lily to die before me and I knew this day to be the last one I would ever see her again. Yet this sadness of giving up is a necessary part of getting on with life. Even in this minor instance I would be in a pretty pickle if I could not sadly say good-bye, if I got back home still yearning desperately to return to Scotland when, in fact, I was no longer physically able to do so.

This illustrates the reality that kenosis—the withdrawing of cathexes and attachments—is not always a joyous process. Upon occasion it can be virtually heartbreaking. But while always difficult, most of the time it is actually a joyous affair. What could possibly be sad about emptying oneself of irrational anger at a foursome in front of you or irrational anxiety over the foursome behind you? Mind you, I am not saying that kenosis is easy; only that, when put in perspective, it is usually exhilarating.

The fine points of time and balance have to do with rhythm. Only recently have I become aware that playing good golf has a distinct rhythm. Not too fast or jerky; not too slow or perfectionistic. Only a year ago I would seemingly fall into the right rhythm by accident, and whenever I did, I would play well. Today I have mostly learned how to start with that rhythm on the first tee. But I still can lose it. A bad bounce into a sand trap, a fast foursome behind me or a slow one in front of me, and I am off my rhythm and have to work psychologically to regain it. This may seem like a small matter. But to me it seems only slightly short of miraculous that, at the age of sixty-three, with almost crippling arthritis and increasingly questionable memory, I am actually becoming better at rhythm.

NOTES

1. Einstein would probably have lumped space and time into a single dimension.
2. Actually, you can lump all the dimensions into one: creation. But that's not terribly helpful. Still, the distinctions blur. For instance, do we include plants, animals, and the entire environment under the category of "others"? Or does it deserve a separate category of its own? We mystics do not concern ourselves too much with such niceties, but we do insist that *everything* be included.
3. Marijuana is notorious and fascinating in this regard. Once, out of deliberate scientific curiosity, I played golf while stoned to see if the drug might improve my game. It didn't. It also didn't seem to make it any worse.
4. One might imagine that while waiting on the players ahead, golfers could spend the time conversing with one another. So they do. But the golf course is not a suitable place for serious conversation. As soon as you begin telling your partner a fabulously good story, the foursome ahead will move on, and even if your partner is truly interested in it, by the time you finish the story you will be holding up the foursome behind you. Most discourse on the links is limited to: "Good shot," "Bad luck," "You were robbed," or "Oh, shit!"
5. Yes, this is a real word, not unique to golf. *Wiggle-waggle* is not something invented by Dr. Seuss. *Waggling* is traditionally used by students of insects to designate a signaling dance of bees, and by pilots as a signal made by wiggling the wings of their plane.
6. The business of beginners can be tricky. Houseguests who express an interest in playing the local course are apt to add, "But you have to realize I haven't played in twenty-five years." Several such guests have then proceeded to play nine holes well under 50. Several others well over 150.
7. Waving vigorously is an ambiguous symbol. When done at players behind you, it generally means "Please play through." When done at players ahead of you, it can either mean "Hey, for Christ's sake, let us play through" or else "Hey, one of your guys left your pitching wedge at the side of the green."
8. Refer back to hole 2.
9. One under par, or a 4 on this particularly challenging par 5.
10. An eagle, or 2 under par, is the best score one can ever get on a hole. For a par 3 it's a hole in one. On this particular par 5 the young man would have had to hit his difficult chip shot not only onto the green but into the cup for his eagle.
11. These workers are often referred to as "greenskeepers." Yet they do much more than keep the greens in top shape. I myself tend to think of them as "terrain engineers."

12. In charge of both groups is the chief golf professional. Whether he does any teaching of golf is immaterial; he is primarily a top executive, responsible for managing at least two dozen people, for having expertise ranging all the way from different types of grass seed to accounting systems, for negotiating tournaments and construction contracts, and for doing all the work involved in being accountable to a board of directors.

The two or more pro shop staff sell balls, equipment, and expensive golfing clothes. They make the tee time reservations and man the phones. They check players in and collect the greens fees. They coordinate with the starters and marshals and adjudicate complex situations or complaints such as the one I just recounted. Often they are in training with the PGA and may give lessons in their spare time. Where there are carts, there are one or more cart "boys." They not only check the carts in and out but help oversee their maintenance.

13. I am told that the standard in Scotland is shorter and therefore even stricter.

When players are moving more rapidly than the standard, the marshal is unlikely to press them. When moving more slowly, he will request that they speed up their play. If they are beginners and cannot speed up, he will require that they let the golfers behind them play through.

The marshals also perform many additional tasks, ranging from rescuing players with heat stroke, broken carts, and other crises, to reporting incidents by radio to the pro shop. They will pick up clubs that players have inadvertently left behind and return them to their owners. They will chat with players who are waiting or even help them look for lost balls. Some of them—but only when I've asked—have given me good tips on my game.

14. Although the rules allow up to five minutes for a player to search for a lost ball, they also demand that such players let those immediately behind them play through while the search lasts.

15. M. Scott Peck, *The Road Less Traveled* (New York: Simon & Schuster, 1978), pp. 66–67.

*Politeness may be profoundly superficial, but it can be
relinquished with civility only by those who have learned
the rules of civilization to their core.*

H O L E 1 2

CIVILITY

We have arrived back in the desert on the leeward, windless side of Mount Intrepid and are faced with a different sort of par 3. We must hit from the tee not across a mere gulch but a 100-yard-wide canyon, 200 feet deep, and to get from the tee to the green, we must ride our carts over an actual suspension bridge.

It is a dramatic but not difficult hole, as long as one's drive gets airborne. Not all drives do get airborne, however, and the bottom of the canyon is almost white with irretrievable golf balls. Although surprisingly nonlinear, golf is simultaneously a continuing flow. The rules of this hole are the same as for every other one, and the flow of the game proceeds along this riverbed of rules. So as we cross the canyon (hopefully after four well-lofted tee shots), let us continue with this ongoing "dance of etiquette," examining it in the context of the entire subject of civility.

A dance, among other things, is a sequence—in particular, a sequence of steps. For instance, it is an ancient custom that the best-scoring player on any one hole has the "honor" on the next tee—meaning he gets to hit first. The second-best-scoring player on the last hole tees off second, and so forth.

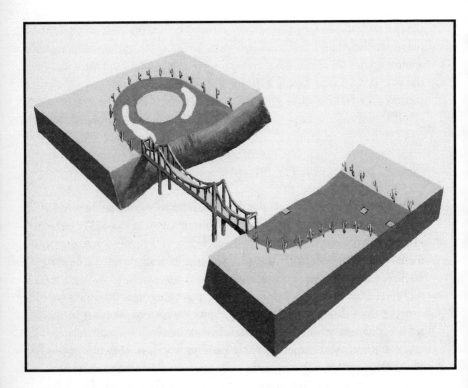

Sometimes the system of honors can seem complicated, but in reality it is quite simple.[1] Indeed, its simplicity is its reason. The system relieves golfers, insofar as it is possible, from having to make decisions about the sequence of their tee shots. They all know where they stand, so to speak, and the prescribed order allows them to move ahead with maximum efficiency—without any waste of time.

Once you're off the tee, the sequence of shots is totally dictated by the distance of one's ball from the green. Whether male or female, the player farthest from the green hits first, with her or his fellow players standing laterally. Then the next farthest player, and so on. Distance is the sole determining factor. For instance, if it is Joe's turn to make his second shot and he looks up while doing so, topping the ball with the result that it dribbles but a few feet ahead, it is likely that his ball will still be farthest from the green. This being the case, Joe doesn't lose his turn. To the contrary, he is next up once again. He must now hit his third shot while his fellow players stand to the side and may yet be waiting to hit their second.

Safety is the primary reason for the order of this dance down the fairway. Anyone who stands ahead of a hitting player is putting himself in jeopardy. Even at an angle. Remember, a golfer can shank a shot as much as 70 degrees to one side of where he is aiming. I once saw a woman hit in the face by just such a shanked shot. She was lucky to lose only a tooth. A golf ball is very hard and moves very fast.

On the green, the sequence of shots is again determined by distance—this time distance of the ball from the cup.[2]

On the fairway I spoke of how poor Joe, who dribbled his second shot, might well be required to immediately make his third according to "the law of sequence and distance." The same phenomenon is also unfortunately common on the green—particularly with downhill putts. Let's say it is now Mary's turn to putt, and her ball lies twelve feet past the cup on the uphill side of a steeply sloping green. Knowing all the perils involved, she gives her ball the most delicate of taps with her putter. The ball very slowly moves in the direction of the cup while Mary and her fellow players hold their breath. It may happen that, through a combination of grace and Mary's genius, her ball will meet the very center of the cup and plop into it, with one of the most beautiful sounds in the world.

What is much more likely to happen, however, is that the ball will ever so slowly skim past the edge of the cup and ever so slowly continue to roll foot after foot after foot until finally coming to a stop 24 feet downhill from the cup—twice as far away from it as when she started. At this point, if a fellow player is gauche enough to speak, she will probably hear one of the most horrible sentences in the language of golf: "Well, Mary, at least you didn't lose your turn."

Since putting and short shots are 60 percent of the game, everything becomes more condensed the closer we approach the green and its cup. The dance of etiquette naturally spirals inward, and its precision becomes ever finer and more elegant. You may perceive the soul of the matter if you imagine yourself to be an angel, hovering 50 feet in the air over the green. It won't take you long to discern the elegance. Unless they are beginners or narcissists, all the players know their moves, and they make them smoothly with an efficiency that is quite lovely and a privilege to observe from on high.

On the last hole I noted that the etiquette or proper sequence of golf may occasionally be waived in the interest of speeding up play— particularly when another foursome is hard on your heels. Let us suppose, for instance, that I have the honors on a particular tee, but I also happen to be the designated scorekeeper for our group. I may be so busy writing down our scores that I haven't even pulled out my driver yet while Tom, Dick, and Harry have their clubs already in hand. Without a "by your leave," they tee off ahead of me. Are they being rude? Uncivil? Not as far as I am concerned. We have played often enough together for them to know that being the first to tee off is an empty honor for me; the real honor is that I was lucky enough to get the lowest score on the preceding hole.

But exactly how are such decisions to waive the rules made? They are made by consensus. Virtually never can consensus be arrived at by inconsiderate, egotistical, rugged individualists. To the contrary, it requires delicacy, sensitivity, and a reasonable capacity for selflessness on the part of all concerned. It is a highly civil process. And it is a measure of the civility of the game and most golfers that consensual decisions are arrived at by foursomes with remarkable speed and facility.

I must acknowledge that most of the cooperative decisions made while playing golf are relatively simple, compared with the far more complex decisions that must often be made in business or family life. And that in these arenas other decision-making styles may be more appropriate. Whether a three-year-old should be allowed to run out into the street is not a matter for consensual decision making. A ten-year-old is not likely to volunteer to take out the garbage, but in many families he may properly be required to do so as an assigned chore. Families are not democracies. Still, as children get older, there is more and more room for negotiation, as in matters of allowance or what time an adolescent should get home from a party. Such decisions can merge into consensual decision making and should be encouraged whenever possible. As for spousal relations, consensus will be the norm in a healthy marriage. Marital partners who know how to struggle well toward consensus will generally be winners; those who do not will generally be losers.

In the business world the majority of decisions are not made consensually; executive fiat of one kind or another is far more efficient. Nonetheless, the more important decisions, such as those of morale, strategic planning, or broad policy, are best made by consensus—if possible. For consensus to be possible in these more complex situations, however, the participants are likely to require formal management training in the various parameters of consensual decision making.[3]

Bending the rules in golf is a relatively benign affair. After all, it is a game. But bending the rules in other aspects of life may have far more serious consequences. Generally it should not be done. If a child whose assigned chore is to take out the garbage fails to do so, he will become a confused child should his parents routinely relieve him of his responsibility. Generally speaking, consistency is one of the great parental virtues. And as far as business is concerned, bending the rules can be disastrous. Whole financial institutions have gone down the tubes when they have violated their own criteria for extending credit or have otherwise looked the other way. Healthy business organizations also have an internal consistency. Yet there are always exceptions. As a mentor of mine, a lawyer and ethicist, once put it, "Sometimes it is possible to know the rules so well that one can come up with new and creative solutions."

• • •

Of all the many possible consensual decisions to waive the formal rules of golf, my two favorite concern the issues of mulligans and gimmes.

What is a *mulligan*? Most precisely, it is the option of taking a second shot—without any penalty whatsoever—off of the first tee when your first drive has gone awry. Particularly when your first drive has gone so awry that it is out of bounds, in the water, or obviously lost in deep rough so that it would ordinarily incur a penalty of two strokes.[4]

I am told the Scots are strict about their golf. If true, the point is well made by the popular little story of an American man on the first tee of one of the great courses of Scotland. He hits his drive way wild out of bounds. Turning to his ancient caddy, the American inquires, "Do you have what's called a mulligan here? Do you know what a mulligan is?"

"Oh, aye," the caddy answers, "only here we call it a three."

It is not uplifting to start off your round with a two-stroke penalty so that you're hitting three while you're still on the first tee. Consequently, it has become the custom in soft-hearted America for one to take a mulligan when his first shot of the day gets him into trouble—as long as it is not tournament play. Still, it is proper to ask your fellow players whether they will permit you the option before you take it. If you and your fellow players constitute a foursome that plays together regularly, you will not have to ask; the matter will have been consensually decided so long ago that it has become a tradition among you. But as a consensual tradition, it will generally be understood that a mulligan is a "right": namely, that each of you can take one if he chooses.

America is so soft-hearted and liberal, it has even become almost customary in nontournament play for American golfers to take as many mulligans as they want. Hit a bad first shot, take a second. Hit a bad second shot, take a third. And so on. Don't leave the first tee until you've had a drive that you feel good about. Occasionally such excess is justified on the basis that the particular course you are playing doesn't happen to have a "practice range" where you can "warm up." I find this argument specious, however. It is also customary to take multiple practice swings just behind the first tee (without a real ball) to loosen up. For reasons I shall eventually discuss, it is all too common to hit lovely balls on the range and almost immediately flub your shot off the first tee. The real reason for mulligans in America is that we are a "feel good" culture, and it just doesn't seem right to us to leave the first tee without feeling good—particularly since we've paid our greens fees for the supposed pleasure that will result.

But my poking fun at my culture doesn't mean I don't take advantage of it. In fact, I have even contributed to the invention of a new kind of mulligan. I have a golfing buddy, Wally, with whom I fortunately get to play at least once a year. In his own way, he is perhaps as competitive a man as I. We play for a dollar a hole. The sum is of no consequence to either of us, save for the pure joy of winning it or the symbolic distress of losing it. Our invention is what I call a "floating mulligan." Each of us is entitled to one extra tee shot without penalty every nine holes. The reason it is a "floating" mulligan is that we don't have to use it on the first tee; we can use it on any tee we want. For instance, if Wally hits his very first shot out of bounds and I hit a straight drive out into the fairway, he will take his mulligan but I will reserve mine. Using his mulligan, he will feel good (as long as his mulligan shot is a good one) because he's started out on the right foot. I will feel even a little better not only because I've started out well but because I've still got my mulligan in reserve. Then when I drive out of bounds on hole 4, I don't have to feel so bad because I can try again "for free."

There are fine points to all this. It is not a total giveaway. We allow ourselves one—and only *one*—mulligan every nine holes. If Wally hits a second bad drive off the first tee, he will be penalized for it, just as I will be penalized if I hit a second lousy drive on hole 4. We also do not accumulate our mulligans. If Wally hasn't used his on the front nine, that doesn't mean he then has the option of taking two mulligans on the back nine. The back nine is a fresh start, and we start it the same way we started the front. Implied in this is the fact we do not *have* to take a mulligan. Indeed, we've played several eighteen-hole rounds without either of us taking any. But that's rare. Neither of us alone usually plays so well, much less the two of us together.

We enjoy making decisions about such fine points—consensually. And whenever we get back together, we have fun reviewing our self-made rules to see if we want to make any new intricate and consensual ones. Furthermore, while we are both as competitive as all get out, we also like to give a little. Perhaps through mulligans we have learned the paradox of how to simultaneously compete and lighten up.

If anything, I enjoy gimmes even more than mulligans.

A *gimme* is a very short putt that the players agree you do not have to make. They give it to you on the assumption that it is so short and easy, you would make it anyway.[5]

In our "feel good" culture, strangers playing informally together will frequently take gimmes without even asking. Doing so is something of a breach of etiquette. When Lily and I play together, it is most informal. Seldom are we betting, and if it's not a great day, we're usually not keeping track of our scores. Unless we're so disgusted that we "pick up," however, we will still ask each other, "Would you be willing to give me that putt?" or else one of us will volunteer, "I'll give it to you," or "It's a gimme as far as I'm concerned."

In tournament play the ball is *never* close enough to the hole to be a gimme. Otherwise, there's no firm and fast rule. If Lily's having a bad day, I may give her a three-foot putt just to help her feel better about it all; if she's on fire, I'll make her putt it out. And she, me. How can there be a firm rule when gimmes are inherently illegal?

Nonetheless, there is a convention: A ball may be considered a gimme when it is "within the leather." One simply takes a putter, places its blade in the cup, and lays it down on the green with the shaft of the club alongside the ball in question. If the ball lies alongside the grip, it is not "within the leather"; hence, no gimme. If it lies next to the exposed shaft, however, then it is considered within the leather and, therefore, an automatic gimme.

This all sounds a bit absurd, even as I write it, but when I'm actually involved with it on the course, I find it to be great fun. One reason I love golf so much is because it does have for me a kind of *Alice in Wonderland* quality, filled with arguments of no consequence. When we play together, Wally and his wife, Barb, and Lily and I have consensually adopted the "within the leather" convention. But what happens when the ball is precisely at the juncture of the leather and the rest of the shaft? And whose putter do you use to make the measurement?

Because I'm the tallest of the four, for instance, my putter can add as much as two inches to what is within the leather. Oh, delight! The four of us have consensually agreed to abide by the convention, but what fun we have either interpreting the convention or trying to stretch the consensus minusculely! Particularly when a whole dollar lies on the outcome of the debate!

The supposed reason for gimmes is that they speed up play. This they do. But the real reason, at least for me, is this business of feeling good. When I am putting from a distance, I am reasonably relaxed. While it is lovely if my putt happens to drop into the cup, I have no expectation that it *should* do so. My limited goal is that the ball will come to rest within gimme range. But when I am making a 20-inch putt, I feel I should sink it, as if I had a moral obligation about the matter. Certainly I will look like a perfect fool if I fail. Suddenly I become extremely self-conscious, my hands start to shake, and I am filled with doubt. The result is that I miss more short putts than any other human being I know. It does not feel good to miss a 20-inch putt. The custom of gimmes in golf is the nicest, most humane custom I know.

From all that I can ascertain, the Scots probably consider the customs of mulligans and gimmes to be nothing more than consensual cheating. I do not agree. Certain groups do consensually decide to defraud the public in one way or another. But when a group of four consensually decide to take mulligans and gimmes, who are they defrauding? No one, not even themselves. They know perfectly well that they're not playing by tournament rules. Were they in a tournament, they would behave differently, but they're not in a tournament; they're just out on the course to have as much fun as possible. By virtue of all its rules, golf has plenty of agony as well as ecstasy. I see no harm—not to anyone else and not to their own souls—for golfers to bend the rules a bit to minimize the agony slightly, as long as it is consensual. I doubt that God does, either.

I have not exhausted all the little dance steps of civility that constitute the full extent of etiquette in golf, nor shall I. But it might help make the point to mention a few of the other rules of what the Buddha would have called "right conduct."

- Replace your divots, the large slices of fairway turf that golfers often take in making their iron shots. A divot may fly as much as 20 feet ahead of you. Don't just leave it lying there. Pick it up and put it back where it belongs.
- After you have succeeded in hitting out of a sand trap, rake your ball marks and footprints so the players behind you don't have to hit their ball out of some pocket you have made in the sand. Rakes are positioned at the edge of almost all traps. They are there for a purpose.
- Repair your ball marks on the green. A high or hard-hit ball will make a significant dent in the turf when it lands on the green. It is not nice for others to have to putt over such a dent. They are easily repaired, and experienced golfers will be happy to show you how.
- If you are standing near someone who is making a shot, don't talk or move; it can be quite distracting.
- Watch your shadow on the green. If it is in the line of a player's putt, move yourself and your shadow to a position where it could not possibly bother her.
- Replace the pin in the cup when all are finished putting. The reappearance of its flag is a signal to the golfers behind you that you are leaving the green and they soon can hit.
- As you leave the green, look around to see whether you or any of your fellow players have left a chipping or pitching wedge on its edge. Inexperienced players tend to forget their clubs. This can be expensive, and one of the ways the experienced can quietly help out the inexperienced is to do this little remembering for them.

I have elsewhere defined *civility* as "consciously motivated organizational behavior that is ethical in submission to a higher power."[6] I do not know whether any of this has to do with God or a "higher power." Certainly it is organizational behavior. All golf is. Even when you are playing alone, it is in the context of an organizational dance with the golfers behind you, the golfers in front of you, and the organization of all the people who have worked long and hard to create and then maintain the course. Certainly the behavior I have just described is ethical— that is, considerate of others, as if they were somehow precious. And perhaps above all it is consciously motivated behavior. Once again, it is a measure of the civility of the game that golf is the only sport I know where one properly needs to be conscious of his or her own shadow upon the earth for the sake of others.

What about incivility in golf? It is, of course, the failure to do the kinds of things I've just mentioned. And the failure to do some of the things I discussed previously, such as speeding up your play when you're delaying the players behind you or else waving them through.

These failures do not exhaust the list. We have friends who own a home on the edge of the fairway of the course I mentioned that we love to play on the northern California coast. Their garden is not only roped off but, like those of the other homes, is marked by white stakes, the traditional signal that the territory is out of bounds. The course is owned in common by the householders of this semiresort community. It is also open to the public. On any given day approximately half the players are homeowners and their guests, and half are "public players." Signs are clearly posted to the effect that players are not to enter the homeowners' gardens to search for their balls. This rule is also written on the back of the scorecard. Public players are also informed of the rule by the starter.

Naturally, the homeowners obey this rule. So also do the majority of the public players. The minority who do not, however, are substantial. This minority (most of whom are male) can be divided into three types:

1. The golfer who will not step over the rope but will reach across it to fish for a nearby and visible ball with his club.

2. The golfer who will step over the rope and roam about the garden searching for his ball, but who does so gingerly, taking care not to step on the flowers or otherwise damage the property.

3. The golfer who not only roams the garden at will, trampling the flowers, but hacks away at the bushes with his five-iron in search of this ball, usually damaging the garden's watering system in the process. If he does find his ball, he may even try to hit it out of the garden as if he could somehow avoid the legal penalty of being out of bounds.

There is a name for this latter type of golfer: brute. Although he may know a little bit about how to play golf, he has not yet become civilized.[7] Certainly his behavior is grossly unethical, if not criminal. I do believe that there are evil people in the world, yet when I have spoken with such uncivil golfers, they have not struck me as frankly evil so much as unconscious. Remember that civility is "consciously motivated" behavior. To be consciously motivated, one must be conscious. It is not simply that these brutes are narcissists—although they are that—who cannot or will not think about the needs of others. They don't think about much of anything. I might label them "borderline conscious." I hope they will keep playing golf. Lots of it. They have a lot to learn from the game.

The consensual giving of putts and mulligans does not constitute cheating, yet one hears much about cheating in golf. And cheating is obviously unethical, uncivil. In my experience, however, precious little cheating occurs on the course. In tournament play, where all the rules are rigidly adhered to, you will be observed too closely to cheat. In informal competitive play, where there may be consensual mulligans and gimmes but where there's money involved, you will also have no room to cheat. That doesn't mean you won't be tempted to do so; just that the person or people you're betting with won't let you get away with it. For instance, if I tell Wally that I got a bogey on this hole, number 12, the conversation might go as follows:

"What do you mean you got a bogey?" Wally asks.

"Well, I had a pretty good tee shot," I answer, "only it bounced sideways into the trap. I hit out of the trap onto the green, and then two-putted. So that gives me a bogey four."

"But you took two shots to get out of the trap," Wally responds. In truth I may have forgotten this fact. But whether I repressed it or suppressed it doesn't matter. Wally remembers it, and now I do, too, and I have no choice but to say, "You're right. I'm sorry. Put me down for a double bogey five."

More important, if it isn't already clear, it very shortly will be that the primary person you are competing with in golf is yourself. It is no accident, therefore, that when people do cheat at golf, their only victim is themselves.

Some years ago Lily and I were playing with our son Christopher, the illustrator of this book, on a resort course in Arizona. To fill us out as a foursome on this busy course, the starter linked us up with a fifteen-year-old single lad. He was fifteen in every way, shape, and manner. Typically scrawny, he still had more muscle mass than I, and when he connected well, he hit by far the longer ball. But as often as not, he didn't connect well. After every bad or wild shot, he went into a spasm of excuse making: "Usually I don't play this poorly"; "I had a horrible lie"; "I'm not used to greens being this fast." This didn't bother me. From personal as well as professional experience, I was agonizingly familiar with the fragile self-esteem of fifteen-year-old boys. It's a tough age.

Nonetheless, by the end of the front nine, my game had seriously begun to deteriorate, and I realized why. The lad had asked me to keep his score. I soon realized he took as many mulligans as he wanted without asking, he didn't count any penalty strokes, he counted no more than one shot out of sand traps, and he gave himself every putt under eight feet. Toward the end of the back nine, as my game remained poor, I commented to my son, "That kid is really pissing me off. There isn't a hole he hasn't cheated on."

"I suspect you're angry," Chris responded, "because he's getting away with all the things you wish you could."

My son, although it is not his profession, is frequently a better psychiatrist than I. His diagnosis was accurate. It pointed to my shadow—not my bodily shadow but that part of the mind that contains all those traits of character we would rather keep hidden from the light of day. We humans have a profound tendency to get irrationally angry at whoever exemplifies a trait that lies within our own shadow sides. Although I was not actually a cheater, Christopher was clarifying that there was still a mostly unconscious part of me that wished I could be one.

The term *shadow* was first coined by the great psychiatrist Carl Jung more than half a century ago. Since then a number of books have been written about the subject. This is no accident: The concept is the key to defining the nature of good and evil—and the distinction between civility and incivility. Every person on the face of this earth has a shadow. But, as Jung himself put it, human evil has its genesis in "the refusal to meet the shadow." By this he meant the absolute unwillingness of those who are evil to become *conscious* of their darker impulses, such as the impulse to cheat. Because of their unconsciousness of them, they are unable to restrain such impulses. I repeat, everyone has a shadow side. Even the saints. But what characterizes the saints is the depth of their consciousness of their shadows and hence their extraordinary capacity for self-restraint and true civility.

To be the best golfers possible, it is necessary that we be conscious not only of our physical shadows but also of our psychological ones.

Several years later, on a less crowded course, I was paired as a twosome with another fifteen-year-old boy who was the spitting image of the previous one just described. Only this time, thanks to the psychotherapy I'd received from Chris, I was not perturbed. At the end of the front nine, which was all I could play, I added up our scores. I had shot a 50—just about my average. The scores the boy had given me totaled 47. Although I was not the least bit angry that he'd beaten me on paper, I felt something needed to be said. Out of a place of calmness and, I believe, compassion, I said, "Thanks for the game. I enjoyed it. I do sort of hope one of these days you might think about including your penalty strokes."

"I intend to," he replied. "As soon as I'm sixteen. Or maybe when I'm regularly hitting in the eighties."

"That's a neat idea," I told him as we parted.

NOTES

1. One example of a complication is when two men and two women are playing together in what is called a *mixed foursome*. The men tee off first, even though one of the women may have had the best score on the previous hole. This is not dictated by sexism but by the simple fact that the women's tee is in front of the men's. A woman on the red tee would be endangered by a man hitting from the white tee.
2. There is a "sort of" exception to this rule. Quite frequently a ball on the skirt of the green, on the fairway, or even in a sand trap or cultivated rough may lie closer to the cup than one or more of the balls already on the green. The sequence of these *off-the-green* shots, even if they are made by a putter, is again determined by distance from the cup—the exception being that they are made before anyone on the green putts.

There are a few other wrinkles as well. The general rule is that the pin is left in the cup for any off-the-green shot. Sometimes this is an advantage and sometimes a disadvantage. A well-aimed shot may hit the center of the pin so that it is stopped dead and falls into the cup, whereas it might have sailed over any empty cup. On the other hand, a slower-moving ball that might have dropped into an empty cup may hit the side of the pin in such a manner that it is deflected one or two feet away. It is purely a matter of luck, good or bad.

As soon as everyone's ball is on the green, the pin is removed and placed aside, presumably by the player who happens to be closest to it. If requested, this player may temporarily hold the pin in place for another who is putting from such a distance that he cannot clearly see the cup, but she then must "pull" the pin as soon as the ball is struck and before it comes near.

If one's ball lies relatively close to the cup and "in the line" of another's putt from a greater distance, the putter will ask him to "mark" his ball. Indeed, experienced golfers will do so without even being asked. In fact, they will routinely carry with them specially designed markers for this purpose—little pieces of plastic or metal that can be embedded in the turf of the green so as to be visible but offer no obstruction to a putt passing over them. It is also quite proper for a player making an off-the-green shot to ask one or more players on the green to mark their balls. Usually it is not to either player's benefit when their balls collide on the green.

This marking of balls on the green is the sole instance I know whereby golf has been made easier over the past century. Many years ago if another player's ball on the green lay between your ball and the cup, that was just tough for you. You were what was called "stymied." You had no option but to putt around your fellow player's ball (without hitting it—otherwise you would incur a severe penalty). Usually being stymied would cost you at least an extra stroke. But somewhere along the line the rule-makers conceded that this business of being stymied was basically unfair (and often confusing, as in the case of multiple stymies), and they allowed the marking of balls. Since then, whenever golfers speak of being stymied, they are merely referring to having an unplayable lie, as when their ball is "stymied" amid the roots of a banyan tree.

3. Readers who want to explore deeper aspects of civility are referred to my book *A World Waiting to Be Born: Civility Rediscovered* (New York: Bantam, 1993). If their interest is restricted to the issue of consensual decision making in situations more complex and challenging than golf, they are recommended to pages 271–98 for a narrow consideration and pages 271–366 for a broader one.

4. The word *mulligan* is of obscure origin. Like so many terms in golf, it probably arose out of Scotland, although the Scots would disavow it. The word is also used to describe a particular kind of stew. There is no known connection between these two usages. Indeed, the Scots would probably say that a mulligan has everything to do with a meat dish and nothing whatsoever to do with the game of golf.

5. The word *gimme* is not limited to golf but is used as slang throughout the English language. It is a contraction of *give me,* and sometimes, as we shall see,

players will actually ask each other, "Will you give me that putt?" I am somewhat struck by the similarity in sound between gimme and the word *gimmick,* meaning a sort of advertising ploy that may be attractive to the unsuspecting but that is not truly representative of the product. I imagine the Scots may also have noted the similarity, since they consider the gimme to be a gimmick unrepresentative of real golf.

6. See again *A World Waiting to Be Born.* This definition is a real mouthful, but the entire first section of the book is devoted to paraphrasing it (pp. 3–92).

7. The words *civility* and *civilization* of course come from the same Latin root. Indeed, civility is the foundation of what we call civilization.

Competition is a choice in all aspects of life—even in business. The healthy or whole person will know when and how to compete—and when or how not to compete.

H O L E   1 3

COMPETITION

Although the variety of a great course, like Exotica, may be stunning, it is not limitless. Golf course designers must operate within the limits of geography—the limits of the terrain that they have been given to ply their unique trade. So here we have another long par 5, winding down along the side of Mount Intrepid, much like hole 9, looking like another segmented worm on the map, quadrisected by another four gulches and again traversing three climatic zones.

While there may be limits to golf course design, the varieties of competition in golf are virtually infinite. This may come as a surprise to nongolfers whose only experience of the game has been watching pro tournaments on TV. With but few exceptions the breathtaking competition of these tournaments follows a single, simple design called *stroke play.* The sole determinant of who wins such a tournament is the total number of his or her strokes. The player with the lowest total gets the "purse" or at least the largest portion of the apportioned monetary winnings. And he or she very much deserves it.

The stroke play of the pros is occasionally called *gross play.* This is because the gross total score is all that counts, not because the play is ugly. But it is brutal. Most of the time we amateurs compete in a far gentler fashion that is commonly referred to as *match play.* What's the difference? Match play, sometimes called *low hole play,* is based on hole-by-hole competition. You get a lower score than I on this hole, and you get a point. I get a lower score on the next hole, and I get a point. The two holes have evened out for us. Our total sum scores have nothing to do with it.

Why is match play so much gentler? Let's suppose you play this hole perfectly, avoiding all of its gulches and sand-trapped narrows, ending up with a par. And let's say that I land in about four of these hazards with an eventual resulting score of 11. In gross stroke play my "sextuple bogey" 11 to your par 5 means that I would have lost six strokes to you, not only enough to keep you in the running, but probably enough to put me decisively *out* of the running by virtue of this one hole alone. But in match play I have merely lost the hole to you. Assuming we started the hole even, I am only "down one" to you. Were I to get a par and you a bogey—just a one-stroke difference—on the next hole, then we would be even again. The pros, who hit so bloody damn well almost all the time, probably prefer stroke play. But we amateurs, who are often so erratic that we can totally blow it on a single hole, are quite naturally inclined to match play with its almost ever-present opportunity for redemption.

The most authoritative book I know on the subject, *Golf: Games Within the Game,* lists 196 different ways one can play competetive golf (divided into twelve broad categories) along with thirty possible styles of betting—and even I know a few games the authors forgot to include.[1] These games range from ordinary low-hole match play, such as I've just described, to some variations that are more or less bizarre (albeit great fun).

As an example of a common tournament variation, consider the Scotch foursome. Here the foursome is divided into two pairs of partners. Each pair plays only one ball, with the partners alternating their shots. One reason this form of country club amateur tournament is popular is that the play moves fast since only two instead of the usual four balls are being hit. In a common variation of Scotch, both partners drive from the tee; they then select the better of their two drives and thereafter alternate shots for the remainder of the hole. This variation is called Acapulco.[2]

Of the more bizarre "games within the game," let me cite four of my favorites.

• Amigos. The two players who hit their tee shots farthest to the left are paired as partners (or *amigos,* Spanish for "friends"), and for the rest of the hole, they compete with the two who hit their tee shots farthest to the right. On the next hole the partners will likely be reshuffled in accordance with the same meaningless criterion. This game isn't even included on the list of 196 in the book I've cited.

• Groundhog. On two holes so designated by the tournament chairman, one on the front nine and one on the back, all players must hit their tee shot using an upside-down Styrofoam cup for a tee. This produces some unusual shots. It is unclear how this game got its name. Probably it is an annual event at some southern country club on February 2, Groundhog Day.

• My One and Only. Players are allowed to carry only two clubs on the course: their putter and the one other club they feel they're most likely to succeed with. (The normal number of clubs one carries is in the neighborhood of twelve; fourteen is the maximum number allowed by the rules.)

• Humility. This is my overall favorite because of its spiritual implications. As soon as you lose a hole, you have to carry your opponent's bag until he loses a hole and then he must carry yours. It is also my favorite because my bad back excludes me from playing it.

To my knowledge, no other game in the world can be played in at least 196 different ways. The phenomenon is so remarkable, we need to look at it more deeply. Why such variety? Not surprisingly, I believe, the answer is again another paradox: Golf is simultaneously the most and the least competitive sport in the world. It is so competitive that golfers over the centuries have stretched their minds to construct ever more ways in which the game might be used to fulfill their competitive instincts. Yet golf is also so noncompetitive that they have been free to do so. Were it nothing but brutal competition, golfers would be stuck with the gross stroke play of the pros.

The paradox of competition/noncompetition in golf has been captured in the system of handicapping. This system makes it possible for golfers of distinctly unequal ability to compete against each other with intensity. Other than golf itself, handicapping has been golfers' greatest invention. As we shall soon discern, it has profound relevance not only to the sport but to our whole society.

It has been said that "God is in the details." In order that we might discern the true godliness of handicapping in golf, we must first comprehend the major details of the system. To do so, we will look at formal handicapping.

Formal handicaps range from 0 to 36.

A player with a handicap of 0—meaning no handicap at all—is referred to as a *scratch golfer.* On a reasonably good day a scratch golfer will shoot par (a total score of 72 for an eighteen-hole round on a standard course) or better. He or she is very, very good and might want to consider quitting a more ordinary job to take up golf as a profession.[3]

On a reasonably good day a player with the highest possible handicap, 36, will shoot an average score of 108 on the same course. He or she would be considered a mediocre golfer at best. How can she or he possibly compete with the excellent scratch golfer?

Simple. In gross stroke play this high-handicapped player will simply subtract 36 from his score of 108 to make a *net score* of 72. If the scratch golfer shoots par exactly, he and his high-handicapped opponent will end up exactly even. If the scratch golfer has a particularly good day, shooting a 4-under-par 68, he will beat his opponent by four strokes. If he has a slightly bad day, shooting a 76, and his mediocre opponent a slightly good day with 106, then the mediocre player will win the round by six strokes.[4]

How do you get a formal handicap?

First, you must want to get one. Second, you need to play golf with some regularity at a legitimate golf club of which you usually must be a member. Finally, each time you play an eighteen-hole round at this course, you must post your score for the round. At some clubs you do this by writing it against your name on a public scoreboard; at others you do it more discreetly simply by dropping your scorecard into the slot of a locked box that may look, for all the world, like a postal box.

At this juncture the administration of the club—or more likely its computers—takes over. Typical of golf, there are a variety of ways in which the club may then compute your handicap. The simplest and most common is to average the best ten of your last twenty posted scores. For instance, if your last twenty scores ranged from 82 to 99, but your ten best averaged 86, and par for the course is 72, then your handicap will be 86 minus 72, or 14.

What's the point of all this effort? Actually, there are four points deserving of note:

1. Your formal handicap reflects you at your best. Whatever system your golf club uses in determining it, your handicap is always just a bit lower than your usual score. Yes, it gives you a considerable leg up in competition, but it is also designed to challenge you and keep you on your toes.

2. Your handicap will eventually be withdrawn if you don't continue to post scores with reasonable frequency. This means that it is routinely recalculated so that it will decrease as your game improves or increase if your game deteriorates.

3. Your handicap instantly allows other golfers to have a good idea of the quality of your game. If you and I, as strangers, were paired by a starter on the first tee, you might modestly say, "I'm not very good. I hope I won't drag you down." Having watched you idly taking a few practice swings behind the tee, I am skeptical and may even be so bold as to inquire, "What's your handicap?" When you answer, "Fourteen," it will be my turn to say, "I'm the one who will be dragging you down."

4. Your handicap will permit you to play not only in amateur tournaments at your club but also as a visiting guest in similar tournaments at most clubs throughout the world. Like science, the system of handicapping is an international, cross-cultural phenomenon. The only wrinkle is that when you play a course that is easier or more difficult than your home course, your handicap may be adjusted slightly lower or higher. This adjustment is made by a mathematical formula taking into account the different slope of the courses.

On the last hole I noted that in competitive play you will be watched too closely to cheat, even if you wanted to. But is it possible to cheat in regard to this business of handicaps? Golf lore holds that it is and even has a specific name for such cheating: *sandbagging*. To sandbag is to deliberately hit poorly in ordinary play so that you can post high scores and obtain a high handicap. With this unrealistically high handicap, you can then supposedly enter tournaments and clean up by playing the game according to your true ability.[5]

Despite the lore I doubt that anyone ever has sandbagged. Certainly I've never seen anyone do it. But the concept remains useful in the construction of backhanded compliments. If you are playing atrociously on a particular day, we, your fellow players, are likely to comment, "Oh, you're just sandbagging." Our true intent is to make you feel a bit better through the hidden message "We know you're just having a bad day and you're a much better golfer than this." Or if you win a tournament, we may exclaim, "Well, you old sandbagger, you!" actually meaning, "Congratulations, you must have been really hot."

Riding in a cart between holes one day, Lily, with her characteristic genius, casually remarked, "Handicapping is just a form of affirmative action."

Of course! My mind practically exploded with the possibilities. Among other things, it occurred to me that handicapping in golf is relevant to the issue in the following ways.

• There is a limit to handicapping. To have even the highest handicap of 36, one must have at least some ability. If your average playing level is triple bogey or worse, then you're out of the running. You may be ready for training and practice, but you're not yet ready for formal competitive golf.

• Your handicap is based not on your average performance but on your average *good* performance. A few might consider this to be a burden. Most golfers, however, look at it as a challenge they need to live up to and even exceed.

• Indeed, if you are at all serious about golf, it is expected that you will *work* on your game and that your performance will thereby gradually improve over time. Sandbaggers, if they exist, might see the result as a detriment to their handicaps, but all the golfers I know are proud and pleased when their handicap is diminished.

• No one is simply entitled to a handicap in golf. You must work to get one and work to keep it.

- Whether they are high handicapped, low handicapped, or scratch, all golfers play by the same rules and must abide by the same laws. A high handicap in no way relieves you from having to take your due penalty strokes.

- Golfers are not ashamed of being handicapped. No low-handicap player ever looks down on a high-handicap one. We do not expect ourselves to be equal. We know we have differing abilities both on and off the course.

Consider the implications for business organizations. Although a range of competencies would be acknowledged, everyone couldn't just walk in the door expecting a job. Employees would have to be at least minimally qualified on the basis of their personal, relative, above-average performance at the time of hire. While minimally or only moderately qualified, they would not be looked down upon by their fellow employees. They would clearly be expected to work on improving their job performance and be rated accordingly. In no way would they be exempted from any of the company's rules. If they failed to improve, they would not be promoted despite their longevity of employment, and should their performance decline in any sustained fashion, their "handicap" would in no way exclude them from being laid off.

I do not mean to imply that the system of handicapping in golf, elegant though it is, could or should be directly transposed to the workplace. Nonetheless, affirmative action is a highly debatable issue these days, and sometimes the debate seems to generate more heat than light. I seriously think that if those on opposite sides of the debate were to take a good look at the phenomenon of handicapping in golf, the light would increase and the heat diminish.

I have spoken of formal handicaps and formal tournaments. Does this mean there are informal handicaps and tournaments? Oh, yes.

Actually, whenever two or more players bet with each other, it is a tournament of sorts, with or without handicaps. I have played in only two formal tournaments over the course of my life. I have, however, played golf for money on more occasions than I could possibly count. Without even attempting to give a dissertation on the thirty different styles of betting in golf, I will describe my three most common experiences with this pleasant practice.

One has been with several long-standing men's foursomes who invited me in for a round because one of their members was absent and they knew my game was roughly equivalent to theirs. They played for skins, greenies, and sandies. A *skin* is when one of the foursome scores lower than the other three on any hole, for which accomplishment he gets a point. The player whose tee shot comes to rest closest to the pin on the green of a par 3 gets a point for a *greenie*. Any player who gets a par or better on any hole from which he had to shoot out of a sand trap also gets a point for what is called a *sandy*. Back at the clubhouse, over beer in the "nineteenth hole," the points are added up. In my league each point represents a dollar. This means I owe any player a dollar for as many points he has accumulated more than I— and if I should have any points, then one or more of the players might need to pay me.

There are, of course, variations. The skins, for instance, may be *carried over.* This means that if no player has the lowest score for five consecutive holes, the points are accumulated so that the first player to get another skin after such a hiatus may get six points. Handicaps are often computed in. For instance, if it is a hole we all par but on which you all owe me a stroke by virtue of my high handicap, then I will get the skin. Some foursomes have even been known to add *barkies*—a point for any player who hits a tree but still manages to par the hole.

You might think with all this it would be necessary for the players to carry around laptops along with their bags. Usually, however, the one of the four who is the consensually designated scorekeeper won't find it a mental chore and will perfectly recollect everyone's score on every hole if challenged at the end. Moreover, you need not worry about losing your shirt. As long as points are kept to a dollar, I'm not sure I've ever seen anyone have to pay out more than twenty dollars or so in total—or what you'd have to pay for a very cheap new shirt.

Since neither Lily nor I have had any desire to play in formal tournaments for more than twenty years, we've not bothered to maintain formal handicaps. Several years ago, after we'd entered semiretirement, I was working hard to assist Lily in regaining her lost enthusiasm for golf. I thought some money might help. I gave her a handicap stroke on par-3 holes, two such strokes on the par 4's, and three on each par 5. If she had a bad day we'd break even or I might even win one or two dollars. Usually, however, we'd finish our nine-hole round with me owing her three to four dollars.

It worked. Shortly she became so serious about her golf that we discontinued the practice. "I don't want to be distracted by betting," she announced. "I want to feel free to experiment more with different clubs and swings."

Needless to say, Lily's game has improved. Recently she remarked that someday in the not-too-distant future she might want to resume betting with me. But even she acknowledged that when that day comes, we'll need to work out a more equitable and competitive handicap system. Like maybe I'll give her two strokes on the par 4's and 5's and she'll give *me* a stroke on the par 3's.

When Wally, my best golfing buddy, and I get together, it is usually with our wives to play as a foursome. Lily and Barb, under these circumstances, choose not to bet at all. I'm not sure Wally and I could make such a choice, we are both so compulsively competitive.

He is the better player. He even has a formal handicap. I believe it is 18. Long ago, as I recounted, we decided on gimmes and a floating mulligan each nine. But since I don't have a formal handicap, how many strokes should he give me? On the eve of our first round, we argue vociferously about this. Usually he gives me around ten.[6] If either of us wins handsomely that next night, we will argue again over how much this number should be adjusted up or down. Then we'll argue later again about readjustments. Playing simple low-hole match play in this way, I can't remember either of us ever winning more than five dollars, but the arguments can go on for hours. It is the cheapest entertainment I know—not golf, but our arguments.

Usually in these informal tournaments of ours, he gives me my handicap strokes on those holes that are rated the most difficult. If I know the course well, however, my personal ranking will likely differ from the formal one. In this case I'll ask him to give me my handicap strokes on the holes I designate. Then we get to joust over whether he should accede to my request.

And occasionally we'll *press*.[7] The most common form of a press in golf occurs at the turn. If I'm five strokes down already after nine holes, it's virtually a foregone conclusion that I'll lose the match. This means the pressure is pretty much off. To keep it up, I'll press—meaning I'll pay you off now for the front nine if you're willing to start fresh on the back nine. But this is not my favorite variety. My favorite is a double-or-nothing eighteenth-hole press. If Wally is four up on me after seventeen holes—and he should accept this press—it would mean I'd pay him four dollars if we tie hole 18, eight dollars if I lose it, but nothing at all if I win the hole. I love this sudden, last-minute escalation of the stakes. But Wally may not feel like it that particular afternoon. If so, there will be no argument. He and I may be a little loose about our golf, but we are not loose about our betting, and it is a general rule of betting in golf that no one is required to accept a press.

To conclude this discussion of betting *in* golf, it should be noted that one need not be a golfer to bet *on* golf, any more than you need be a horse to bet on horse racing. People bet on golf in all manner of places, ranging from Las Vegas to their living rooms. Only one place and time did this ever surprise me. It was on Okinawa, where, as noted, players had to hire women caddies to "carry double." Lily and I were playing with another couple as a mixed foursome. We were not betting—we were out just for fun.

Only we didn't have that much fun. Both Lily and I happened to be terribly off our games on that particular day for no apparent reason. It also didn't help matters that our caddy, who had been remarkably pleasant at the beginning, became progressively sulkier as the afternoon wore on. Indeed, by the last three holes, she was downright nasty. Such a mood change was dramatic in and of itself, all the more so given the fact that the Okinawans are a notably friendly and gentle people. We were puzzled.

Our puzzlement ended as we came out of the locker rooms and headed for our car. There at the edge of the parking lot we spied our caddy handing several dollars to the caddy of the couple we'd played with. It suddenly dawned on us that they'd been betting. They may have been carrying our clubs, but we were their horses. Our caddy had bet on the wrong horse. It's kind of silly to get angry at a horse, but we now understand that in her mind we'd let her down.

. . .

No discussion of competition would be complete without mention of *gamesmanship*. The term was coined by Stephen Potter to denote the use of perfectly legal (albeit sometimes vicious) ploys to psychologically unnerve or demoralize your opponent in any form of competition, whether money is involved or not.[8]

Insofar as I might be excessively competitive, it is probably a partially genetic phenomenon. It is a measure of my father's goodness as a parent that when I was a child, he frequently played tennis with me although he would have much preferred both of us to be out on the golf course. It is a measure of his competitiveness that the time, at age twelve, when I finally beat him was the last time he ever picked up a tennis racquet.

My father was not only an internationally famous litigation lawyer but also a master gamesman. When I returned from Okinawa, I told him that I had taken up golf there, and he immediately arranged for us to play together at a course on Long Island where he had "privileges." Being still well practiced and at the youthful age of thirty-four, I was in my prime as a golfer.[9] I had no intention for that afternoon beyond having fun. We weren't betting, and I don't believe I even considered the occasion a match. On the fifth tee my father announced, "We've only played four holes, and you're already two up on me."

I was dimly aware of the fact, although until that moment I'd not attached any consequence to it.

But my father continued, "I had no idea you were this good. Why, you're probably going to beat the pants off me. Certainly the way you're shooting now. Certainly the way you're swinging. Not a hook! Not a slice! Now, you just keep it up. Keep it up, my boy."

Of course I immediately and completely lost it.

I never did beat my father at golf, even when he was in his advanced old age. But then I never tried to. God knows I didn't want him to put down his clubs forever.

If anything, my father was a negative role model in this respect, and I have mostly gone through life trying to restrain myself from practicing gamesmanship. Occasionally, however, I slip up, and my shadow pops out. The most recent occasion centered on tee markers.

Tees are designated blue, white, and red because each has markers of that color.[10] These bilateral markers are moved a few yards ahead or behind each day, primarily in order to protect the turf. The rule of golf is that you should tee your ball up either exactly on an imaginary line between the two markers or else within two club lengths behind that line. It is illegal to tee up in front of the line, even if doing so places your ball only a few inches closer to the hole.

When your opponent violates this rule, you have four options. The only kind one is to overlook the violation. The most vicious is to let him go ahead and hit, but then point out that he has violated the rule and that in doing so, he has either incurred a penalty stroke or forfeited the hole entirely. Although some might consider this option to be gamesmanship, I deem it something worse: the most crass form of *rulesmanship*. A third option is to point out to your opponent that he is about to be in violation of the rules the very moment he tees his ball ahead of the markers. You could look upon this gambit as gentle teaching or—since it will likely slightly unnerve your opponent—a possibly mild form of gamesmanship. On the occasion in question, however, I took the fourth option.

Phil, both a friend and business associate, visited us a couple of years ago. The primary agenda was to discuss mutual philanthropic concerns. But the time was somewhat flexible, and he demonstrated interest in a nine-hole round on our local course with the disclaimer, "I haven't touched a club for twenty-five years."

So we went out to play. By the second hole it was clear he'd retained all his skills over the supposed generation he'd been away from the game. While gamesmanship has everything to do with competition, it may have nothing to do with betting or formal competition. In this case we weren't betting at all. The agenda was pure fun. Nonetheless, by the eighth hole I was conscious of being pissed that he was so good after all this time. On the eighth tee he teed up his ball at least three inches in front of the markers. I waited. I waited until he addressed the ball. I waited until he had almost finished his waggle. And then, just as he was starting his backswing, I coughed loudly and announced, "Phil, you've teed up wrongly."

His drive, when he finally made it, was horrible.

I do not recount the incident because I am proud of it. To the contrary, I believe it was a moment when my shadow side, my competitiveness, got out of hand. It was good gamesmanship on my part, but it was also unkind and less than civil. Neither of us had acknowledged that we were competing in the least. He was clearly annoyed. I wish I had it to do over again so that I could say nothing at all. Nonetheless, I must acknowledge that a small part of me still chuckles over the moment. I also hope there is a small part of Phil that can today forgive me and chuckles over it also.

On the next hole we shall consider the enormous internal competitiveness of golf as I focus upon my titanic battle with my own anger and narcissism on the links. Our entire discussion for this hole has been upon *external* competition—namely, the battle in which we engage with or against others.

It has not been a comprehensive discussion. I've not said anything about the possible origins of the competitive instinct in us humans or in other species. Nor anything about the possible perversions of that instinct.[11] What I've most wanted to get across is the wonderful paradox of competitiveness and noncompetitiveness in golf. The paradox relates to our free will as humans. We are free to compete or not compete. There is no other sport or game I know in which we have such complete freedom. And most of the time when I am playing golf, I am not competing with another human being in the least.

Then why externally compete in golf at all? There are three reasons.

One is to make a livelihood. As I've made clear, this is not an option for 99.9 percent of us. We are better off competing for our livelihood in some other field of endeavor.

The second is that competition with others can be great fun. I emphasize "can be." If it's not fun for you on the golf course, then stop it! When you are feeling up to it, competition in golf is more fun than any other competition I know. Still, in order to remain fun, delicacy is required. There is sometimes a fine line between thoughtless competitiveness and viciousness. If you find a few points here or a few dollars there obsessing you or causing you to behave in ways you'd rather not, don't cease playing golf; just cease competing. At least for a while. At least with that particular person. Practice some kenosis. Empty yourself of your excessive competitiveness. For the moment, however, Wally and I seem to be able to mutually walk the fine line, and I look forward to nothing more than our next reunion on the course.

There is for me a final reason for external competition in golf: Generally, I play a little bit better when I am involved in external competition. The phenomenon may even be explained by the expression "It keeps me on my toes."[12] Most pros will tell you that the best stance for hitting a golf ball is not when your weight is on your heels or when you're flat footed, but when you're ever so slightly balanced on your toes. Yet this stance is not quite natural. It doesn't happen when we're feeling lazy. And since our original sin is to be lazy, our natural inclination is to forget to stay on our toes. Yet once again it is a matter of paradox. We need to relax, but not too much. We need to concentrate, but not too much. Mild competition spurs me to remember all the things I know about golf but tend to forget. With such competition I am helped to stay on my toes, not just literally but in all the other respects that the game requires of me to play at my best.

NOTES

1. Linda Valentine and Margie Hubbard, *Golf: Games Within the Game* (Crest, 1987). The authors are among those who got seduced into golf by their husbands and then became fascinated by its variety. Although they went to an enormous amount of trouble to do thorough research and to self-publish their book, they apparently never dreamed it might sell because they never put a publishing address on it. Consequently, as best I can ascertain, it is currently out of print. It is my hope that some publisher will hire a private detective to find its bashful coauthors, because it is a lovely little book that deserves republication and a broader circulation.

2. I have no idea why Scotch is called such. Possibly it was invented in Scotland. My more probable fantasy, however, is that the game is an American invention and was so named because of the American (usually inaccurate) stereotype of the Scots as "cheap." Certainly it is slightly less expensive to play golf with one ball than two. As to why the variation of Scotch is called Acapulco, I wouldn't even hazard a guess.

3. The word *scratch* is used differently in several sports (cricket, billiards). In golf its use possibly comes from the old expression *up to scratch,* for "meeting a high standard."

   Handicapping is used somewhat similarly in certain other sports, such as horse racing, as well as for burdens or disabilities. Although it is a word in broad usage, its etymology is obscure.

4. It may be equally simple in match play. Our scratch golfer will simply "give" his 36-handicap opponent two strokes on every hole. If he gets a par on any given hole

and his opponent a double bogey (2 over par), they come out "even." Similarly, if he gets a birdie (1 under par) and his opponent a bogey, they will also be even for the hole. If he gets a birdie and his opponent a double bogey, the scratch golfer will win the hole. If he gets a par and his opponent a bogey, then, there being only a one-stroke difference, his opponent wins it.

But it is not often that a scratch golfer gets paired against such a high-handicapped one. Let's consider a more typical pairing of opponents, one with a handicap of 10 and the other with one of 20—a ten-stroke difference. In gross play it is again simple. The higher-handicapped player merely subtracts ten strokes from his total score at the end of the eighteen-hole round. In match play, however, there is a major wrinkle: On which of the eighteen holes does the better player give the lesser his or her ten strokes?

The dilemma has been resolved by committee—often the same committee of visiting professionals who have formally determined the *slope*, or level of difficulty, of a particular course. On the same sorts of grounds the committee will rank each of the eighteen holes according to its difficulty. This ranking will then be listed on the course scorecard under the category "handicap." On Exotica, for instance, this hole 13 is ranked number one in terms of its difficulty, meaning the officials consider it the most challenging hole of the entire course. With the ten-stroke difference in our handicap, as the better player you would have to give me, the lesser player, one of my ten strokes on this hole. Hole 8, on the other hand, is ranked seventeenth, meaning that it is not a hole on which I would get a handicap stroke from you in formal match play. You par it; I bogey it; I lose it.

5. Although the term is used in a somewhat similar fashion in the game of poker, it is unclear how it got into either poker or golf. By now it must be indubitably clear how much I wish some real scholar would eventually come along with the patience to thoroughly track down the origins of the remarkably rich language of golf.

6. You've been dying to know, haven't you? If I did have a formal handicap, I suspect it would be in the neighborhood of 26.

7. In golf this term reflects the emotional pressure involved.

8. Stephen Potter, *Gamesmanship* (New York: Henry Holt & Co.). The book is long out of print.

9. Yes, at that point—the only point in my life—I did have a formal handicap of 18. Although I play just as much since my semiretirement, I'll never be that good again.

10. There may also be gold tees. These are located between the ordinary men's white tees and the women's red tees. They are designed for short hitters and are often referred to as "old men's tees." I am increasingly using them these days. Indeed, one of our arguments, when Wally and I are playing, is whether he'll give me the same number of handicap strokes if I'm "playing from the golds." Since he's thirteen years younger, it is proper that he should do so. On the other hand, if I am ahead, it is also proper—and less humiliating—if I return to the whites.

11. I will, however, offer an observation. Whenever I've encountered a human who despises playing games (and virtually all games are competitive), it has been someone who is probably excessively competitive. Such individuals refuse to play games simply because they cannot bear the pain of losing; it is such agony for them.

12. As far as I know, the expression did not originate with golf, but it surely might have.

If we are to grow out of our natural human narcissism into full humanity, then we must wrestle with personal demons along the way. No one can force us to do such wrestling. In other words, it is a choice to become humane.

THE HUMAN CONDITION

We have returned to the island's coastal plain and now get to play Exotica's second-easiest hole. So it is assessed, at least, with its handicap rating of 17. Certainly slightly under 300 yards from the white tee, as par-4 holes go, it is quite short, the shortest such hole on the course. Nonetheless, it has its quirks.

Is it an accident that Exotica's most difficult hole should be followed by one of its easiest ones? Perhaps, but it strikes me as somewhat symbolic of the human condition. Certainly we are continually bouncing back and forth between periods of ease and periods of difficulty. Someone once said that we are all manic-depressives. As a psychiatrist, I think that is an exaggeration. But it does reflect the reality that even the healthiest of us tend to vibrate between feelings of relatively mild elation (when everything seems to be going our way) and feelings of mild depression (when everything seems to be conspiring against us). And a frequent effect of a round of golf is to speed up the vibration.

Why such opposing feelings of elation and depression? We humans are creatures with a will of our own living in a world that often doesn't behave the way we want it to. This is frustrating. It means we spend a fair amount of our time being angry. Anger on the golf course is such

an important topic that we need to look at its permutations and combinations more deeply in the light of the human condition.

As we need also do with narcissism. The crux of the human condition is that we are inherently narcissistic creatures. The reason we get
angry, you see, is that we somehow believe that the world *should*
behave the way we want it to. What hubris! What extraordinary self-
centeredness![1]

If we are all born narcissists, then the spiritual journey is all about
growing out of narcissism. But the failure to grow out of it is extremely
common. Indeed, certain adult golfers are so self-centered that their
psychospiritual development has obviously been arrested.

The arrest of one's development out of narcissism can be even
more serious than chronic inconsideration. I refer to what might be
called a "narcissism of the will." If the world doesn't behave as we
want it to, it is natural and healthy to attempt to change it through
humane means. If and when it becomes clear, however, that the world
cannot be so changed, then most of us properly begin the work of
changing ourselves through acceptance. This process has been captured
in the famed Serenity Prayer so important to Alcoholics Anonymous:
"Lord, grant me the courage to change the things I can, the serenity to
accept the things I can't, and the wisdom to know the difference."[2]
Some, however, cannot or will not practice such acceptance. Instead,
they continue attempting forever to impose their narcissistic will upon
the world, not caring who they hurt—even kill—in their attempts.

But few golfers are grossly inconsiderate, much less lethal. This
doesn't mean, however, that they aren't still bedeviled by shreds of narcissism they haven't yet outgrown. So let me turn to the milder varieties
of narcissism, about which I am an expert. I am an expert not from my
experience as a psychiatrist but from my experience with myself, particularly on the golf course. Ultimately I shall be speaking of my own personal demons. I shall be doing so, however, because I suspect they are
also many of your own demons, since we share the human condition.

First I need to make it clear that not all narcissism is bad. Within
bounds it is the normal and healthy psychological side of our survival
instinct. There are times when it is most appropriate to "look out for

number one." It is as important that we wisely love ourselves as it is that we should so love others; indeed, we must do so in order to wisely love others.

Second, it should be understood that a narcissistic trait may be used either for good or for ill. Let me tell you about Major General John Milton "Micky" Finn.

As soon as I arrived on Okinawa in 1967 the army psychiatrist I was replacing said, "Boy, wait until you meet the commanding general of this island! He's the damnedest phallic narcissist I've ever seen." By *phallic narcissist* my colleague meant a type of man whose predominant and unconscious motive in life is to be admired for the size of his penis. It is a dynamic that frequently drives men toward high and famous positions.

When I did meet General Finn, I indeed found him to be a flashy type of leader, one who even carried a "swagger stick." I also found him to be wise, caring, and flexible. Over the course of the next two years, he became a mentor to me. During that time I witnessed him repeatedly behaving with genuine heroism. I also learned he had a golf handicap of 2!

The day before he left Okinawa on reassignment to the United States, he came to my office to say good-bye. I used the occasion to satisfy my curiosity. "You know how much I've come to love you, Micky," I said. "You're an extraordinary man. What do you think is the secret of your success?"

Thoughtfully, he sat back in the chair. Finally, with a grin, he answered, "I would say that the greatest desire throughout my life has been to be admired."

Micky was able to put his finger squarely on his own psychodynamics. He was conscious of his narcissism. Had he not been, he might have wrought all manner of havoc. Instead, being conscious, he had long ago given up a compulsive need to be admired by people. His primary desire had come to be that of being admired or pleasing in the sight of God. In so doing, he had become one of the most admirable people I've ever known.[3]

The least of the reasons I so admired Micky was his golf handicap of 2. But it was a sign of how much farther he'd come than I in mastering narcissism. Earlier I mentioned that a very large number of golfers tend to hit their first shot of the day poorly off the first tee. I noted they frequently explain this by saying that they "really haven't had a chance to warm up yet." I have no trouble allowing them that rationalization, but I can't use it myself. The reason I tend to hit my first drive badly is because I am being *watched*. The first tee is a busy place. I am being watched not only by the others in my foursome but also by the starter, possibly by a marshal, and probably by two or more members of the foursome to follow. This can feel like quite an audience. Being watched, I want to look good. I want them to admire me. So I strive to make a particularly great shot—and I flub.

The varieties of my flubbing sometimes seem almost infinite. One I haven't yet mentioned: Having made five or six easy practice swings without my driver even touching the ground, when I do tee off for real, I am likely to lunge at the ball, digging my club into the turf before I even hit it. This produces a topspin, which may be quite useful in tennis but has virtually no place in golf. On this hole, for instance, a topspin makes for a very low drive that, instead of sailing over the hillock of lava and coral a mere 100 yards ahead of the tee, embeds itself therein.

I frequently attempt to teach a basic principle of psychiatry: "All things are overdetermined." By this principle we psychiatrists mean that all symptoms—all sins, illnesses, flubs, or failures—have more than one cause. So I do not mean to imply that a desire to be admired is the only reason so many golfers tend to hit a poor first drive. There is a great psychological difference between taking a practice swing at an imaginary ball and actually "addressing" a real ball. In the first instance nothing is at stake. In the second it may feel like everything is at stake, and the accompanying emotion can border on terror. All golfers will know what I mean. Regardless of narcissism or pride, there is an inherent gulf between practice swings and swings "for real."[4] This gulf seems to be at its greatest with our very first real shot.

Nonetheless, when I am on the first tee, among the complex of feelings I am experiencing, I must admit that the primary one is the desire to "look good." This desire is not necessarily all bad, as I noted with Micky Finn. But when it is not in control, it can cause great harm, particularly to one's golf game. Because underneath it lurks pure panic at the prospect of "looking bad."

The point was brought home to me a decade ago when, as a member of the board of directors of a foundation, I was coerced into taking something called the Myers-Briggs Personality Type Indicator test.[5] This potentially most useful test divides humanity into some sixteen categories. The results put me very clearly into what is called the INTJ category.[6] As our expert consultant took pains to point out, each personality type has its virtues and vices, upside and downside. I beamed with pride when he noted that us INTJs—a relatively rare type—tend to be found in the highest positions of executive management. But then he proceeded to really hit the mark when he added, "If you want to psychologically demolish an INTJ, all you have to do is tell him that he's incompetent."

It is my terror of appearing incompetent that so often makes me flub on the first tee—and that causes my hands to shake on the putting green. They will shake more the closer my ball is to the cup. No one will think me incompetent if I miss a 30-foot putt, but I am certain they will think me so if I miss a three-foot one. Then I proceed to miss it. I've already told how psychologists call this a self-fulfilling prophecy. My terror of looking bad produces a prediction in my mind that I probably will look bad; my hands start to shake and cause me to fulfill the prediction.

My terror is a purely narcissistic phenomenon. If all I desired was to appear average, there would be no problem. But you see, I want to look as beautiful as a narcissus; I want to look perfect. Unlike thoroughbred narcissists, I know that I am not perfect. Yet enough fragments of my narcissism are left that I still want other people to think I am. I want to be admired. I want it too much.

It is obvious that I am caught in a vicious cycle. But neither you nor I should despair about such cycles. For one thing my desire to be admired is under much better control in the rest of my life. Indeed, it can even serve me well, such as by prodding me to keep my audience in mind so that I write with the greatest care I can possibly muster. At the same time I know in my guts that life is much more than a popularity contest. Yet golf is as subtle as it is demanding, and many have noted before me that the game is almost guaranteed to bring to the surface those flaws in a person's character that otherwise might not be visible.

Which is all to the good—at least as long as you choose to think of golf as a spiritual discipline. For it is only when our character flaws are out in the open that we are able to work on them. And such work pays off. I am happy to report that in recent years I've become much better at hitting off the first tee. I've learned how not to let those onlookers concern me much anymore. As for short putts, I've still got a long way to grow, but even in that respect I'm starting to see signs of progress.

When things don't go the way we want them to, our natural narcissistic response is to get angry. The more strong-willed we are, the greater will be our anger. Humans customarily direct their anger either outward or inward. When outward, golfers may blame their shortcomings on any conceivable aspect of the course, cursing the wind, the depth of the traps, the roll of the greens, and on and on. When their anger is directed inward, they blame or curse themselves.

My preferred, although not exclusive, style is the latter. It was Freud who first discerned that anger turned inward is the primary psychodynamic cause of depression. I have spent a great deal of time depressed on the golf course.

One winter afternoon, playing by myself on an almost-deserted muddy course, I was doing badly and typically feeling mildly depressed about it. I then made a particularly poor midfairway shot. Suddenly I heard myself exclaim, "Peck, you asshole, you idiot, you dumb, stupid shit!"

Now, I had been saying such things—and worse—to myself for years, but this was the first time I had truly *heard* myself saying them.[7] I was a bit astonished. From whence had come such depths of self-hatred?

As soon as I asked myself the question, I knew the answer: It was from the depths of my narcissism. Not only did I want to look good in public, I wanted to look good to myself, without spot or blemish. In fact, I wanted to be perfect. But a mere two pages back I wrote, "I know I am not perfect." True, yet here I was enraged at myself for failing to be. What was going on? I realized there were two parts to me: a rational, healthy part that knew full well I could never be perfect, and an irrational, narcissistic part that expected unending perfection from myself nonetheless. It was this latter sick and narcissistic part that gave rise to such intense "anger turned inward" and to depression.

As I've noted, anger—whether turned outward or inward—is poisonous to golf. Depression can interfere with one's performance of any task. But since golf is such a subtle task, depression is particularly deadly to one's game. I knew this from long experience. Now I knew more specifically that I would need to exorcise myself of my irrational, self-defeating narcissism if I was to play a better game. But how? I hadn't the slightest idea, and it seemed that I was stuck with the pattern. It didn't occur to me that I might need an exorcist of sorts, and I certainly didn't dream that the right one was waiting in the wings.

I've recounted how we may be paired up on the course with obnoxious people; more frequently it happens that we can be paired up with uniquely delightful women and men, sometimes even the teacher we particularly need at the moment.

One such time, shortly after I'd gotten in touch with my capacity for self-hatred as recounted, I was paired as a twosome with a man my own age. He was a top-ranking executive of a golf products corporation and, befitting his profession, a superb golfer with a single-digit handicap. He was also a gentleman, literally as well as metaphorically. He was a gentle person and therefore one I was unusually open to learn from. He taught me several worthwhile things about golf that day, but the most valuable was on the fifteenth hole, when he noticed that I was depressed after a triple bogey on the previous hole and, as a result, continuing to play poorly. "You know," he commented mildly, "we have an expression in golf: 'One hole at a time.'"

A lightbulb went on for me. Of course! I well knew the spiritual wisdom of the famed Alcoholics Anonymous saying "One day at a time." But I had never thought of applying it to golf. What this gentleman was suggesting was that I needed to put the previous hole behind me emotionally just as an alcoholic needs to put the previous day's—or week's or month's—slip-up behind him.

But how? How does one set aside anger at oneself? I turned the question around by asking myself how one puts aside anger at somebody else. This answer I knew: We get over such anger by forgiving the person. We can relinquish it only through the difficult process of for-giveness. Another lightbulb went on. I could put aside my anger over my performance on the previous hole only by forgiving myself. I had never before considered myself in need of self-forgiveness.

Yet I clearly was. Somehow, by Her grace, I knew that God didn't consider me to be an "asshole . . . an idiot . . . a stupid shit." Then what was I doing leveling such epithets at myself? Was I smarter than God? That smacked of arrogance. Of narcissism. I realized that God had no expectation that I should be a perfect golfer—or a perfect any-thing—and since She was quite willing to forgive me my imperfections at the game, I might have a certain obligation to do the same. Only my pride stood in my way.

At that point the exorcism was over, and I began the process of quite ordinary self-psychotherapy. I am still engaged in that psy-chotherapy today. There has been some progress. The concept of self-forgiveness that I needed to learn from golf must be practiced every time I play. The most important thing I have since learned is that the AA maxim "One day at a time," translated into golf as "One hole at a time," needs to be further translated into "One shot at a time." Forgive yourself each and every bad shot—as long as you have learned what it had to teach you—and then get on with it, free and unencumbered.

I have mentioned the words *demon* and *exorcism*. Surely I must be speaking metaphorically, am I not? Well, yes and no.

Contrary to prevailing public opinion, some very rare human beings do become demonically possessed and may require a successful exorcism before more ordinary psychotherapy can be fully effective.[8] I know this from professional experience, but let me begin with a story that is more than two hundred years old.

It was told to me at least a dozen years ago by Wayne Oates, a famed pastoral counselor and one of the saints of this century. A dozen years is a long time, and I apologize if my memory has failed me in regard to some of the details, but the gist of the story is this.

About two dozen years ago Wayne was traveling through the British Midlands. In the course of his travels he not only happened to stumble upon an old, and pretty, small Protestant church but also was able to read the church minutes dating back to the early 1700s. Toward the very beginning of those minutes, he noticed an unusually large section. Curious, he read it. It proved to be an extraordinary account of an exorcism that the church had performed on one of its parishioners in its early days.

The parishioner in question had been a single man in his fifties. Previously quiet, placid, and apparently sane, he rather suddenly went visibly bonkers. The minutes described him as being "afflicted with a Way of Despairing." It must have been severe because the entire church met at great length to decide what to do with him. Approximately half the members thought he should be "sent into the fields" (that day's equivalent of the state hospital, which is not much different from today's). The other half of the congregation felt they had a greater responsibility and should attempt an exorcism. The matter was heatedly debated back and forth. Finally it was decided that those in favor of an exorcism would try it, working in shifts, while the remainder of the congregation, also in shifts, would meet to pray for the exorcism's success.

At the end of a week the team succeeded in identifying and casting out "a spirit of fear," the minutes recounted. But since the patient was still bonkers, albeit in a somewhat different way, they continued their work. At the end of the second week they succeeded in exorcising him of "a spirit of rage." Whereupon he remained crazy in yet another way. Finally, at the end of the third week, they exorcised him of "a spirit of shame." At that point he was as good as new, and both he and the congregation then went about their more ordinary business.

For me personally the most powerful message of the story is the amazing community of that little church way back then—a community of caring and commitment that I doubt one could find in any church or anywhere else today. We have lost something extremely precious. But that is not my message for this book.[9]

Here my concern is with the notion of demons or spirits. From this distance I cannot tell whether the parishioner in question was suffering from demonic possession or from a more ordinary (but equally devastating) condition that today we would call a psychotic depression. Either way, he was apparently healed. And either way, in his despair, he was undoubtedly afflicted by spirits of fear, rage, and shame.[10] I have never seen a serious depression when these three emotional dynamics were not present in tandem. Indeed, the account could and perhaps should be used as a teaching case in training programs for psychiatrists.

While few golfers ever become so seriously depressed, I expect that every one of them, at one time or another, has had to wrestle with a spirit of fear and/or rage and/or shame, either on the links or off. Such wrestling can be good for the soul, and the golf course is a potentially ideal place for successful self-exorcism. I am reminded of the famed Saint Anthony (ca. 251–356 A.D.), one of the early Desert Fathers. In his twenties, as a hermit, he is reputed to have been violently tempted by demonic spirits, but he successfully overcame them and went on not only to live an unusually long life but also to become one of the great spiritual leaders of history. I wonder if Saint Anthony shouldn't be considered the patron saint of the golf course and of golfers everywhere.

Cases of genuine demonic possession are *extremely* rare. You would be ill advised to go around seeing true demons lurking in all corners, including sand traps. Nonetheless, a very few real cases have a great deal to teach us.

For one thing genuine possession is not an accident. The primary fault of William Peter Blatty's novel *The Exorcist,* and the movie adapted from it, was to depict a possessed, early-adolescent girl without offering even a hint of an explanation for her condition. This omission led some people to believe that you could go walking down the street one day, and suddenly, without reason, a demon would jump out of a bush and simply dive into you. This is not the way it works. In a later book, *Hostage to the Devil,* Malachi Martin began to correct this misperception.[11] In recounting five cases of possession, he offered at least a smidgen of evidence in each case that the victim had "cooperated" with the demonic. Certainly this was clear in my own two cases: Their possession began when they both "sold out"—one more or less to the devil directly and the other by choosing to believe a lie, not because she knew it to be true but because confronting it was, at the time, the more painful option. Great myths exist because they embody great wisdom. The myth of Faust (and others) making a pact with the

devil reflects reality. Those who become possessed have made a pact of sorts with the demonic. Usually they make it under considerable duress, but the fact remains that there is some kind of cooperation.

But what on earth has this to do with ordinary life and golf, with ordinary rage, shame, and fear, whether on the course or off? Remember the concept of emotional investment, or cathexis. The golfer who refuses to correct a bad habit, such as slicing, despite his despair over the matter, does so because he has a strange investment in the habit. He is cooperating with it, just as much as the habitual wife beater. The latter may despise his own behavior, but he persists in it because it has some kind of payoff for him. It may seem very strange that someone should have a cathexis in wife-beating or slicing a golf ball, but we humans are strange creatures in this way. Examine yourself honestly, and you will discover that you have at least one such cathexis. It may be to smoking cigarettes. It may be to hating smokers. It may be to almost anything. It is hard to give it up—we don't empty ourselves of our cathexes easily. It is not our human nature.

Patients who come to "deep" psychotherapy with proper intent do so because they recognize that they have one or more self-destructive cathexes of which they cannot empty themselves without external assistance. The very few who end up in a full-scale exorcism do so for the same reason, save that their harmful cathexes are to distinct "spirits" that are blatantly evil and demonic. As one patient said to me after her healing, "All psychotherapy is exorcism of a sort." But the somewhat different and more dramatic flavor of an exorcism can enrich our understanding of ordinary healing. With my love of etymology, I find great teaching in the term *exorcism* itself.

The word is derived from the Greek noun *horkos*, meaning "oath," and the verb *horkizein*, "to make one swear an oath." Contrary to the popular understanding, this does not mean that exorcists (who should always work in a team) swear at the devil or through other incantations "drive" the demons out. Save for the strange power of ordinary prayer, no magic is involved in an exorcism. I know. I have seen the incantations used to no effect, attempted as a substitute for or shortcut to the real work.

The real work of the exorcism team consists of gentle, almost tedious confrontation, clarification, and persuasion, to the point where the patient "swears an oath" to renounce his cathexes to the diabolic.

If the exorcism succeeds, it does so by enabling the patient to drive out or expel his own demons. In other words, it is ultimately the patient himself who is the exorcist through a change of will. Through his own free choice. An exorcism is indeed essentially little different from ordinary psychotherapy.

What all this has to do with golf or everyday life is that whenever we make any significant change, we do so by swearing an oath to change. We empty ourselves of our destructive fear, shame, anger, or other emotions—even our narcissism—only by vowing to do so. Of course, as I have suggested, we often break these vows or "oaths" like New Year's resolutions. This is quite normal. It too is a part of our human condition. Generally we must repeat our vows again and again.

The word *exorcism* is additionally instructive because its Greek root, *horkos*, or "oath," is closely related to two other Greek nouns: *horkane*, meaning "enclosure," and *herkos*, meaning "fence." This is important because whenever we resolve to give up something—to empty ourselves of it—we fence ourselves in. We relinquish some part of our freedom (even though greater freedom will eventually be the result). That this is so was eloquently expressed to me by two men who had once been close to evil and underwent a deep psychotherapy somewhat akin to exorcism. In the course of their therapy, each experienced a significant depression of some duration. I asked them why this was so when they were obviously in the process of getting better. One answered, "I used to make commitments without any sense of obligation to follow through on them. Then for the first time in my life, I realized I had to keep my promises. It was like being trapped." The other man, who had undergone a religious conversion as a part of his healing, replied, "Now that I have a real relationship with God, I simply no longer have as many options as before."

Should you wish in golf to exorcise yourself of your slice, then you must swear an oath to do so. And keep it. If you cannot change your swing accordingly, then you must ask your friends for advice. And if that doesn't help, despite your distaste for it, you must go to a golf pro. You have no other option.

I suspect that exorcising the demons of anger turned inward (depression) may be easier than exorcising the demons of anger directed outward. At least when we blame ourselves for the difficulties of golf, we hold ourselves responsible for them. Then we may be able to do something about the matter. But when we blame the wind, the traps, or the greens, we are absolving ourselves of responsibility. Yes, we can curse the wind, but there is precious little we can do about it.

This may be why my primary style has been to direct my anger inward. Directing it elsewhere—at least on the golf course—from the very beginning has struck me as rather hopeless or helpless. Yet while it has not been my style—priding myself as a realist—to rail against the sand traps or the weather of life, I do get angry at other people. So I have been involved in a few personal mini-exorcisms of my anger outward. The principle has been the same. I have needed to learn how to forgive these people, and before I could do so, I needed to see my judgmentalism as a fault—my own wickedness and not theirs.

My greatest learning in this respect has not been on the golf course but in hotel and retreat center rooms. As a member of the Foundation for Community Encouragement (FCE), I have participated in dozens of community-building workshops. My learnings have been many: how much we human beings are all different; how everyone has both vices and virtues; how much we need one another's different gifts; and how often I can take an instant dislike to someone, only to discover with experience that she or he is a saint. In a basic sense what I have to forgive is the human condition. It isn't that I don't have to do as much forgiving these days as before; it is that I have learned to do it more rapidly, whether the human condition is my own or someone else's. I have become more adept at emptying myself of anger through the practice of kenosis.

Still, it is at times necessary to chastise or rebuke someone before we can forgive him. Indeed, anger is a precondition for forgiveness. Let me make this very clear by quoting from a chapter on "Blame and Forgiveness" in one of my earlier books:

A great many people suffer from the problem I have come to call "cheap forgiveness." They come for their first session with a therapist and say, "Well, I know that I didn't have the greatest of childhoods, but my parents did the best they could and I've forgiven them." But as the therapist gets to know them, he finds that they have not forgiven their parents at all. They have simply convinced themselves that they have.

With such people, the first part of therapy consists of putting their parents on trial. And it is a lot of work. It requires briefs for the prosecution, and briefs for the defense, and then appeals and counterappeals, until a judgment is finally brought in. Because this process requires so much work, most people opt for cheap forgiveness. But it is only when a guilty verdict is brought in—"No, my parents did not do the best they could; they could have done better; they committed certain offenses against me"—that the work of real forgiveness can begin.

You cannot pardon someone for a crime he hasn't committed. Only after a guilty verdict can there be a pardon.[12]

What I did not point out in that book is that the same principle holds true for self-forgiveness. While some people, like myself, tend to suffer from an excess of self-blame and shame, others suffer from a lack of it. They forgive themselves too facilely, as if each and every mistake they might make were of such minor consequence that it can and should be glossed over and instantly forgotten. This too is "cheap forgiveness" and yet another permutation of the narcissism that is so much a part of our human condition. Remember I said, "Forgive yourself each and every bad shot—*as long as you have learned what it had to teach you*—and then get on with it free and unencumbered." You cannot learn what that bad shot had to teach you unless you recognized it to be "bad," and its badness hurt you enough to give it some thought. Otherwise you will never really get on with it. You may feel fine as a result of your cheap forgiveness, but your game will not improve.

Beyond that, chronic blaming is almost always an encumbrance. I concluded the "Blame and Forgiveness" chapter by stating:

The process of forgiveness—indeed, the chief reason for forgiveness—is selfish. The reason to forgive others is not for their sake. They are not likely to know that they need to be forgiven. They're not likely to remember their offense. They are likely to say, "You just made it up." They may even be dead. The reason to forgive is for our own sake. For our own health. Because beyond that point needed for healing, if we hold on to our anger, we stop growing and our souls begin to shrivel.[13]

Yet bear in mind that anger, in its right place and time, is a God-given emotion—given for the benefit of our souls. Not all anger, whether directed inward or outward, is an encumbrance to the human condition. It is our anger that allows us, when required, to draw a line in the sand.

I addressed this matter toward the conclusion of a highly successful Foundation for Community Encouragement workshop. Having "achieved community," the hundred participants were feeling very mellow. There was much talk about how nonjudgmental with one another we had become. This was true, but as the talk went on and on, it became a bit too sweet for my taste, and I was moved to speak. I told the group that I was an INTJ, emphasizing the J, which designated me a judging type of person. I expressed my gratitude to FCE for teaching me to gradually become much less judgmental. But I also noted that it was still useful and necessary that I make negative judgments about the behavior of myself and other people from time to time. Then to add a note of humor, I ended my little speech by quoting an ancient Irish prayer (or is it a curse?):

> *May the people love us;*
> *And if they don't love us,*
> *May the Lord turn their hearts;*
> *And if their hearts won't be turned,*
> *May the Lord turn their ankles,*
> *So that we can know them by their limping.*

I spoke of "drawing a line in the sand." When? Where? How do we know when and where to draw the line in our human relationships, to say, "This far you can come but no further"? Or "Beyond this point I will no longer tolerate and continue to condone your behavior"?

I don't know.

I have written about the issue in half my books because the most common request I used to receive before retiring from the lecture circuit was: "Dr. Peck, would you please give me a formula so I can know if what I'm doing is right?" This desire was articulated in thousands of particular ways. How do I know when I'm being loving or a masochistic doormat? How do I know when to interfere with my children or trust the way that they're growing? How do I know when to blame and when to forgive? And on and on.

But my response has always been that there are no formulas to relieve us from the agonies of making fine judgments. This too is part of the human condition. My only advice has been fully to experience the agony and ultimately to act out of uncertainty. It is yet another way in which we must continually practice kenosis in order to become and stay fully human, fully humane. We must empty ourselves of this almost diabolic need for certainty. If we can do so, if we can act out of "the emptiness of not knowing," then it is likely that our decisions and actions will be the right ones. In trying to explain this, I would often use its converse by saying, "Virtually all of the evil in this world is committed by people who are absolutely certain they know what they're doing."

So we have to continually make difficult judgments about how to deal with life. Consider the matter of friends. What new people do we deal into our lives? What old acquaintances do we deal out? This issue used to be particularly tangible for Lily and me as Christmas approached and we annually had to "prune" our Christmas card list. Had to? Yes. She and I are in the fortunate position of having been blessed by more friends than we can handle. (Thirty years ago we used to worry about how few friends we had!) Had we not pruned and repruned the list, I'd have to spend all my time writing cards instead of books. But I apologize to all those good people I pruned, and more recently to everyone, since ultimately Lily and I decided to stop sending any Christmas cards at all.

It is the human condition that we need to continually prune our lives in many respects to keep our balance. For any new activity we take on (even retirement, as Lily and I can tell you), it is necessary that we discard some other. And it is seldom quite clear which activities we should deal into and which we should deal out of.

Take golf, for instance. It is often expensive and always time-consuming. Despite my preaching, it is but one of the paths to salvation, and I will hardly judge you negatively for not taking it.

Nonetheless, I have a concern. I know a great many people who have the money and time for golf but who, on the basis of a little experience with the game, have dealt themselves out because it is so difficult. It held too many demons for them. This is fine. A decade ago I dealt myself out of playing the violin because I decided its difficulties were not worth my time. We can't do everything. My concern, however, is that the multiple demons and difficulties of golf constitute the least of the reasons you should deal yourself out of it. To the contrary, it is these very difficulties and demons that should cause you to reconsider the matter and possibly deal yourself back into the sport.

NOTES

1. Most are aware that the term *narcissism* comes from the Greek myth of Narcissus, a beautiful lad who one day looked into a pool and fell in love with his own reflection—so much so that he dove into the pool to embrace himself and drowned as a result. One version holds that he was then turned into the flower that today we call a narcissus. But the real meaning of the myth is that such extreme self-centeredness and self-absorption can be fatal—if not to the narcissist himself, then to the poor people who have to live with him.
2. Although this very great prayer has been justifiably made famous through the auspices of AA, it is also often attributed to the famed theologian Reinhold Niebuhr.
3. I recounted a version of this story in *A World Waiting to Be Born: Civility Rediscovered* (New York: Bantam, 1993), pp. 256–57.
4. This is the reason for the previously mentioned Japanese koan "Hit second ball first."
5. Trademark of Consulting Psychologists Press, Inc., Palo Alto, CA. Copyright 1976, 1987 by Isabel Briggs-Myers.
6. Meaning the "introverted, intuitive, thinking, judging" type.
7. Generally it is nicest to golf with company, but one of the advantages of occasionally playing by yourself is that you may notice things you otherwise wouldn't.
8. Most of my personal experience is recounted in a general way in my book *People of the Lie: The Hope for Healing Human Evil* (New York: Simon & Schuster, 1983), pp. 182–211.
9. For those interested in exploring the subject of community more deeply, I am happy to refer them to my earlier works *The Different Drum: Community Making and Peace* (New York: Simon & Schuster, 1987) and *A World Waiting to Be Born*. They may also contact the Foundation for Community Encouragement, P.O. Box 17210, Seattle, WA 98107, tel. (206) 784-9000.

10. This is not the place to get into the fine points of the difference between guilt and shame. Suffice it to say that they are close relatives; that in modest degree both are normal, healthy, and even necessary emotions; that in pathological degree both can be not only crippling but very much related to narcissism; and finally that our ultimate battle may be that against the "spirit of pride."

11. Malachi Martin, *Hostage to the Devil* (New York: Bantam Books, 1977).

12. M. Scott Peck, *Further Along the Road Less Traveled* (New York: Simon & Schuster, 1993), pp. 41–42.

13. Ibid., p. 46.

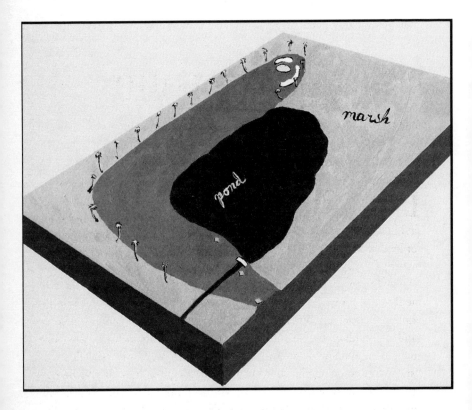

Eros is the spirit of creativity, and wherever you do not perceive the intimations of sexuality will be for you a spiritual desert.

HOLE 15

GOLF AND SEXUALITY

It seems appropriate to begin this discussion of sexuality and golf by saying a bit about passion. These days my personal passion is no longer for sexual activity; it is for liberation. This passion of mine has a long history.

Over the years that I practiced psychotherapy, it became clear to me that my primary role was to assist my patients in the process of liberating themselves. When they first came to me, they were all in some kind of bondage to false ideas. Each was suffering from at least one such idea. One way or another these ideas were all "shoulds" or "should nots": You should always be a caregiver; you should be heterosexual (or occasionally even, you should be homosexual); you shouldn't assert yourself because you don't want to be domineering like your father . . . or because you're black . . . or because you want everybody to like you; you should want to get married and have children because that's what women are supposed to do . . . et cetera.

Until they could be liberated from such false self-admonitions, my patients were not free to be themselves. They were not free to seek, discover, and ultimately express what another author, Joseph Sharp, has called their unique "sacred identity" or "sacred individuality."[1] What

Sharp is implying by "sacred" is that one's core identity is her soul. The soul is sacred because it is created by God; it is the essence of what God designed us to be. But bear in mind that, in Her love of variety, God fashions each soul to be different, unique. You were not designed to be like me or anyone else in the world. Consequently, there is no formula that prescribes what a soul should be. And herein lies the problem, you see, because parents, schools, friends, the media, business, and even churches are all, one way or another, trying to impose formulas upon us, and we are usually doing our best to live up to them. It's what we feel is expected of us. In other words, the whole burden of culture mucks up our sacred identities. Psychotherapists are not in the business of soul-making; only God makes souls. But they are in the business of trying to clean away all the muck.

Many of the false ideas that bedeviled those who sought my ministrations were cultural stereotypes, and many of these were specifically sexual stereotypes. I became a firm supporter of the women's liberation movement even before there *was* a women's liberation movement. And of the "men's liberation movement." Throughout my career as a psychotherapist, I needed to spend a good deal of time with at least half my male patients, helping them to get in touch with their feminine sides (as my own psychoanalyst had had to do with me) and an equal amount of time teaching my female patients how to nurture their masculine sides.

In these more recent days, when most women are not only *free* to work (the word itself is stereotypically loaded) but *have* to work outside the home, some think that the women's liberation movement is a fait accompli, a done deal. Some of what follows may seem dated to them. But I tell you that the liberation of men and women from sexual stereotypes has only just begun. A sign of the earliness of it all is the stridency involved—a stridency that in some external cases is still very much required but in other cases represents still-unresolved internal issues. There remain hot buttons galore, and if I should happen to push some of them, please be gentle with me and with yourselves. At the very least, as I have elsewhere written:

We still suffer from a lack of understanding of the individuality of vocation and from our tendency to stereotype. The one downside of the women's movement is that it has led a few women to feel uneasy with their calling to heterosexuality, marriage, and motherhood and some men to feel guilty over a lack of vocation to housecleaning and child raising. This is stated not to denigrate the movement in the least, but simply to warn that stereotypical liberation becomes its own variety of imprisonment.[2]

What makes this hole "sexy," so to speak, is its lagoon. Geographically the lagoon is the meeting place between the ocean water, as it runs through the salt marshes of the coastal plain, and the fresh water, as it runs off the windward side of Mount Intrepid. It has been there since time out of mind. The genius of Exotica's developers was simply to design this hole around it. One of this lagoon's interesting features is that if you look closely, you can see a fair number of crocodiles lazily floating in its brackish waters.[3] You might think of them as symbolizing some of the dangers that can lurk in the darker aspects of sex.

The crocodiles are not likely to influence your play, but the lagoon itself will totally determine how you handle this hole. There are three options. The expert will likely elect to "go for the green," hitting across the lagoon in its entirety. Although dangerous, the option has been deliberately designed to be enticing and seductive.

So has sex. The summer I was fifteen, my family belonged to a golf club on Long Island. At the end of an evening of dancing in the clubhouse, if she was willing, my date and I would wander off across several dark fairways to "make out" in a sand trap at the edge of one of the greens. By making out, I mean that I would get somewhere between first and second base (to mix in a nongolf metaphor) on those balmy summer nights. For some reason it was always my date who afterward would steal the flag off the pin of the adjacent green to take it home with her as a symbol and memorial of sexual conquest. In retrospect it all strikes me as relatively innocent. I can remember feeling at the time, however, that it was extremely seductive, enticing, and somehow dangerous.

Although it is surely possible even to "go all the way" and actually have sex on a golf course, that is not the purpose for which courses were created.[4] So it is not my purpose here, beyond what I've just done, to discuss the sex act. Yet sexuality—the psychospirituality as well as

the physiology of sex—is so pervasive and important that I cannot do justice to golf as "life condensed" by excluding the subject.

There is still an extraordinary number, men and women alike, who continue to think of golf as primarily a "male thing." Golf far surpasses any other sport in the plethora of jokes it has given birth to. Naturally, some of them are about this matter.

According to a popular golf joke, Joe, Tom, Dick, and Harry are playing their usual Saturday round on the local course. Just after eleven o'clock in the morning, they tee off on hole 7, a lengthy par 4 running alongside a highway. As they reach the middle of the fairway, a funeral procession begins to pass by, all lights on, hearse in front. Seeing it, Joe takes off his cap, holds it to his chest, and facing the highway says to his companions, "I wonder if you wouldn't mind joining me in a moment of silence."

So Tom, Dick, and Harry take their hats off also and stand at silent attention. As soon as the funeral procession moves out of sight, Joe replaces his cap. His companions do likewise. As they return to their game, Harry comments, "Gee, Joe, I didn't know you were a religious man."

"I'm not, really," Joe responds. "It's just that on Monday we would have been married for thirty-five years."

Essentially it is a very sad joke. One does not hear of tennis widows, skiing widows, or even poker widows. Yet everyone has heard of golf widows. The term invariably refers to women. It bespeaks not only the amount of time golf can take their husbands away from them, but also the passion for the game that allows "their men" to take such time. It also bespeaks the darker issues of sexuality and marriage.

There are lots of stereotypically bad marriages, but few stereotypically good ones. Yes, when the partners spend a great deal of time apart, it may be a sign of sickness in a marriage. But it may also be a sign of health. "Let there be spaces in your togetherness," Kahlil Gibran began his great poem on marriage.[5] Many healthy couples come to make a goodly amount of space for each other to "do their own thing." And golf may not be a healthy wife's "thing" at all. Such a woman, however, is unlikely to refer to herself as a golf widow.

The woman who does consistently refer to herself as a golf widow is proclaiming herself to be a martyr: a martyr to golf and a martyr to her husband. But there is no room for martyrdom in a healthy marriage. Not even for feelings of martyrdom, except very occasionally.

The golf widow may be accurate in thinking herself a martyr—if she would like to play golf but her husband discourages her. A few men, in fact, do want to play golf only with other men, do not want to play it with their wives, and do not even want their wives to play it at all. They want their wives in the kitchen. Such men are indeed chauvinist, and their sexism may be the primary determinant of the sickness of their marriage. I say "may be" because their wives do have options. One is to defy their husbands and take up golf anyway, joining the ranks of women who enjoy playing it among themselves. Another is to seek a divorce. These are not necessarily easy options, but they are preferable to chronic martyrdom. In any case, the sexist husband is in desperate need of psychotherapy.

In a different, equally common and sad scenario, the husband would be truly happy for the wife to play golf either with him or without him. But golf is not her "thing." Yet she has no "thing" of her own, no activity that she enjoys by herself. She wants her husband to stay home to somehow keep her amused. She refers to herself as a golf widow in order to make him feel guilty for not staying home. Yet she is driving him away. Thankfully, as the women's liberation movement proceeds, such marriages seem to be on the decrease. Yet Lily and I met one of these stereotypical couples just recently. As far as we could tell, the wife had earned her golf widowhood, and her martyrdom was mostly self-imposed.

In any case, golf is not necessarily a "male thing" at all. Perhaps it was, more than a hundred years ago, although one sees Edwardian paintings depicting women at golf in huge hats and long skirts. If they could play golf back then with all those encumbrances, think what they can do now! In my recent years on the course, I would estimate that a third of my fellow golfers have been women—women playing with women as foursomes, threesomes, and twosomes; women playing with husbands, boyfriends, or just friends in all the same permutations and combinations; and even nowadays occasional women playing by themselves or with whomever the starter happens to pair them with. It is not just an American phenomenon. I have been impressed and delighted by the huge numbers of Japanese women playing golf with each other or, more commonly, with their men. I love women, and one of the many reasons I so love golf is that it has become one of the least sexist sports in the world.

Lily (who is Chinese and the human being I know best) took up golf on Okinawa shortly after I did. She very much enjoyed playing with a particular woman friend, but she also enjoyed playing with me. I thought she was as hooked on the game as I.

After Okinawa, for the next twenty years we were so busy, we had relatively little opportunity to play golf. When the opportunity did arise, sometimes she would play and sometimes not. She was quite unpredictable about it. But at least one of our children was still underfoot, and I simply assumed her unpredictability to be the result of her intense involvement in motherhood, as well as her own practice as a psychotherapist.

Six years ago, as we moved toward semiretirement and the children were no longer underfoot, we began to have ever more opportunity for golfing. Yet Lily remained unpredictable about it. If I asked her whether she wanted to play the next day, she'd usually respond, "I'll tell you in the morning." And when morning came, as often as not she'd say, "No, you go play by yourself." I was puzzled. Why this strange reluctance to commit herself to the game? It was a total mystery.

It was also annoying to me. I would have preferred routinely playing with her rather than by myself or putting myself at the mercy of the starter. Lily's unpredictability also made for a bit of a problem getting tee times. But I swallowed my annoyance. She was her own person. She was quite entitled to do with her free time as she pleased. And I wasn't about to try to push her, knowing from long experience that pushing her was likely only to be counterproductive. So I was very patient about it, gently encouraging her but always respecting her space to be separate and different.

The strategy (if you can call it that, along with the betting I described on the last hole) eventually paid off. Three years ago Lily became rehooked. Whoopee! It is perhaps the greatest delight of my life these days that I am routinely and predictably able to play golf with my very best friend.

It is also a delight that the mystery has been solved. The more you play golf with someone, the better you are likely to know that person— or the more she will choose to reveal about herself. Gradually I came to realize that the reason Lily had been so hesitant about becoming recommitted to golf was her hesitation to deal with her demons on the course. And what are those demons? As we shall soon see, pretty much the same as my own.

When I was young, I used to bounce back and forth between thinking that women were aliens from outer space and that they were, except physically, no different whatsoever from me and "us men."

The longer I've been married (thirty-nine years now), worked closely with others in a not-for-profit organization, and practiced psychotherapy, the more impressed I've become by the power and paradoxical mystery of sexuality. The paradox is that men and women are simultaneously human *and* profoundly different. The power resides in the profundity of the difference and the mystery in the obscurity of its depths.

The essence of sexuality is difficult to pinpoint. The fact of the matter is that I cannot put my finger on the essence of sexuality, any more than I can on God. Each man and each woman is unique. No one's sexuality is totally stereotypical. Indeed, the *mystery* of sexuality is so deep, so profound, that my treatment of it here in a single chapter will inevitably be superficial. So because it is easier, I shall begin by focusing not on the differences of sexuality but on the facets of the human condition that we women and men have in common.

By the end of my career as a psychotherapist, I had reached, I believe, a most important conclusion about the matter. Different though their roles might be and the cultural stereotypes with which they were raised, and different though their sexuality is, women and men share the essential dynamics of the spiritual journey. Only the superficial flavor might differ. Men and women alike have to deal with the issues of growing up, of sexuality, of becoming independent from their parents and learning to think for themselves; issues of competence and incompetence, of interdependence and collaboration, of giving and receiving;[6] issues of God and religion; issues of death and separation and loss; issues of their own aging and dying, of losing beauty, mobility, and power, and ultimately of losing independence and needing to hand over the reins, to give up control.

The list is not meant to be exhaustive, but I hope its point has been made. The truth is that despite our differences we women and men face the same major psychospiritual hurdles in life. The timing might vary slightly, and some of the external circumstances, but men and women alike must either overcome these hurdles or fail to do so with disastrous consequences. And although I have great respect for the Catholic Church, there is one aspect of its practice that I cannot countenance. Since the dynamics of the spiritual journey are the same for women and men, there is absolutely no spiritual reason for the Church's refusal to ordain qualified women as priests.

Because the dynamics of our spiritual lives are essentially the same, women and men are afflicted by the same demons—both on and off the golf course. What were the demons that made Lily so hesitant to recommit herself to golf? Fear of failure, fear of not looking good, anger at slow players, rage at deep sand traps, shame at flubbing, and the demon of competitiveness.

Only this last came as a surprise to me. You see, until these past couple of years, I'd not thought of Lily as competitive. After all, hadn't she made a point of losing all those card games to the children? But then I also hadn't considered the cultural pressure on women in our society to hide their competitiveness. Nor was I fully aware of my own stereotypical thinking that women should somehow not be quite as eager "fighters" as men. Lily is quite competitive, and I admire her for her courage in recently choosing to reveal that fact to me. Playing one day not long ago, she confessed that she resented me for being able to hit my long shots so much farther than she could hers. She's even acknowledged resenting me for being a foot taller and God for creating her short.

As I've revealed, I am just as competitive. The mature part of me rejoices when she is playing well. Yet when she gets a par on a hole and I get a bogey—as increasingly happens these days—another part of me feels a bit irritated. This is the shadow side of my somewhat excessive competitiveness. Lily has a similar shadow side. She appreciates my delight in her game, but she *loves* it when I get irritated for this reason.

Although they may have exactly the same demons, women and men do not always behave exactly the same when playing golf. The differences are noticeable, but it is usually quite unclear to me what they mean—to what extent they are determined by cultural pressures or by real, honest-to-God sexuality.

I've already mentioned, for instance, that a woman is unlikely to trample through somebody's out-of-bounds garden looking for a ball, whereas it is common for men to do so. Is this because women are more inherently rule-abiding or less ridiculously attached to their balls? Or is it because the man may be looking for her ball as often as his own, and she's just letting him do her dirty work for her—as she may have been culturally taught to do?

I'd like to delve more deeply into these ambiguities by using another example. About one time in ten, when playing with ladies, I've heard a woman ask another on the tee of a short par 3, "What club do you think I should use?" Approximately one time in four, when playing with a man, the woman will ask, "What club should I use, hon?" I have never yet heard an adult male turn to a woman or a man (unless it's his infinitely experienced caddy on a course totally new to him) to inquire, "What club should I use?" Why this dramatic difference in behavior? My belief is that most such behavior represents a "sexual game" akin to flirtation.

Men love to feel competent, and consequently they tend to be quite strongly sexually attracted to women who seem childlike, helpless, and incompetent—at least in such relatively minor matters as choosing which golf club to use for a particular shot. But are women actually incompetent to make the decision for themselves? No. Not unless they are beginners, but I'm not talking about beginners here. They are only pretending to be incompetent because it will be a sexual turn-on for the man in this little dance.

I call it a game because it is a pretense; it is not for real. All games involve an element of pretense—even golf. I am delighted when I get a par or take a couple of dollars off Wally, as if the matter were of great importance. Indeed, part of me even feels it to be important. Yet at the same time I know perfectly well that it is of no import whatsoever. God doesn't give a damn whether I get a par, and I'm quite aware that Wally will win back his two dollars in a day or so. I'm only pretending that it's important when it's "just a game."[7]

Most games are harmless pastimes. However, I do not think this to generally be the case with sexual games.[8] In large part it is a matter of consciousness. When we are at other sports, we are quite conscious of the pretense involved and aware that we're playing a game. But with sex this is often not the case. The man who is all too happy to instruct his girlfriend or wife about which club to use may not be the least bit aware that she is pretending to be incompetent.

But sometimes my concern in this instance is more for the woman than the man. Often she will not even be conscious that she is pretending, that it's just an act. Often she herself will believe she is incompetent to choose the right club. How can this be? It is because she has been taught from an early age that the appearance of incompetence is sexually attractive to males, so the pretense has become natural to her. At this point incompetence has indeed become part of her nature. I do not believe this to be good or healthy. I believe it is an actualization of a lie that has become destructive to her self-image and to her very being. Her self-induced incompetence is not a fact of her true sexuality but a harmful consequence of her unconscious enculturation.

Now, back to the male and his role in this not-so-playful sexual game. Women wouldn't be taught to play up to the "male ego" if there were no such thing. I honestly don't understand all the ins and outs of why so many men, myself included, have such an ego investment in appearing potent and competent. It is too complex. The best I can do in this limited space is to offer but one personal vignette.

I mentioned that my own psychoanalyst had to work to help me get in touch with my "feminine side." Had you asked me when I first entered psychoanalysis whether I was a dependent sort of person, I would have responded: "Scott Peck dependent? Why, he doesn't have a dependent bone in his body!" Indeed, I was so independent, I was one of those men who couldn't even ask for directions. Whenever we were lost, I'd pull into a gas station (I was the driver, of course) and require of Lily, "You do it, hon."

My psychoanalysis succeeded precisely because it taught me not only that I did have a few dependent bones in my body, but that having them was quite okay. As a result, I have no trouble asking for directions these days (which, in this respect, has paradoxically made me *less* dependent upon Lily).

Looking back after all these years at my terror of even appearing to be dependent—to others and to myself—I am still amazed at the depth of its roots. Some of those roots were cultural. I believe, for instance, that my identification of my dependency with "femininity" was primarily such. Other facets of the terror were primarily rooted in very particular family psychodynamics. Yet this distinction is itself potentially specious. Those family dynamics were definitely related to the sexual cultural stereotypes to which both my parents had themselves submitted. Yes, it can be quite complex.

It needs to be pointed out, however, that the lies of sexual stereotyping go much deeper than flirtation on the golf course. While encouraged to flirt, women are also taught from an early age that "good" girls should "play hard to get." This could be looked upon as either a healthily paradoxical sport or a grossly deceptive inconsistency. I think it is a bit of both. Underlying the inconsistent part, however, is a huge complex of cultural falsehood. I know. I somehow learned all the lies before I even reached fifteen and was first attracted enough to girls to go out into the sand traps with them at night.

Falsely, I learned that women aren't really interested in sex; that sex isn't nearly as important to them as it is to men; that men are *obsessed* with sex; that a man's brain lies between his legs; that men are animals and women are pure; and that both men and women who do not behave in accord with these respective cultural stereotypes are either "sick" or "bad."

But sex, like golf, is not all that it appears to be. And since the age of fifteen, I've had to gradually and painfully unlearn all these strange lies I unconsciously picked up, to empty myself of them. Somewhat oversimplifying the matter, it is now my perception that sex is much *more* important to women than men in our culture. Indeed, too important. It is women who are the more likely to be obsessed with sex, and our culture pushes—almost forces—them to be so.

Consider the media. Men will sneak into "dirty" bookstores for pornography that they will later look at in private, primarily for occasional masturbatory stimulation. But the production and sale of such media do not generally constitute a particularly successful publishing enterprise. You will not see them being perused on airplanes. What you will see on the planes is vast numbers of ladies reading "women's magazines." What is their content? Mostly disguised sex. Oh, there are no blatant pictures. But the most common article titles will be something like "How to attract a man," "How to keep a man once you've caught him," "How to revive your marriage," "How to enhance your beauty" or "your breasts," "How to slim your waist" or "take inches off your hips," "How to pick the right man," "Ten danger signals that your sexual relationship is in trouble," "What the smart bride should wear," and on and on and on, including tips about asking your man on the golf course, "What club should I use, hon?" These magazines are obviously big business.

Or consider TV advertising and how much of it is devoted not only to women but specifically to their sexual behavior: to their dresses and their jeans, their shoes and their hairdos, their undergarments, their perfumes and deodorants, their skin creams—above all, to an apparently compelling need to look younger. "The medium is the message," as Marshall McLuhan so properly pointed out.[9] What is the message of this media blitz? It is that women are first and foremost sexual objects, that their primary aspiration should be to "catch" a man in marriage, and that beyond keeping him caught, there really isn't that much point to their existence.

It would be ridiculous were it not for the fact that so many women—and men—consciously or unconsciously, totally or partially, buy into it. I cannot imagine a more demeaning and limiting message. Sexuality is most literally a vital part of the human condition. But whether female or male, we are human beings first and sexual creatures only secondarily. Although not entirely separable, our spiritual lives are infinitely more important than our sexual lives. Indeed, our spiritual lives often begin to "take off" only after we've become more or less dis-illusioned with the importance of our sexual lives. We need to counter-act the cultural media messages with which we are bombarded, which may be an even more pressing task for women than for men. I suggest that looking younger than we truly are is, if anything, even less impor-tant than scoring a par. Let's keep things in perspective.

In no way do I want to imply that sex is—or should be—the same for women as for men.

I have been impressed by split-brain research, which has recently demonstrated that the two halves of our brain tend to operate differ-ently in regard to perception and even thinking. Specifically, the left brain seems to be more involved in deductive, analytic reasoning, where we take things and analyze them into their component *parts*. Conversely, the right brain seems to be more involved with inductive reasoning, where we take parts and integrate them into *whole* con-structs or ideas.

Although less certain, some further research suggests that the right brain *tends* (only a tendency) to be more active or dominant in women and the left brain in men. Extrapolating, we might suppose that men are generally more comfortable dealing with parts and women with wholes.

If this supposition is correct, it would go a long way in explaining at least one aspect of the "battle of the sexes." Men do seem more likely to be interested in parts, such as breasts, penises, and vaginas, while women do seem to be more interested in the whole picture—the total "gestalt" of an evening—which might include not only sexual stimuli but also a candlelight dinner. It is natural then that women would fre-quently have difficulty understanding why men are so focused on these silly concrete physical parts, and that men would likewise have difficulty understanding why women might want to waste time with all this romantic candlelight stuff before getting down to the "real business."[10]

Although what I have just described are but tendencies with many exceptions, the subject has begun to move more toward differences of biology than differences in enculturation. We men and women are dif-ferent biologically, and I am not just talking about different parts like breasts and penises—or even brains. We move differently. We carry ourselves differently. Being a man, I love to watch women, and I particularly love to watch them at golf. They may not be able to hit as far as men (although a number of them can way outdrive me), but so what? I do not believe the advantage of the red tees represents blatant sexism; it is a minimal and realistic adjustment to a biological reality. And when it's good, a woman's golf swing is even more beautiful than that of any male pro.

Please do not think that this mixture of biology, psychology, and culture that we call sexuality is either simple or clear-cut. Like God, it is profoundly mysterious. I have knocked women for pretending to be "childlike, helpless, and incompetent" as part of a sexual game when they ask a man what club to use. I do not think that women are inherently helpless or incompetent. Yet I do believe they may be more innately childlike. Not child*ish*—they may be as wise as the wisest man—but child*like,* as in a child who loves to play. I have reason to suspect that women generally like to play more than men.

Take their fascination with clothes and makeup. Unquestionably, as I've suggested, this fascination is partly driven by cultural stereotypes of what constitutes effective mating behavior. But only in part. As I have written elsewhere,

> I also suspect that the predominant motive of most women using make-up is more obscure than the simple desire to be sexually attractive. As an efficiency expert regarding the extraordinary amount of time, energy and money such women expend on their make-up and clothes, I would have to conclude this practice of self-adornment the most wasteful activity on earth unless . . . unless I regard it as art. For many women, make-up is a kind of creative play whereby they make an art form of themselves.[11]

But painting themselves is hardly their only form of play. Just this very morning while I was reclining in bed, my feet comfortably ensconced on a heating pad, shaving with my electric rechargeable razor, Lily and our entire staff of two, Gail and Valerie, came bounding into the room and onto the bed. The reason for this violation of my space was to propose an even greater one: They had decided that they wanted to rearrange the furniture in my office. I was not enthusiastic about the idea. I know of few men who *ever* want their furniture rearranged. I know of few women who can ever tolerate a room for more than a decade without totally rearranging it. This deep-seated need to rearrange furniture clearly has nothing to do with sex per se. Consequently, it would be somewhat misleading to label it "sexual" behavior. Yet surely it is motivated by a rather profound "sex-based" difference that I can only ascribe to the feminine delight in play.

But what has this to do with *playing* golf? Everything, upon occasion. When the circumstances are right—when the demons are at bay—my experience is that women will take even more delight in golf than men. Indeed, I have never seen such joy as when Lily makes a great shot.

Finally, a few words about love—a subject even more profound and mysterious than sex or sexuality. There can be sex without love and love without sex. Nonetheless, it is generally sex and sexuality that leads people not only to mate but also to marry.

Most marriages are failures. Even a substantial number of those that last a lifetime seem to survive more on hate than on love. The stereotypical golf widow and her husband we so recently met were older than we. It struck Lily and me that they would likely go to their graves despising each other.

A successful long-term marriage is not an accident; it takes a lot of work—work that can be far trickier than playing golf. It is an awesome and arduous journey. In her classic work *On Death and Dying*, Elisabeth Kübler-Ross, M.D., elucidated the emotional stages people tend to go through upon being diagnosed with a rapidly fatal illness.[12] In sequence they are: denial ("They must have gotten my lab test mixed up with someone else's"); anger (at the doctor, the nurses, the hospital, their families, and, most of all, at God); bargaining ("Maybe if I go back to church and start praying again, my cancer will go away"); depression (when they work on facing the fact that the jig is really up); and acceptance (when they have truly accepted their imminent death; a stage of philosophic calm and spiritual light). It is important to realize that these stages can get mixed up; seldom are they completely linear—

just as golf and life are never completely linear. Even more important, you should realize that relatively few people ever die in the beautiful fifth stage of acceptance. This is because the depression is so painful that, when they hit it, they usually retreat back into denial, anger, or bargaining.

Although Kübler-Ross didn't realize it at the time she wrote *On Death and Dying,* we humans tend to go through those same stages in the same order anytime we make a major psychospiritual growth step. It is as if any significant change requires of us a "minideath," even though it is a death into new life, into a more vibrant state of being. The dynamics of such dying are similar to those of the kenotic process, whereby we empty ourselves of the old (kill it off) so as to embrace the new and better. This is true not only for individuals but also for groups and organizations. By way of example, let me recount how ever so gradually Lily's and my marriage did not die but managed to grow into new life.

For much of the first five years of our marriage, Lily and I spent a great deal of energy attempting to deny the reality that we were no longer romantically in love with each other. The next five approximately were years of anger at each other's glaring faults, with each of us trying to "fix" or "heal" the other. Our efforts were unsuccessful. It was a turbulent time. For roughly the next ten years we attempted to bargain it out with each other. "I'll try and change in this way if you'll change in that way," we'd say to each other. The process was sterile, unproductive, and joyless. The next ten were perhaps the worst, certainly the most painful and seemingly hopeless. Read "depressing." Each of us had precious little hope that the marriage could survive and even less wisdom that it *should* survive. Nonetheless, both of us were blessed with certain character traits that might be considered rather old-fashioned virtues, such as loyalty and pertinacity. We hung in there. Finally, around ten years ago, something rather miraculous happened: We began to *accept* each other. I began to see Lily's supposed faults as flip sides of her virtues. She began to see my weaknesses as necessary concomitants of my strengths. More and more we stopped trying to change each other, and paradoxically, each of us started to change more rapidly. Ever since it's been mostly wonderful.

You may discern that depression is the most crucial (as in *crucifix-ion*, or "hanging in there on a cross") of the stages, whether they be the stages of death and dying or the stages of a long-term marriage. Depression is the stage of kenosis, when—wittingly or unwittingly—we empty ourselves of our expectations, even our hopes. You may also discern that the stage of acceptance that follows is akin to resurrection.

I do not mean to imply that all lengthy marriages do or should pro-ceed in order through these stages, as Lily's and mine has done. That would be a formula, and I repeat that goodness is never stereotypical. Nonetheless, it is my impression that in those decent marriages that survive beyond the twenty-five-year mark, somewhere after about twenty years the partners learned how to stop trying to change each other and started learning to accept each other. (Isn't it amazing how rapidly we human beings grow?!)

I also do not want to imply that this is all there is to marriage. Among other things, there are issues of plain luck and instinct and even grace. As I have elsewhere written in a sort of verse form:

I thank You for my friends
And, most specially,
For my best friend.
Thirty-seven years ago,
When Lily and I were wed,
I did not know who she was.
Nor she me.
Nor much about ourselves.
Nor anything about marriage at all.
The learning was often to be painful,
Although without it
There would have been nothing.
Somehow we made it through,
And it would be wrong not to give ourselves
Any credit. But tell me this:
Utterly innocent back then,
How did I know
In my blind ignorance
That Lily—more different

> *Than I could imagine—*
> *Was right for me?*
> *I cannot explain it*
> *Unless You were invisibly at my side,*
> *Guiding me while I, like Jacob,*
> *Was unaware. And I,*
> *Like Jacob, must also now exclaim:*
> *"Surely God was in this place, and I,*
> *I did not know it."*[13]

As I've suggested, at times Lily and I were unsure we even should complete this journey of love together. But we got through those times, and now we are enjoying the payoff in the mornings at work, in the afternoons on the course, and during the quiet evenings at home. I hardly mean to suggest that golf is an essential ingredient for a successful long-term marriage. We know nongolfing elderly couples who have achieved the same payoff. Nonetheless, whenever I am relaxing my sore bones in a hot bath at the end of an afternoon of golf with Lily, I am aware that, by God's grace, our marriage has become a thing of mystical beauty—a beauty rooted in sexuality yet simultaneously transcending sexuality. It is love, but it is even more joyful than romantic love, and at such moments of awareness, my heart is filled nigh unto bursting.

NOTES

1. Joseph Sharp, manuscript in progress.
2. M. Scott Peck, *A World Waiting to Be Born: Civility Rediscovered* (New York: Bantam, 1994), p. 63.
3. How do I know they're crocodiles? The question reminds me of a poem by Ogden Nash about an aging professor of zoology who married a pretty young lady and immediately took her off to the tropical jungles on a field trip. One morning as he was working on his notes, his native assistant frantically ran up to him, announcing that his new bride had just been eaten by an alligator. Nash ended the story with the words:

   > *The Professor could not help but smile.*
   > *"You mean," he said, "a crocodile."*

Anyway, these creatures have sharp-featured snouts and particularly knobby heads. I can assure you that they're crocodiles.

I am not the first to note a potential relationship between golf and either crocodiles or alligators. In one of his relatively early cartoons, Charles Addams depicted a golfer (male, of course) in the rough attempting to pry open the jaws of an alligator to reach into its stomach for a ball. Standing on the adjacent fairway, his partner is saying, "Oh, for goodness' sake, forget it, Beasley. Play another one."

Actually, I have played on several tropical or semitropical courses with lagoons containing either crocodiles or alligators. I have never yet seen one of these creatures on the fairway. Nonetheless, I found it reassuring when a caddy once explained to me that while they can move very fast—far more rapidly than humans—they are very clumsy at turning. When you're trying to escape from an alligator or crocodile, he told me, "Don't run away in a straight line. Just zigzag, and you'll be fine."

4. Still, some might have a field day in doing so: for instance, in exploring such things as the vaginal symbolism of "cups" and "holes," the phallic symbolism of "shafts" and "clubs," and the whole notion of "scoring."

5. Kahlil Gibran, *The Prophet* (New York: Alfred A. Knopf, 1955), p. 15.

6. I used to think, for instance, that receiving was much more of a problem for men than for women, and so it might appear superficially. But my work both as a psychotherapist and in community-building groups eventually made it clear to me that on a deep level women are likely to have at least as much trouble being recipients of gifts as men do.

7. When pros are competing for tens or hundreds of thousands of dollars, the matter does become truly important in their lives. But for them (unlike their TV viewers) golf is frankly no longer a game or "play"; it is business.

8. Prostitutes (male or female) will often refer to their business as "the game." Wild animals killed to be devoured we humans call "game" because they have been the object of our hunt. Men who succeed in having sexual intercourse without any meaningful relationship may speak of themselves as having "scored"—hardly a way of dignifying sex.

9. Marshall McLuhan, Kathryn Hutchon, and Eric McLuhan, *Media Messages and Language: The World As Your Classroom* (New York: Simon & Schuster, 1980).

10. See my *The Road Less Traveled and Beyond* (New York: Simon & Schuster, 1997), pp. 28–31, for more elaborate coverage of these concepts.

11. M. Scott Peck, *In Search of Stones: A Pilgrimage of Faith, Reason, and Discovery* (New York: Hyperion, 1995), pp. 348–49. Or see the entire chapter on art, pp. 345–59.

12. Elisabeth Kübler-Ross, *On Death and Dying* (New York: Macmillan Publishing Co., 1976).

13. Peck, *The Road Less Traveled and Beyond,* p. 302.

Throughout the entirety of your life, try to remind yourself
to remember to remember.

H O L E   1 6

REMEMBERING

Because of giant winter storms, the course on the northern California coast with which I am most familiar has no trees. Relatively barren in this way, it properly refers to itself as a "Scottish links course." Introducing a group of business executives to it, I told them, "It has no trees and no water hazards. So no problem, right?" Of course I did not mention the fierce winds or the rolling greens, the salt marshes, the canyons, or the cavernous sand traps.

Except for the initial avenue of Australian pines on hole 1 and the banyans of hole 4, trees have not obstructed Exotica's fairways—until now. On this hole my beloved coconut palms become a major challenge. Two of them bracket the front of the men's tees, so you had better drive dead straight or else. We've dealt with what I call "fairway narrows," which can be created with sand traps. Here they are created by trees, one 200 yards out and the other 320 yards. Because the trunks of coconut palms are thin and their fronds appear insubstantial, these trees may look like less of a hazard than sand. But if your ball hits one of them and is deflected sideways into the marsh or bounces backward or falls at its base, you will feel differently about the matter. Sand traps are not the greatest of evils.

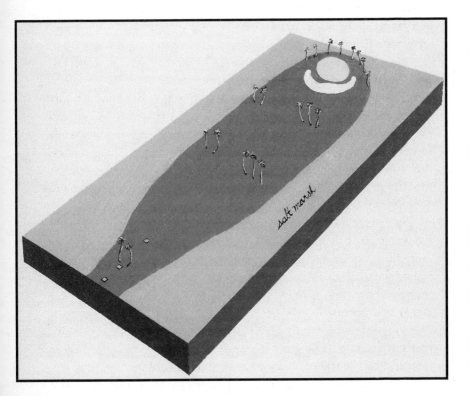

salt marsh

Exotica's greens are not atrociously fast. Still, if you are so eager to avoid the massive sand trap guarding its front that you hit to the far side of this green without backspin, your ball will probably roll among the trunks of the palms guarding its behind. You may have an easy pitch or chip between these trunks. Or your ball may be blocked by one of them, in which case you've lost yet another stroke. So it is on this hole, as on all the others of Exotica, and on almost all beautiful courses anywhere: If you are to play decently, you must stay alert.[1]

But what does it mean to be alert? More than simple consciousness. There has been a tendency in recent years to extol the virtues of "living in the moment." It can indeed be pleasant to be conscious only of the present, enjoying sniffing the flowers to the fullest, and we can even envy the capacity of the insects and the animals to do so. But while this may be consciousness of a sort, it is not complete alertness. A wonderful nun once pointed out to me that what makes us human is our capacity to bring to the moment both the imagination of the future and the remembrance of the past.[2]

So on this hole it may be quite useful for us to imagine what might happen if our ball were to hit the palm trees ahead of us. I am also more likely to imagine this when I have a memory of my ball stuck behind the trunk of a tree on a previous round I once played. Now, this may cloud our enjoyment of the moment. For instance, many have suggested that because of our capacity to imagine the future, we are the only creatures who are conscious of our impending death. Generally, they have seen this as a curse (although I have much reason to believe the curse can be transmuted into a blessing). Certainly imagining and remembering can be overdone. It may turn us into worrywarts, and it is not good to be too much of a worrywart—definitely not on the golf course. It will make our game worse. On the other hand, it will also make our game worse if we are living purely in the moment, paying no heed to the hazards ahead of us or to the lessons of our past mistakes.

On virtually every hole of Exotica, I have early made note of the hazards in front of us, to emphasize our need to look ahead into the future. Less frequently, until now, have I spoken of remembering. Our capacity for memory is one of the things that makes us human, yet I often refer to us as "the forgetful creatures." A paradox, is it not?

Nowhere is the paradox more dramatic than in golf. Every time I step up to the tee—and if I'm smart, every time I'm hitting from the fairway, rough, or sand trap—I say to myself, "Remember to relax, to swing easy, to keep your eye on the ball and your head down, to let the clubhead do the work, and to follow through to where you're aiming." Why this constant litany? It is because without it I forget to do all these things I know perfectly well I ought to do, all these critical things I know I need to remember but that I forget unless I remind myself over and over again.

Since we are such forgetful creatures, the golf course is hardly the only place where we engage in litanies of remembrance. Indeed, they are a practice of every great religion.

The Muslims seem to me to do it best. In the tiny bit of Islamic theology I've read, I've been struck by the frequency of the word *remember*. As a consequence, it makes sense that the Muslims should build their towns with towers from which to call out to the faithful five times a day to remind them to pray—to remember God. Only the most contemplative (or rememberful) Christian monks and nuns ritually pray the "offices" with such frequency, while for the traditionally religious Muslim, it is the standard practice.

Still, the most central ritual of Christians, whether they practice it occasionally, weekly, or daily, is a distinct ceremony of remembering. Most specifically, Communion (or the Mass or Eucharist) centers on remembering the Last Supper. In it the worshippers reenact the disciples' eating of the bread and drinking of the wine that Jesus gave them at the Last Supper, instructing them that these "elements" were his body and blood. He further instructed them in each case, "Do this in remembrance of me."

The greatest celebration of the Jews is Passover. In celebrating it, Jews very deliberately remember how God "passed over" or spared the lives of their firstborn children while taking the lives of the Egyptians' firstborn. Moreover they do so because God instructed them to celebrate the event as a remembrance of Him for the generations to come. And through the celebration they further remember how God led their ancestors out of Egypt and out of slavery. Another great Jewish holiday (read "holy day") is Yom Kippur, the Day of Atonement, which is specifically set aside for Jews deliberately to remember their sins.

Days of remembrance are not necessarily religious. The most notable in the United States is the holiday of Thanksgiving, where we reenact another feast, that of the earliest Pilgrim settlers celebrating their first harvest in the "New World." Even atheists and agnostics are likely to use their annual Thanksgiving dinner as a brief occasion to remember to be thankful for family, friends, and food. It would, of course, be wonderfully helpful to our souls and society if we could remember our sins and remember to be thankful each and every day of our lives. But being forgetful creatures, most of us are not up to it, and it is better that we should have a few of these formally designated days of remembrance than none at all.

A day of golf (and that is about what a full round takes, from the start of your preparations until you return home) may seem like a personal holiday, but it is hardly a holy day. Yet I wonder. Certainly if it is going to be a good day for you, it will likely, among other things, be a day of remembrance.

I have already recited the basic litany of remembrance upon the course: "Keep your head down, keep your eye on the ball, relax, swing easy, let the clubhead do the work, don't look up, follow through." That's the condensed version. I could add: "Remember to keep your left arm straight, to cock your wrists—but not too much—at the height of your backswing, and above all, to watch your stance. Are you firmly balanced, with your weight just a bit on your toes and with those toes (and heels) properly aligned with the ball (depending upon whether you're hitting a wood or an iron downhill or uphill) in the direction you want your ball to go?" Some could make the litany even longer.

Most of these rememberings have to do with one's swing, and if you are not a golfer, they will seem to have no relevance to your life. I have, however, almost casually mentioned some other principles of golf, easily forgotten, that relate to anyone's game of life.

- Remember to take adequate supplies with you. If you are a mountain climber, failure to do so may well cost your life. Golf is much less likely to be fatal and, to my mind, is infinitely more sane and enjoyable. Still, one needs to remember to take not only clubs, glove, shoes, balls, and tees but also a sweater or windbreaker, perhaps an umbrella and medicines for a possible emergency, as well as enough money to pay your greens fees and pay off the bets you lose. It is a good rule to travel lightly, but with the exception of our final trip into the afterlife, it is advisable to take at least some provisions along on almost any journey.

• Remember your past experience. If you're old enough to read this, you know that some things work and some things don't. Be a holy innocent if you want, but don't be just innocent. In golf many of your rememberings need to be most specific. If you've played Exotica a number of times before, it will help you to remember that the palm trees of this hole can be dangerous and that its green most subtly slants from right to left.

• Remember to adjust. Life is often uneven, and to do it well, you will need to shift with the good times and the rough ones. Consider uneven lies on the golf course. If your ball lies above your feet, you may want to shorten your grip on your club; when it lies below you, you may want to lengthen it. Depending on whether you're hitting uphill or downhill, you'd be wise to think about adjusting your stance.

• Remember to be civil. Don't forget all the little things your parents or others taught you, like how you should say please and thank you (even to your children) and how you shouldn't run red lights or pee on toilet seats. In golf replace your divots, rake sand traps after you've hit out of them, and remind yourself to watch your own shadow on the green.

• Remember your sins as precisely as possible, and then remember to forgive yourself. No one's perfect. Play life one day at a time. Don't forget to play golf one shot at a time.

• Remember to be grateful. Not just at the Thanksgiving dinner table. Cultivate a grateful heart, and you will see blessings where others see curses. You will also likely have better mental health than most and will enjoy life more. Once you are past the beginner stage, try to think of every round of golf as a gift that has been given you by your money, your leisure, your friends, the course personnel, the planet, and perhaps even God.

- Remember to remember. Remember to be alert. Pay attention to the narrows ahead of you and that sand trap guarding the green. Pay attention to whether interest rates are going up or down and when your driver's license expires. Pay attention to what your spouse, children, or others are saying, and to whether it makes sense or not. In his book *Island* Aldous Huxley constructed a fictional utopia.[3] The reason it worked so well was that throughout the island there were parrots that had been trained to squawk "Attention!" every few minutes to remind the human inhabitants to remember to pay constant attention to what they were doing.

If we are to survive decently for a while yet, Lily and I need to pay ever more rather than less attention to what we are doing. For instance, we have recently begun to stumble a bit, both on the golf course and in our own home. When we were younger, we lifted our feet without thinking while walking. Now it takes an effort. And it is easy to forget to make it. The consequences of such forgetting, however, can be as disastrous as a broken hip and an inability ever to play golf again. Or something even worse, which is hard to imagine.

So now I am going to embark upon a paean to the paradoxes of old age. Oh, boring! But pay attention, for three reasons. One is that if you play it right, old age will be the most definable of your own destinations, and it might pay for you to learn something of what's ahead, like tricky trees. Second, you may remember me noting some holes ago that golf is the one sport you will likely be able to play in your old age. Indeed, for that reason even now you may find yourself paired on the course with golfers in their sixties and seventies, if not eighties. You might want to know something about what lurks underneath these women and men. Finally, you may save yourself a regret or two.

I have many regrets. It is impossible to live a full life and not make mistakes, so there are dozens of things from the perspective of age that I wish I'd done differently in all the years past. But like a bad shot or a bad hole, I've learned to forgive myself these mistakes and generally put them behind me. All except one: my lack of empathy for my parents in their old age. They both came from a school of dignity that taught them not to talk about their illnesses and fears, their aches and pains. The fact that they learned their lessons too well, in my belief, still doesn't let me off the hook. Nor does the fact that until their deaths I myself had not personally experienced any of the more significant vicissitudes of aging. Had I paid more attention, I could have observed their vicissitudes and been more empathetic and supportive. And I have trouble putting this regret behind me since almost every day I am reminded of it, now that it is my turn to experience the aches and pains they so seldom mentioned.

But this is a book about golf, not old age, and I am not going to say more about the aches and pains of aging save to note that they require constant adjustments in one's golf swing. I am, however, going to use old age to comment upon some of the many paradoxes and mysteries of memory.

I used to vociferously curse the drivers of cars ahead of me that were crawling along at 30 miles an hour in a 45-miles-per-hour zone. I'd guess that the driver was some ancient person, and when I finally got to pass them, I'd realize my guess was almost invariably correct. I imagined that they drove at such an infuriating snail's pace because of their deteriorating eyesight and reflexes. That is a possible reason. But today I know there are two more powerful reasons for the phenomenon. One is that our sense of time changes with age. Many of us elderly simply aren't in a hurry anymore. It's kind of nice, actually (except for the younger driver behind us, who'd like our licenses taken away). The other reason we drive so carefully is that we remember so many past accidents or near misses that in our old age we are more alert than the young to all the things that can go wrong. Think of that: In certain ways the elderly may be more rather than less alert.

One of several virtues of our still-modest old age and retirement, in addition to playing more golf, is that Lily and I get to travel abroad more just for fun. But packing is worrisome. It isn't a matter of clothes; a ten-item checklist can cover that. The problem is remembering to pack the thirty different medicines we need to take for our various degenerative diseases—and, aware as we are of all that can go wrong, the thirty other medicines we might need "just in case."

With regard to name and word retrieval, it is dramatically evident that Lily's and my memories are not what they used to be. Of course we wonder whether this might represent encroaching senility. But the answer is not clear. Are we more forgetful these days because we've got half as many brain cells left or because we've got five times as much to remember? Lily may forget an ingredient of a recipe she used to cook ten years ago at age fifty-five. It so happens, however, that that was the age she first took up the computer and began learning a whole complex set of new skills. At forty-five it was easy for me to remember everything I'd written in my first book when I hadn't yet had a second one published. Today thirteen of my books are in print, and I find it pardonable that I can no longer cite each one of them chapter and verse.

In worrying about encroaching senility, we've been reassured by the best definition I know of the condition. Someone—of course I can't remember who anymore—once said, "Senility isn't when you can't remember where you put your keys; it's when you find them and can't remember what you do with them." We're nowhere near there yet.

Still, I would be in total denial if I tried to tell you that our memories are no problem. In case there's a possible book in them, I've taken to writing down—lest I forget—some of the more memorable things that Lily says, expressions of her personality that our staff refers to as "Lilyisms." Two of her most recent were: "Everyone's stealing my ashtray, including me" and "It's very easy for me to remember things, as long as you just remind me."

Among the ever-increasing number of things we need to remember are people, both living and dead. Over the last quarter of our lives, thanks to working in the community, our number of good living friends has multiplied at least tenfold. The number of dead is also increasing. Obviously we need to remember the living, and somehow Lily manages to keep track of the birthdays of an amazing percentage of them, even without the help of her computer. But why bother to remember the dead? I don't know really, but remembrance of the dead strikes me as particularly human. Again, most religions have made room for it as a ritualistic practice, such as in "Prayers for the Dead."

Although he was not dead at the time, I'd like to tell you about my mother's older brother, my uncle, George Saville, through a poem—not quite a prayer—I wrote almost forty years ago, when our first children were very young and our youngest child had not yet been conceived:

Uncle George's Visit

Last year his wife died. I suppose he cried
Awhile, and then he left
To go around the world, still a handsome man
At seventy; not, mind you,
Frantic for adventure, but strong enough
To travel further.

He came through the canal at Panama
And talked about the heat and the people on the boat.
But mostly told us of the past: Of Brooklyn
When Italians grazed their goats upon the heights,
Of tennis on New Jersey lawns,
Of how the class of nineteen-eighteen left to go to war.
Now and then he had to hunt for words
And often told the same story twice
But was no bore.

He brought balloons and played with our children
Even though it meant to kneel upon the floor.
We showed him the sights and took him out to dine
Where there was a view out across the bay.
That was all. Five days, and he went
On to Honolulu and then Japan.

What can I tell you of this man?
What shall I say? Something noble?
Something grand? Or shall I merely say
That he has lived, and will you understand?
You see, we took no pictures. Sometime
Our children, passing by, will glance up to demand
"Who was Uncle George?" And we can then say no more
Than "A man who traveled around the world
And stopped to play with you one day
Upon the floor."

San Francisco, California
September 1965

Although the poem doesn't stress it, George had recently had a stroke and, at the time, was having real difficulty with his memory. But he taught me something important. During that visit he carried around with him a little notebook in which he jotted down everything about his travels that he wanted to remember. Uncle George was to remarry within another year and die within another six, but thanks to him I am today, all these years later, writing down Lilyisms and making more and more lists of what to take on which trip. I remember him gratefully.

Bopping around the world on his own, George was hardly senile. Yet were it not for his note taking, he might well have been. What I am suggesting is that much—not all but perhaps most—senility is a choice. Often that choice is made decades before the onset of diagnosable senility, when one opts for a lifestyle of limited awareness, limited alertness. This assessment may differ from the conventional understanding of the matter, but I can offer much to back it up. The cause of senility is often more mysterious than a mere brain defect.[4] Certainly those who work closely with them know how well many of the seemingly hopelessly senile can pull themselves together for at least a few moments when "they have a mind to."

I described my Uncle George as talking mostly about the past. This may have had more to do with his recent stroke and consequent memory problem than anything else. When I saw him a year later, he showed no sign of memory difficulty. But we do tend to think of the elderly as "dwelling in the past." Whatever the cause, that is often the case. Yet not necessarily so.

I am in the process of having my archives established at Fuller Theological Seminary. Why? Is it because I want to be remembered after I'm gone? Yes, that is perhaps one tenth of my motivation. At least 90 percent of my motivation, however, is to get rid of clutter. As I continue to age, I don't want to be hemmed in by memorabilia: different editions and foreign translations of my books; past awards; reviews and articles from long ago; and mountains of obsolete correspondence. I want to be liberated from all this "stuff," to be free to move on—even if it's to a nursing home—and free to pay attention to what's truly important, including the present and the future.

If anything these days, Lily and I are ever more focused on the future, whether it be this afternoon's golf game, next month's trip to Europe, or our not-so-distant demise. We are constantly preparing. Yet even in this there is ambiguity. Our traditional notion is that one looks forward to the future and backward to the past. Someone, however— again, I can't remember who—told me that the ancient Greeks thought of it very differently. They saw us humans as continually facing the past, which we know, while they envisioned the future as creeping up behind our backs, ready to pounce upon us with some unforeseen surprise. In any case, Lily and I know that surprises await us down the road, and whether out of trepidation, excitement, or both, it is these surprises that are our primary focus.

Have I been meandering? We old folks tend to do that. But golf should be in part a meandering sport. Remember how at the very outset I took pains to point out that it is the most deceptively nonlinear of pastimes?

Golf is about not one thing but many. It is as much about anticipation as remembering, as much about comradeship as competition, about failure as success; as much about learning as enjoyment and prayer as performance. It is much more about your psychology than your agility. Half crippled by arthritis, I cannot hit a ball nearly as far as I used to, yet I score much the same. This is because I have become more clever at the game. And that is so because I am more alert than when I was a young man.

While this book is about ever so many things, a single theme has run throughout: the choice to envision golf as a spiritual discipline. It is a choice. You do not have to look at it that way. Many golfers, including many who score far better than I, never think of it as such. Nonetheless, as long as you do think of it that way, golf will never be for you "a good walk spoiled."[5]

If you do choose to regard golf as a spiritual practice, you will learn much about remembering. You will learn that remembering does not come as naturally as one might expect. You will learn that you need to remember to remember, and hence how to remind yourself to remember. You will also learn that as a spiritual practice golf doesn't just have to do with golf, and that if you deeply practice remembering, you will find yourself more alert not only on the links but also in your living room. Indeed, you may even discover a vaccination against senility.

You will remember all the things I have talked about, from remembering to keep your head down to remembering to be civil and mindful of the environment and your own particular demons. You may even begin to increasingly remember all those who have gone before you, men and women like my Uncle George, including the heavenly host of golfers who over centuries, with great pains, designed ever superior balls and clubs and courses.

You may even remember to make out of each and every round you play—no matter what you score—a mystical celebration of remembrance.

NOTES

1. I know of only one exception. Many years ago I was invited down to an obscure area of the tropics where there was then a large enclave of the wealthy because they were exempt from income taxes there. The enclave had a gorgeous golf course, and my hostess arranged for me to play it. Although I'd not picked up a club for several years, I was initially amazed at how well I was doing. I finished the front nine with a 43. Proud and pleased, I continued to do remarkably well but then began to be curious about the fact. Only then did I become alert. I observed that the palm trees never intruded upon the fairway. I further observed that while the course had the usual number of sand traps, they were all situated where one was least likely to hit into them. I took note of the fact that the sloping greens all sloped like a bowl toward a drain, in such a manner that no matter where you hit your putt, it was likely to end up damn near the cup, if not actually in it. Slowly it dawned on me that this enclave of rich people had quite deliberately designed their beautiful course in order to make themselves look good.
2. This tough little Episcopal nun has for twenty years been my spiritual director and a sort of teaching golf pro, save that our concern has not been with the golf course but with the whole course of life.
3. Aldous Huxley, *Island* (New York: Harper, 1989). It will be *remembered* that Huxley was also the author of *The Perennial Philosophy,* about mysticism, as well as the classic *Brave New World* (New York, London: Harper & Brothers, 1982).

4. I am happy to refer those more deeply interested in the ambiguities of senility to my book *A Bed by the Window: A Novel of Mystery and Redemption* (New York: Bantam, 1991). It is a murder mystery set in a nursing home and is much about the subject of mystery itself.

5. *A Good Walk Spoiled* is the title of a recent successful golf book by John Feinstein, subtitled *Days and Nights on the PGA Tour* (Boston: Little, Brown & Co., 1995). The title is taken from an original quotation of Mark Twain's.

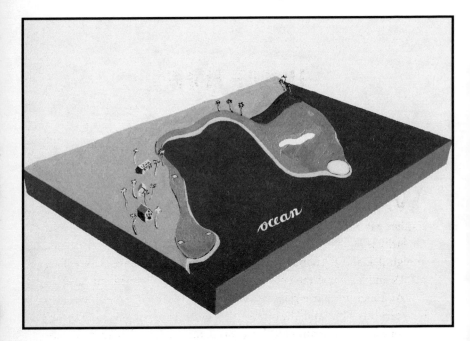

If we are alert to them, we will realize there are moments when our human lives touch upon the divine, and even some when the divine reaches out to touch us.

H O L E   1 7

_____

IN THE FLOW

We have hit the coast again and, as with the third hole, have another par 3 from one promontory to another across ocean water. The similarity is not surprising. Oceanfront property is hugely expensive and in high demand by homeowners as well as golfers. I have played long par 4's and 5's along the oceanside, but they are an exorbitant rarity.

Although both are relatively short for that reason, the differences between this hole and the third otherwise outweigh the similarities. This one is far more difficult. It is considerably longer. There is no way, even for the women—even playing it safe—to get from the tee to the green without hitting the ball over the ocean. Finally, as the course advice booklet takes pains to point out: "Bear in mind that you are hitting to a sharply two-tiered green. When the pin is situated on the lower tier, you will have no chance for a birdie unless your drive comes to rest on that lower tier. For this to happen, since the lower tier is most narrow, you must hit a delicate tee shot indeed."

In other words, you must hit a perfect shot. Way back on the third hole, I said, "Golf has to do with perfection." Ever since, I have been talking primarily about dealing with imperfection, failure, and disaster—quite properly, since we are inherently imperfect creatures and cannot even begin to approach perfection except through imperfection. Nonetheless, as we near the end of our round, it is also proper that we should return our attention to the mystical matter of perfection.

If you were asked at this point how you have been playing, chances are about 50 percent that you would answer, "Lousily." Chances are about 49 percent that you'd respond, "Erratically." Erratic is the norm for even very excellent golfers. A good hole or two will be followed by a bad one or two—and then a couple more good ones and a couple more bad ones. But one time in a hundred, you may respond, "Pretty well." This unusual response will be dictated by modesty. What you really mean is "Very well" or "Extraordinarily well, actually" or "Damn near perfectly."

And what you also will mean is that you have been "in the flow."

Perfection, as previously noted, is relative. I know I have been in the flow if I hit three pars in a row. A scratch golfer may not consider himself in the flow until he has hit four birdies in a row.

With that caveat about relativity, being in the flow refers to a period of time when it seems that you can do no wrong. It is an extraordinary phenomenon. I am told some younger people these days call it "being in the zone," but that is the less meaningful expression.

The phenomenon of being in the flow is not the least bit unique to golf. To the contrary, it occurs at one time or another in the practice of any sport I can think of, ranging from Ping-Pong to chess. On your TV (which is most perfectly adaptable to the sport), you may observe it best when watching professional tennis. There you'll likely see a player in a single match moving into the flow and out of it, then perhaps back into it again. When he is in the flow, a tennis player will not simply be hitting his shots into the confines of his opponent's court (in the zone, so to speak); his shots, one after another, point after point, game after game, will hit whatever tape he wants them to with magical accuracy. I use the word *magical* conservatively. It is not just a matter of him playing very well; it is as if, for that magical period of time, he can truly do no wrong.

But the phenomenon is distinctly periodic; it does not last. I've not personally witnessed a golfer be in the flow for more than two rounds nor a tennis player for longer than a single match. The magic will then be lost for a little while. Yet the great players of each sport will regain it—only to lose it again—and then again regain it.

Similarly, a sedentary activity in which the flow occurs is putting together jigsaw puzzles. Who has not engaged in this inexpensive pastime? Whether you're aware of it or not, if you have been deeply so engaged, you will know what it means to be in the flow. Work on a difficult five-hundred- or thousand-piece puzzle, and you may well stare at it for over an hour without finding a single piece you can put together with another. Then suddenly, without a break or any other apparent reason, you may fit fifteen pieces together in two minutes. It is as if your fingers, eyes, or both were being magically guided. But then it will stop as suddenly as it started, and you will be stuck again. You will know, however, that during those two minutes you were in the flow.

When this happens to me on the golf course, I do not feel that my fingers—or my hands or feet or arms or hips—have been guided. I am usually not aware that I have done anything whatsoever to change my swing. Rather, it seems as if my *ball* is being guided. It not only soars for the distant green and lands on it, but it soars for that particular part of the green where the pin happens to be located. My body is not capable of producing such accuracy. Yet it happens. Not for long, mind you, but when it happens three times in a row, this kind of accuracy is not an accident. The scientist in me, with all my knowledge of probability statistics, is quite capable of distinguishing it from "a bit of good luck." Something strange is going on. What? I cannot explain it, this phenomenon of being in the flow. Nonetheless, there are a few hints.

The expression "being in the flow" is almost undoubtedly derived from Taoism. This ancient Chinese religion usually attributes its origins to the probably legendary figure of Lao-tse (ca. 600 B.C.), although scholars attribute it to a definitive body of writing called the *Tao Te Ching* (ca. 400 B.C.). Typical of religions, Taoism shortly became separated into a mystical minority branch and a concrete majority branch, both of which still exist today, bearing little or no resemblance to each other. Here we shall restrict ourselves to the mystical branch. Over the millennia it gave rise to some profound writings, full of paradox, that have seeped into the modern Western culture.

The primary focus of Taoism is on the *Tao,* best translated into English as "the Way." What is "the Way"? The *Tao Te Ching's* opening sentences begin by declaring it to be indefinable (as all religions do of God). No matter how indefinable, it soon becomes clear that "the Way" refers to a certain basic order in the universe, and the teachings of Taoism are aimed at helping the student to become aligned with that order. In this respect Taoism differs from no other religion. On hole 7 I quoted William James's brilliant definition of generic religion as "the attempt to be in harmony with an unseen *order* of things."

What makes Taoism different from other religions is its unending insistence that the *Tao* is a Way and not some static thing. It is a path rather than a destination. And since the path will meander a bit, this way and that, Taoism most specifically among all the religions teaches a "way" of life that is continuously open to adjustment and readjustment, to change. Life is a "flow," and if you will be in harmony with it, you will need to shift or flow; if you are rigid and unable to adjust, you will quickly and forever be "out of sync" or "out of the flow."

It is no accident, therefore, that in those Taoist writings I have read, the most recurrent image is that of water, and that the Way or *Tao* is most commonly symbolized by a river. The point of Taoism is for us human beings to get into the river and, despite all our natural inclinations, let ourselves just float or flow to whatever the destination might be. At least to us Westerners, the image and teaching are remarkably passive. Indeed, the only enemy in Taoist teaching is our all-too-human tendency to want to control, to want to maneuver—our grasping nature and active desire to clutch onto the roots of the riverbank, lest we be carried off to God knows where.

In regard to golf Taoism would hold that we are all born golfers— that it is within our nature to hit a golf ball that just flows to where the pin lies. We are instinctively perfect, whether at golf or jigsaw puzzles. The major issue to Taoism is not why we get into the flow—that's our natural destiny—but why we virtually always and inevitably get out of it, why we throw our perfect destiny away. Here Taoism has much to teach us golfers.

Much of my work as a psychotherapist, lecturer, and author has been devoted to extolling the virtues of consciousness. This, in fact, was

福壽康寧

what I was doing on the last hole, as I urged myself and others in the direction of ever-increasing alertness. Yet on some relatively rare occasions, I wish to God I could be unconscious. One of those times is when I am in the flow on the golf course. The first giant step I take out of the flow comes with the realization, the consciousness, that I have been in the flow. That is when I usually, immediately, proceed to blow it. And so it is, I suspect, for most golfers. Why?

It is not that I want to get out of the flow. To the contrary, the second I become conscious that I am in it, my greatest desire is to stay there. And that's the problem: my desire. I want to keep things going just the way they are. I have become aware that they might change, and fearful that I might lose the flow, I become clutchy. It is the self-fulfilling prophecy again. Afraid I might blow it, I become sufficiently uptight that I do just that.

I have my own name for this disease: "scoritis." It is an inflammation of the psyche set off by the awareness that one is scoring well. I am severely afflicted by it. Even a single birdie can precipitate an attack in me. *Wow, a birdie!* I think to myself. *Now if I can just par the next hole, I'll really be scoring well.* So the next hole I slice out of bounds and get a triple bogey. It's almost guaranteed.

The most glaring example of my scoritis occurred in the middle of my last year on Okinawa. With the usual fluctuations my game had gradually improved to the point where I was routinely hitting in the low 90s. If I kept improving, it clearly would be only a matter of time until I "broke" 90—a great landmark in a golfer's career when he first completes a full eighteen-hole round with a total score in the 80s. And then one morning I set off in our customary men's foursome. On the front nine I scored an almost unbelievable 38. I'd been in the flow. As we made the turn, my mind was filled with simple additions and subtractions. If I scored another 38 on the back nine, I'd end up with a total score of 76. I'd not only break 90 but break 80 on the same day! But I knew that was just dreaming. I knew all about falling out of the flow and my proclivity to scoritis. Still, I reasoned, even if I did fall out of the flow—and I assumed I would—there was no way I wouldn't score in the 80s. Today was the day—the day I was going to break 90.

I shot a 53 on the back nine.

Although I was to break 90 a few times before leaving Okinawa (never since—it was an easy course), I remain almost as severely afflicted by scoritis to this day. The problem is the treatment for the disease. It is not unconsciousness. We can no more become unconscious of our score than of the fact that we are playing golf. Nor is it forgetfulness. While we may be forgetful creatures, once a golfer becomes aware he is in the flow, he will be unable to simply ignore the matter. Then what is he to do? The answer that Taoism provides is to try not to control the matter, to flow with the flow, to just let yourself drift, not worrying about where you are headed, even if you might end up in a backwater. In other words, don't worry about getting out of the flow. The problem is that this requires you not to care much how you're scoring.

Not care about your score? You must be kidding! "No," the Taoist teacher would answer, "I'm utterly serious. Care too much about your score, and you'll be instantly out of the flow. Which is more important: your score or staying in the flow? I recognize, dear pupil, that you are facing a conundrum. Indeed, the conundrum is so shocking as to take your breath away—or at least your hearing. You have heard us saying, 'Don't care about your score.' But that is not what we said. We said, 'Don't care *much* about your score.' In order to remain in the flow, it is necessary for you to care enough about your score to stay alert, to remember all the things you need to remember, like swinging easily. Beyond that, however, your caring is only obstructive of the flow—and hence self-destructive. By all means care, but not too much. You must learn how to simultaneously care and not care."

Certainly this echos hole 8, where the central discussion was about mysticism and paradox. You will remember the great Zen koan of golf: "Strive and don't strive." It is all the same, all one. This is not simply because Taoism and Buddhism have roots in common; there is also a certain paradoxical oneness to true mystical thought. Indeed, there is a certain oneness to all wisdom.

Still, this paradoxical teaching of "Strive but don't strive; care but don't care" is so difficult, we need any trick we can possibly lay our hands on to help us practice it. I have given you a lot of hints, but I can actually offer you only one "trick." Interestingly, it was taught to me by old age and disability. Whether it will be of any assistance to you whatsoever, I have no idea. But I do believe it has upon occasion helped me to keep myself in the flow longer than I might have otherwise.

It used to be my custom, as it is for most golfers, to take a practice swing every time before I actually hit the ball. Several years ago it began to become exhausting for me to play a full eighteen-hole round. Moreover, my exhaustion by the end was clearly compromising the quality of my game. I moved to a preference for nine-hole rounds. Yet I still wanted to play the full eighteen if the occasion was right. It brilliantly occurred to me that I might conserve my limited old-age energy by forgoing practice swings. Doing so seemed at first like an immense risk. Would it not interfere with my game, my score? But after loosening up on the first two or three holes, I took the risk and began by hole 4 generally to cease taking practice swings on long shots. Neither my game nor my score seemed to suffer.

One afternoon two years ago on the eighth hole, I became aware that I was in the flow. Without any practice swings I'd parred the sixth and seventh and had just hit a lovely drive. Delighted, about to make my second shot, a long fairway wood, I said to myself, "Let's make this a lovely one, too." So I took a practice swing. Then I hit and flubbed.

By God's grace, I was alert. I paid attention to what I'd just done. After two holes of being in the flow without practice swings, I'd suddenly switched and taken one. Why? It was because I wanted to do my damnedest to stay in the flow. But it didn't work. It only seemed to backfire. At that moment of crystalline clarity, it dawned on me how foolish my behavior was. Already playing perfectly well, I had changed my behavior in the desire of continuing to play well. How stupid! Why on earth change what you're doing when you were doing perfectly?

So since that afternoon I have developed a little rule for myself. It doesn't apply until I've loosened up. It also doesn't apply to my putting, chipping, or short pitches—any shot where I'm taking less than a full swing. But when I'm warmed up and hitting all out, I now *never* take a practice swing *unless* I've just hit a poor shot. If I do hit a poor shot, then I *always* take a practice swing before hitting the next one to assist myself in correcting whatever I just did wrong. It seems rather sensible.

Obviously it is appropriate to take a practice swing when a correction is called for. But why take one when you're doing fine without it?

This little rule may not be right for you. Everyone is different. But should it help you, even slightly, you will bless me.

All I have offered is but one little trick for staying in the flow that might help a few. Are there no other tricks? None that I know. But I do have a big hint, which by now should be obvious: kenosis. Emptiness.

I said in relation to this matter of staying in the flow that it is one of the few times I wish to God I could be unconscious—while still awake. I also implied that there are connections between Taoism and Buddhism (two oriental religions or "philosophies" that developed in the same era). So I am reminded of a certain Zen Buddhist practice called "no mind" meditation. The goal is to stop thinking without falling asleep. It is not easy to do. If the goal is achieved, then the mind, Zen teachers instruct us, will become like the smooth surface of a pond on a windless day, unrippled by any trace of thought.

A few of us Christians also occasionally practice "no mind" meditation. Much earlier I pointed out that the reason to practice kenosis is not to have a permanently empty mind but to make room in the mind for the entrance of the new, the unexpected, even the divine. Shortly I shall be speaking of hearing "the still, small voice of God" while on the golf course. One cannot hear that voice, on the golf course or elsewhere, if one's mind is cluttered with the noise of worldly concerns, with scores and other such continual ripples of mental activity.

Do I digress? Yes and no. On the one hand, we can play decent golf only when we are actively attentive to the hazards ahead and the lessons of our past. Paradoxically, on the other, we can stay in the flow only when we get ourselves out of the way, only when we are empty enough to let the Tao (or the divine) flow through us. The fact that this balance is extremely difficult to achieve and downright mystical (read: "mysterious") should not obscure the clear reality that kenosis is the key. So:

- Be attentive to the hazards ahead of you, but empty yourself of your fear of them.

- Strive to do your best, but empty yourself of your concern with your score.
- Learn from every mistake, but empty yourself of any shred of self-hatred for your imperfections.
- Compete, but empty yourself of shame that you are not measuring up.
- Play to win, but if you fail to do so, empty yourself of any remorse.
- Remember every good thing you have been taught, but in that fraction of a second when your clubhead is connecting with the ball, empty yourself of all your remembering. It should be a "no mind" moment without ripples.

I repeat that these paradoxical admonitions of exquisite balance are extremely difficult to follow. If I could follow them myself with significant regularity, I could spent much more time in the flow than I do and would be a much better golfer. It also strikes me that these admonitions of kenosis also hold true for the whole game of life, which is of even greater import than the game of golf.

Being in the flow is such a dramatic phenomenon, some have even wondered whether it isn't a proof of the existence of God. Certainly being in the flow may make one feel almost godlike—for a brief, fleeting span of time, somehow superhuman. Much as I believe in an active God, however, I do not suppose He or She is likely to *put* us into the flow. In this respect I am more Taoist than Christian.

The vision of Taoism, as I said, is essentially a passive one. It posits an unseen, indefinable, but flowing order to the universe—the *Tao,* or the Way. It urges us to attempt to be in harmony with that order. It does offer us some often paradoxical teachings about how we might actively work to achieve alignment with the Tao and even more about how we might keep that alignment. But never does it suggest that the Tao is active in the sense that it reaches out to assist us. The Tao just is, flowing along. It is a "force" of sorts, but a neutral one. Indeed, this neutrality had led some scholars to suggest that Taoism (like Zen Buddhism) should be considered a philosophy, not a religion.

Yet being, in most respects, more of a Christian than a Taoist, I believe not only in "an unseen order of things," with which it is proper that we should attempt to be in harmony (since it is smarter than us), but also that this unseen order—God—*wants* us to be in harmony with it and will therefore on unpredictable occasions actively reach out to assist us in being so. In other words, I believe in an active God who has concern for us. I doubt, however, that God is particularly concerned about our golf scores. Or whether we are in the flow or out of it on the course. Still, as always with God, there may be exceptions.

One such possible exception may be a phenomenon somewhat akin to being in the flow. This hole can be used to illustrate it. Let us suppose that today is one of those days when the pin is placed on the lower tier of the green nearest the ocean. I could hit for that lower tier. Being a short hitter, however, as well as an otherwise mediocre golfer, it is most unlikely that I would make it. I'd just waste one or more balls in the water. So what I will do today is hit to the left and be quite content with a par or, more likely, a bogey. I will play it safe—unless . . .

Unless I have a strong sense of inner certainty that I can make the far more difficult and dangerous shot. I have been in perhaps a thousand such "forced choice" situations on golf courses throughout the world. Approximately nine hundred of those times, accepting my limitations and obeying my natural instinct, I played it safe. They usually worked out reasonably well. Approximately ninety times I ignored my limitations and coinciding instincts. I went for the perfect shot—and failed. But there have been four—and only four—occasions in my career as a mediocre golfer when my instinct did not coincide with my limitations. Instead an inner "voice" within me said, "Go for it," and I felt absolutely certain that I could—that I would—make that perfect shot. On each occasion, obeying that "voice," I succeeded. I remember them well. It is not my nature to forget such experiences.

They were bizarre. They were not only statistically bizarre; they were irrational. It is reasonable to play within the limits of one's game. Failure to do so will be routinely costly. It is not reasonable to have a sense of certainty that you can accomplish something well beyond your ordinary capacities. From whence then comes such unreasonable, irrational certainty, particularly to a man so accustomed to be reasonable? And why should the whole thing work? I don't know.

Yet on a mystical level I do know. Unlike Taoism, Christianity teaches of a strange God who, for mysterious reasons (albeit always to our benefit), will upon occasion actually speak to us—even *reveal* Herself to us. This revelation will be experienced most commonly as a "still, small voice" within oneself, although sometimes more simply as a certain "sense" that is out of the ordinary. It is never experienced as a "booming" voice from the heavens. Still, the voice is so extraordinary and sufficiently frequent that Christian theologians have even hypothetically designated it a specific part of God, with the name "Holy Ghost" or "Holy Spirit" (which Jesus referred to as "Comforter").

As to why God should have "spoken" to me on those four rare occasions, telling me to attempt the impossible, I don't have the slightest idea. She has "spoken" to me with extraordinary wisdom on many other occasions off the links when the stakes were much higher. I have trouble believing, however, that my golf score would be of such interest that She would exert Herself so. I suspect She simply used these occasions to remind me of Her existence. In any case, it worked.

Yes, I have from time to time received a significant, profoundly helpful revelation in my ordinary life—*ordinary life* referring to my existence when not golfing.[1] But what about being in the flow when we are not engaged in a sport or game? Do we ever get into the flow in the course of ordinary life?

The question is not easy to answer. I have called golf "life condensed" because it faces us with so many of life's challenges in such a short period of time. But one of the things this means is that ordinary life is generally more humdrum, and it is difficult to discern whether we are in the flow when we are in the midst of the humdrum. At the same time ordinary life is even more complex and mysterious. If you are a nongolfer, you have probably concluded by now that golf is a most complicated sport. But would that ordinary life were so simple!

For instance, there have been brief occasions in my ordinary life when it seemed I might have been in the flow: I was speaking with a fluidity and eloquence of which I didn't know I was capable or acting with a brilliance that seemed far beyond my own intelligence. Yet they were not necessarily successful occasions. My listeners often didn't understand my eloquence or else they resented my brilliance. I may have been in the flow, but the results were frequently lousy. More often than not those occasions backfired.[2]

Then there have been longer periods of months, or even a year, when I was so taken by a book I was writing that I felt as if I might have been caught up in the flow. Yet during several of these periods, I somewhat neglected my children. I might have been in the flow as an author but certainly not as a father. As far as my children were concerned, I was distinctly out of the flow.

Actually, the subject of writing provides a perfect forum for discussing the ambiguities of being in the flow during ordinary life.

The summer of 1956 I spent living with John P. Marquand, probably the most famous and successful novelist of the day. He was sixty-four at the time; I was a mere twenty. He had no need to make any more money. He could have retired handsomely, but he was born to write, and every weekday morning at the dot of nine, I watched him stride out of the house to his study in a little barn 50 yards distant. There he wrote until he returned for lunch on the dot of one. On the one hand, he taught me nothing about writing that summer. On the other, he taught me almost everything. One does not simply flow by the clock five days a week, and he showed me as much. Mr. Marquand served me as a role model in regard to the simple discipline of writing.

Twenty-five years later, when I was still engaged in the practice of psychotherapy as well as writing my second book, I was treating a young woman I'll call Clara.[3] Clara was an artist of sorts. For some time she had been complaining about how little art she produced. Late one afternoon she came in for her appointment moaning, "When I got up this morning, I thought I'd do some painting. But then the phone rang. Then the mail came. Then I had to feed the dog. Then I got interested in a talk show on the radio. And by that time I didn't feel like painting anymore."

"You *thought* you'd do some painting when you got up this morning," I echoed.

"That's right," Clara agreed.

"Look," I told her, "next Tuesday I don't *think* I'm going to write. It's in my calendar. It says, '*Write.*' Unless I or someone in my family is seriously ill, that's what I'm going to do, and I'm going to do it for eight hours whether I feel like it or not."

Thank you, Mr. Marquand.

Now and then, when I happened to feel in the flow on a particular free evening, I have written a number of poems. A few of them are pretty good. An equal number are pretty awful. In any case, we haven't made any money from them. For the real business of writing, I have to set aside the time whether I feel inspired or not, and I don't know of any professional author who does it differently.

Of course I hope (as in the regular practice of golf) that during such set-aside time, I will get in the flow. But unlike with golf, when I am writing I have no idea whether I'm in the flow or not. I write long-hand on standard yellow pads. On many eight-hour writing days, I've felt inspired. My words just seemed to flow naturally, and by the end of the day, I will have filled as many as fifteen pages. *Wow,* I'll think, *I was really hot today.* Only six months later, when the time for a second draft is upon me, I'll come back to those fluid fifteen pages and they'll mostly strike me as crap—either totally irrelevant or in obvious need of literary reconstructive surgery.

Conversely, with equal frequency, I may begin one of those eight-hour days by staring at my yellow pad for two hours, not writing a word, in a seeming state of mental paralysis. Finally, when I do begin to squeeze out a few words, each of them feels like a tiny, worthless little turd. By the end of my eight hours, I may have filled no more than one and a half pages. And at the conclusion of the day, I'll think, *God, what a waste of time. I was totally constipated. The little bit I did was utterly prosaic and uninspired.* Yet six months later when I come back to those few words, they are likely to strike me as some of the most succinct and glorious prose I've ever written.

I have absolutely no capacity to assess accurately the quality of what I am writing at the time I am writing it. For that matter, I also have precious little capacity to assess accurately any part of my ordinary life when I am in the midst of it. There have been many times other than when I was writing when I was feeling way out of the flow.

Yet these times of frustration and fear and depression and even despair have often in retrospect turned out to be my finest moments.

In any case, there seem to be two morals. One: Much as I love the sport, there is more to life than golf. The other: There's much more to ordinary life than simply being in the flow—or at least feeling in the flow. There the feeling may be deceptive. I'm not saying we never get in the flow as we go about our daily lives. I believe we do upon occasion. But on such occasions we're usually not even aware of the fact—perhaps because we're not keeping score.

NOTES

1. These experiences of revelation have been so personally dramatic that I have written about them in many places. For a recent example, see the section on revelation in my book *The Road Less Traveled and Beyond* (New York: Simon & Schuster, 1997), pp. 261–66.
2. All this talk of fluidity reminds me of an evening in the summer I turned twenty-one. It was in a Bavarian beer garden with a typical German band playing "Oom-pah, Oom-pah." Somehow I had fallen into the company of two German youths about my own age. The three of us had consumed an enormous amount of fluid—namely beer. The alcohol had loosened me up and loosened my tongue. We were standing, engaged in some abstract discussion of philosophy, a subject I couldn't ordinarily handle in a foreign language. Only on this evening I seemed to be in the flow. I was amazed at my sudden fluency in German, in comprehension as well as speaking. I fluently finished making a complex point. One of my compatriots opened his mouth to answer. But no words came out. What came out was a cataract of fluid—of beer—and vomitus—that sloshed all over my pants and shoes. It is the most tangible example I can recount of a moment when I felt myself to be in the flow but that literally backfired on me.
3. Not her real name.

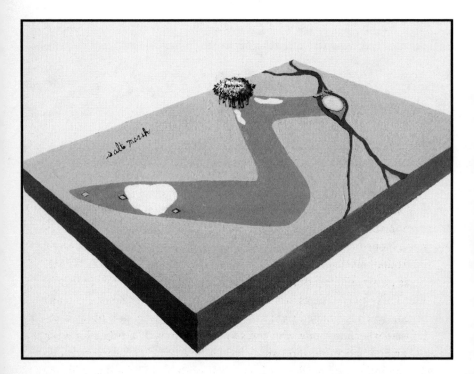

Belief is a free choice. I believe God is a Person.
By this I mean that He has a personality
and we have a personal relationship.

H O L E   1 8

GOD

We have now come to the final hole. Since golf is so nonlinear, seldom in the sport is there ever anything that could truly be called a climax. Nonetheless, a certain sense of climax comes with the last hole of the round, and on Exotica this hole has been designed to be as climactic as possible. It is a dramatically difficult 610-yard par-5 double dogleg. These two doglegs wend their way through a salt marsh to the green, which is situated right in front of the long verandah of the clubhouse—where anybody who cares to can watch your finish. Moreover, the green is surrounded on all four sides by channels of water that create the inflow (or outflow) of the pond on hole 15 (the one with the alligators). Consequently, the green is actually a tiny island—a dramatic finish indeed.

On the circuit they sometimes refer to this as the "pro's hole." That is because it is possible to hit an unobstructed shot from the bend in the first dogleg, totally bypassing the second, directly toward the green—a 270-yard shot, and if you are to hit 270 yards across the marsh so that the ball lands on a little island, you must indeed be a professional.

Should you manage to make such a phenomenal shot, landing on the green in two (one under regulation), it will be a moment of glory.

But remember that perfection is relative, and hence so is glory. For me, were I to hit my third shot from the bend of the second dogleg and make it to the green, that would be glory. In fact, I would be so exhilarated and surprised by the glory, I would probably screw it up by three- or four-putting.

Glory is not only a relative but a profound phenomenon. Whenever we "achieve" some kind of glory, we are likely to think of it as ours. But we will be mistaken. I think that we are spiritually and psychologically off base—and in grave danger—whenever we think of glory as our own. Glory is an attribute of God. If we happen to end up this last hole "in glory," the glory should properly belong to God.

I have upon occasion vaguely wished that I could write something that was not about God, but I cannot. When I come down to the essentials, there is no part of life in which I do not see the hand of God. To cover virtually any subject fully, I simply cannot leave Him or Her out of the picture—even if it is golf.

Now, it is not my intention, on this last hole of the round, to cram God down anyone's throat. I dislike vomit, and only vomit would be the result of an attempt to do so. With but a few caveats, I am a deep believer in the First Amendment to the U.S. Constitution, which provides for the free exercise of religion. What that amendment means, among other things, is that not only are we free to believe in whatever kind of God we choose, but we are also free to not believe: to have no truck whatsoever with any notion of divinity. The amendment accepts, even encourages, religious diversity.

But why is there such diversity? The basic reason, I suspect, is mystery—and the different ways we handle mystery. For some of us life is such a mysterious business that we have difficulty handling it without resorting to notions of the divine. For others the behavior of God is so mysterious that we have difficulty handling the facts without discounting notions of divinity altogether. And some of us fall in between.

Perhaps the only intellectual sin is to proclaim that there is no mystery at all. Few serious golfers have been guilty of it. In the best compendiums of quotes about golf that I know, appreciation for the mystery of the game is the predominant theme. One of them begins by quoting a PGA veteran, Dave Marr, as saying: "You can never own the secret of golf. You just try to borrow it from time to time."[1] Or as another great golfer, Ben Crenshaw, said about the game, "There's no way you can ever get it."[2]

Certainly you do not have to believe in God to play golf—even great golf. Nonetheless, I suspect it helps—at least to justify the extraordinary amount of time you may expend upon the sport. How else to justify it except to believe that it's somehow good for the soul? And how might you justify the existence of the soul without resorting to the existence of some kind of divinity?

But there is all this diversity. Adlai Stevenson once put it this way: "Some of us worship in churches, some in synagogues, some on golf courses."[3]

Most would probably think that God and golf have absolutely nothing to do with each other. Yet were you to analyze all the jokes about golf, I suspect that you would find at least half of them are religious. The most typical ones have God, Christ, and the Holy Spirit teeing off as a threesome on the first tee. Or perhaps it will be a Protestant minister, a Catholic priest, and a Jewish rabbi teeing off on the fifth. These jokes mostly seem to center on luck, either good or bad.

This is not surprising. Nowhere are good and bad luck more apparent than on the golf course. Luck is the norm. On the one hand, you may land one inch short of the green and have an unplayable lie in a cavernous sand trap. Just one inch more, and you would have "had" glory. On the other hand, you may hit an atrocious hook way to the left of the green, which hits the trunk of a tree and bounces not only onto the green but conceivably even into the cup. The luck involved may be so dramatic that it is only natural to assume either heavenly or demonic intervention.

But I think that such an assumption would be wrong. Attributing good or bad luck to spiritual forces is, to my mind, a most primitive form of religious thinking. Unlike subtler phenomena, such as being in the flow, luck—good or bad—is just that: luck. Chance. And I myself doubt that God has anything to do with it.

Then where does God fit in? I don't know. It is trite to say that God is mysterious, but the reason that I keep saying it is that in absolutely no area of golf—or life—can I be totally certain of God's involvement. The only thing about God of which I can be totally certain is the places where He is not involved, where He doesn't fit in. And so it is in this regard—not luck—that I will tell you my favorite religious joke about golf.

A golfer loved golf more than anything in the world. Consequently, he was very good at it. But he was also obsessed by the game, and he therefore generally neglected his family, his friends, and his spiritual life. It is hardly remarkable, therefore, that when he died he went to Hell. At the entrance to Hell, he was greeted by the devil. The devil, dressed in a smart sports coat and slacks, could not have been more urbane. "Welcome to Hell," the devil said to the golfer. "We're delighted to have you here. It's my purpose to make your stay as comfortable as possible. Anything you need, just ask for it. I and my whole staff are entirely at your disposal."

Although the golfer realized that he was in Hell, he was astonished by the pleasantness of it all. Unlike his stereotypes, the devil seemed such an obliging chap that the golfer was emboldened to inquire, "You don't happen to have any golf courses down here, do you?"

"Golf courses?" the devil echoed. "Of course we have golf courses here in Hell! We have the best golf courses in the entire universe! Here, let me show you." And so the devil led him off to a golf club, which looked for all the world like a magnificent southern plantation, with four eighteen-hole courses going off in each direction—a north course, a south course, a west course, and an east course—all perfectly trapped and manicured.

The golfer was now encouraged almost to the point of ecstasy. "You don't happen to have clubs down here in Hell, do you?" he inquired.

"Clubs?" the devil responded. "Why, of course! We have the most exquisitely balanced clubs in the universe. Come, let me show you."

And so the devil led the golfer into the clubhouse to a huge room that was lined by set after set of golf clubs. The golfer tried several. They were indeed exquisitely balanced. He could have picked any of them, but he chose one that felt particularly right. Next to the door was standing a whole group of young lads eagerly ready to caddy. He put his newly selected set of clubs into a lovely bag, handed it to the brightest-looking caddy, and then said to the devil, "Now if you would just give me a ball, I will be off."

"Ball?" the devil responded. "Ball? We don't have any balls here. That's the hell of it."

The story may be funny, but it is as pointed as any one I know. The golfer who went to Hell did so because he was an addict, and in his addiction he had neglected his family and other important matters. Particularly he had neglected God.

All forms of addiction may be looked upon as varieties of idolatry. The heroin addict makes an idol of heroin and the pleasure it gives him. The alcoholic makes an idol of the bottle. The golfer in question made an idol of golf. Idolatry is the violation of the first commandment, which is very specific: "I am the Lord thy God, and thou shalt not have any other gods before me." But golf had become his god, and what greater poetic justice could there be for him than to have all the accoutrements of golf except a ball?

After saying I didn't believe that God had anything to do with luck on the golf course, I asked the question "Then where does God fit in?" The problem with the golfer who went to Hell was that God did not fit into his picture. He had lost his sense of perspective. As long as we think that God fits somewhere into the game, and we remember to have no other god before Him or Her, we will seldom allow ourselves to let golf get out of perspective.

Now for a story that seemingly has nothing to do with golf.[4] A wealthy New York City man died, leaving a large estate. Part of that estate was some land in Louisiana. The prestigious New York City law firm managing his estate wrote to a law firm in New Orleans asking them to do a title search on the Louisiana property. Three weeks later the New York City firm received a report tracing the title back to 1803.

At this point the New York lawyer handling the estate wrote back to the New Orleans lawyer that the estate was more complicated than he had first assumed, and would the New Orleans firm be so kind as to trace the property title back before 1803. One week later the New York lawyer received the following letter:

Dear Sir:

We are in receipt of your request to trace the title of the property in question back before 1803. The property was acquired in 1803 by the U.S. through purchase from France. France in turn had acquired the property from Spain in 1801 as a part of the spoils of war. Spain had originally obtained the property in question through discovery made by a Genovese sailor sailing under the aegis of Queen Isabella of Spain and with the blessing of Pope Innocent VIII, who was the Vicar of Christ, who is the Son of the Almighty God who, gentlemen, created Louisiana.

As we hit down this last fairway, it may help us to remember that God created the island of Exotica. Such remembrances will also help us keep matters in perspective. Indeed, we might want to go a bit further. While the majority of authorities believe that golf was invented in Scotland, there are two minority views. One traces it back to at least the thirteenth century, when the Dutch used to play a similar game on ice. The other holds that we really don't have the foggiest idea who invented the game. Sometimes I like to toy with the notion that maybe it was God who invented golf.

The concept of God as Creator—of the universe, of the world, of Exotica, and perhaps even of golf—does not necessarily imply a currently active God. A very large number of people think of God—if they think of Her at all—as a clockmaker who designed and created the whole scheme of things, wound it up like a clock, set it in motion, and then retired on Her pension plan some hundreds, thousands, millions, or billions of years ago.[5] As I indicated, however, my own version is that of an active God, although I can in no way tell you precisely how my mysterious God might intervene on the golf course. While I mildly discounted the notion, I still cannot prove that God has nothing to do with it when we get in the flow. And while I am uncertain, I did suggest that God may well be involved in those rare moments of certainty when we believe that we can pull off a difficult shot, and then against all odds proceed to do so.

But God may intervene in other ways as well. For instance, although I have been paired with some disagreeable partners on the course, I have also been paired with a few great teachers at just the right time for me. It is an old mystical saying that "when you are ready for your next teacher, he will appear." This has been my experience too frequently to ignore. There are some other ways to explain it, but on these occasions it has seemed to me that I was feeling the hand of God at work.

On the last hole I offered a little trick about how I may help myself to stay in the flow by not taking any unnecessary practice swings. There is another possible "trick" to stay in the flow that I have never tried: simply to pray.

The reason I have never tried it is that on one level it does seem like a trick. God has enough on Her mind without me bothering Her with such a prosaic and utterly unimportant matter. No less a religious light than Billy Graham has addressed the issue by saying: "I never pray on a golf course. Actually, the Lord answers my prayers everywhere except on the course."[6]

Nonetheless, the next time I am in the flow, I may very well remember to pray for God's help to stay in it. The fact is, it would not be crass for me to do so; it would be humble. I have a big tendency to pray to God from only a very mature position, without wanting to seem childish about the whole thing. Yet Jesus said, "Except ye be as little children, you shall not enter the Kingdom of Heaven." Oh yes, as the world sees it, it would be most childish for me to pray for such a simple thing as to stay in the flow. But Jesus also said, "Ask and you shall receive." We mature men often have problems asking for things, like directions. I think it is just possible that it might be good for my spiritual life to be childish and humble enough to ask God to help me along a little bit on the course. And I think it is possible that God might even be sufficiently pleased in my doing so. She wouldn't regard it as a trick but rather as a mutual opportunity for the two of us. Anyway, I'm trying to screw up my courage to ask the next time I'm in the flow.

While I've not yet been childlike or courageous enough to ask God for help on the golf course, I do talk with Him. I do so out loud on those occasions when I'm playing as a single, when I'm alone and no one can hear me or think me weird. "Well, we didn't do so well on that one, did we, God?" is what I say most frequently. But sometimes I also get to say,

"Well, we managed to pull that one off, didn't we, Lord? Thank you." Does God listen to this sort of "dribble"? I honestly don't know. The reason I wouldn't talk out loud in this way if I was playing with anyone else is that I wouldn't want them to think I have an "imaginary companion." We are supposed to leave our imaginary companions behind along about the time we are five or so. Actually, I don't think God is my imaginary companion—I just don't want other people to think so. Still, when I am playing alone, there are times when God and I have a lot of fun together.

Why shouldn't God have fun with me on the course?

One of the few things I know about God for certain is that He has a sense of humor. As soon as I think I've got something all figured out, God (or life, if you will) comes along and says, "But what about this, Scotty?" And I'm more or less back to square one. Indeed, God confounds me with such regularity in all aspects of my life, I can only assume He takes certain playful delight in doing so.

This experience of being confounded is one that all golfers share—at least on the course. As but one example, as soon as I start hitting my long irons well, my woods go to hell. Or vice versa. And if by some chance I begin hitting both well, then I can no longer putt worth a damn. The commonality of this complaint is such that it echoes through the locker rooms of every golf clubhouse on the face of the earth.

Earlier I quoted the pro Ben Crenshaw as saying about golf: "There's no way you can ever get it." He was referring to this confounding. Actually, what he said in its entirety was: "Golf is the hardest game in the world. There's no way you can ever get it. Just when you think you do, the game jumps up and puts you into your place."

The notion of God as a "trickster" of sorts—particularly on the golf course—was explicitly expressed by another famous pro, Tommy Bolt. Once after missing a number of putts during a major championship, Bolt turned to the sky and cried, "Come down here and fight like a man."[7]

In any case, a significant number of very serious theologians of many different religions have reached a tentative supposition that the universe in general and humanity in particular are God's "play." Certainly we humans are most likely to be cocreators with God when we can envision life as a "game." Sometimes it is a very serious game.

Sometimes it can and should be quite lighthearted. In any case, we might look at golf as the symbol of God's play. He is having fun with it. Yet on the serious side He is also teaching us a great deal. At the risk of being repetitive, let me say that I cannot think of any game better calculated to teach us the very spiritual virtues that God most wants us to learn: humility, patience, precision, balance, and alertness, as well as the never-ending practice of kenosis.

I began this chapter with a brief mention of glory, describing how, if I were to hit from the bend of the second dogleg a 180-yard drive to land on the green, I would experience just as much glory as the pro hitting from the first bend of the dogleg.

I doubt that I would be able to make such a glorious shot. But little in golf is predictable. Many are the beginners who have played dreadfully yet made one good shot on the last hole, thereby forever becoming hooked on the game. (Maybe the commonality of this occurrence is yet another example of God's playful intervention.) I myself, however, am not a novice. A typical mediocre player, my game is highly erratic. Chances are that during this round I've had a few good holes and a few bad ones. It may well be that until now I've had a string of bad ones. Indeed, I may have already judged the round to be a terrible one. But in the words of Yogi Berra about baseball, "It's not over until it's over." So also with golf. No matter how lousy my score, I may make one last good shot. Maybe just one last good putt. I will not end up in glory in the world's terms, yet I may still return home feeling a tiny touch of it.

The feeling of glory is so thrilling, it is addicting. Way back on hole 4 I noted that the flight of a well-hit golf ball will give us that thrill and suggested it as a major reason for golf's addictive quality. This addiction is not necessarily bad, but it can be dangerous if it becomes uncontrollable. Remember that full-blown addictions are forms of idolatry. The addict of whatever kind is chasing after some relatively cheap and easy substitute for the real God. But the real God cannot be captured—not in a bottle, not in sex, not in political power, and not in golf. God is bigger than us. He is not ours to control.

So we cannot "get" God on a golf course. What we can get on the course are certain intimations of Him. One of those intimations comes from the fact that we cannot "get" golf either. Or life, for that matter.

Someone once said, "Life is not so much a problem to be solved as a mystery to be lived." The same could also be said of golf and God. Nonetheless, an intimation of God and Her glory in the game of golf comes in confronting obstacles.

Much of golf—and hence this book—is about obstacles. The list I have mentioned is almost endless: sand traps, narrows, out-of-bounds marshes, trees, forests, moguls, gulches and canyons, uneven lies, deep rough, cultivated rough, ocean water, pond and stream water, pitched or rolling or tiered greens, rain and wind, et cetera, et cetera. Even more, this book has been about the host of all-too-human internal obstacles that prevent us from easily sailing past, through, or over those external ones. Again the list seems endless and torturous: our eagerness, excessive striving, pride, shame, laziness, anger at others, anger at ourselves, depression, perfectionism, narcissism, obsession with score, fearfulness, overconfidence, underconfidence, inattentiveness, lack of alertness, et cetera, et cetera.

Among its many other permutations, glory seems to have at least something to do with overcoming obstacles—particularly those that are within ourselves. Yet true glory, I remind you, is more God's than ours. As with a pro who has just won a major tournament, we may experience a fleeting moment of glory—without any reference to God whatsoever—whenever we temporarily end up with an exceptionally good score. A greater feeling of glory, however, can come only in relationship to God.[8] It can come even to a mediocre player like myself, when I have done no more than break 90 but know I have done so not just through blind luck but through some overcoming of obstacles. It comes at the end of a long round—or a life—when a strangely quiet yet definably exterior voice says to us, "Well done, good and faithful servant. In you I am well pleased."

NOTES

1. Ryan Herrington, *Golf* (Kansas City: Ariel Books, Andrews McMeel, 1996), pp. 9–10.

2. *Golf: Life on the Links* (Kansas City: Ariel Books, Andrews McMeel, 1996), p. 12.

3. Ibid., p. 118.

4. This story has been attributed to a famed Methodist preacher of the 1940s and 1950s, Dr. Ralph Sockman.

5. This version of God as a no-longer-currently-active original Creator is often given the name *deism.* It is to be distinguished from *theism,* which allows for the possibility of ongoing revelation. By revelation, theists mean that God continues to "reveal" Herself to us through various, often mysterious interventions in our lives.

6. *Golf: Life on the Links,* p. 148.

7. Herrington, *Golf,* p. 95.

8. This partial, even minor, elucidation of glory is hardly original. It was perhaps most clearly stated in an extraordinary sermon by C. S. Lewis entitled "The Weight of Glory," delivered to a large crowd in Oxford in June 1941. Lewis was very aware that many in his audience were on their way to war and soon to die as a result. C. S. Lewis, *The Weight of Glory and Other Addresses* (New York: Macmillan Publishing Co., 1980), pp. 3–19.

Hope would not be realistic were there no such thing as real progress, and there would be no real progress unless there were those who chose to be pilgrims.

H O L E   1 9

CLOSURE

Like virtually all golf course clubhouses, the most frequented part of Exotica's is a simple bar and grill, containing two dozen tables where parties of four can consume all manner of drinks and simple snack food. This informal place is named the Reef Room, but no matter what its local name may be, golfers the world over refer to it as "the nineteenth hole."

There is no requirement that you ever visit the nineteenth hole. More often than not, at the end of a round, golfers will simply change their shoes, stow their clubs, and return home or to their hotel room for a hot bath. After all, the game's over. For better or worse, the round has been completed.

So why bother with the nineteenth hole? There are three reasons.

The least is that you may be hungry or thirsty or both. What could be more prosaic and earthy? Yet that golf-course-owning sect of Zen Buddhists we mentioned on hole 8 customarily referred to the nineteenth hole as their temple. It was also noted on hole 16 that the most outstanding religious celebrations are *feasts* of remembrance. Drinking and eating may seem utterly secular activities. Try doing without either for a single day, however, and they will likely strike you as very close to holy.

Still, in the interest of efficiency and economy, most of us would happily defer an overpriced beer or hot dog for an hour. If beverages and victuals were all that was involved, I doubt that the nineteenth hole would exist as a tradition, much less as a "temple" of sorts. But a greater reason is the food—the sustenance—of companionship. Four-somes almost customarily repair to the nineteenth hole after their round because they don't want their companionship to suddenly end; they want to prolong it—even sometimes the competition of companionship through throwing dice for the drinks.

Companionship is another fascinating word. From its derivation of *com* ("with") and *pan* ("bread"), it most literally means "the process of people eating together." This is not to say that family meals or dinner parties are always *companionable* affairs. They can be vicious. And they can be miserable, as may be one's workaday life in a particular business *company*. It is interesting to speculate upon some of the subtle changes that could be made in the workplace if business executives literally defined their company as a place where the employees "break bread together."[1]

In any case, amid its food and drink, the nineteenth hole is a place of true and pleasant company. Yet while a major purpose of the place is to prolong companionship, paradoxically its greatest purpose is also to bring that companionship to a fitting end. It is in many instances somehow unfitting to play a four-hour round of golf with others and then, simply because you've sunk your last putt of the day, to say, "Thanks, guys, it's been great. See you around." Such abruptness does not afford proper dignity either to the companionship you've enjoyed or to the drama of the game you've been playing. Something more is needed.

That something more is closure.

Closure is yet another most interesting word. Originally it was used simply to refer to the process of enclosing something, as with a fence or wall. Later it came to be used for the process of bringing some competitive activity to an end, such as the application of parliamentary rules for the closure of a debate. Most recently—only over the past few decades—it has come to be extensively employed to describe a psychological process. Both group therapists and management consultants have noted a destructive tendency for group activities—meetings of any kind, for instance—to end abruptly, by the clock, without issues having been adequately dealt with, leaving the participants feeling incomplete or otherwise dissatisfied. We are being properly urged these days to do it differently. We are being taught before the conclusion of meetings to set aside time for closure: a time when we can tie up loose ends sufficiently to part from one another with dignity and good feeling.

The nineteenth hole is an ancient institution. It would seem that golfers long ago instinctively knew the modern wisdom of group therapists and consultants. It is not just that with food and drink they customarily set aside time to add up their scores and pay off their bets. Nor is it simply time to make plans for the future—when and whether they will play again together. Primarily this time of closure is a time of remembrance, a time for recollection.

A round of golf may be an event of little or no significance. If it is to be given any substantial significance, however—and I believe it should—then it needs to be analyzed and remembered. "Do you remember how on the fourteenth you hit out of the deep rough and landed on the green for a gimme? God, that was a shot!" is the sort of thing one hears at the nineteenth hole. Or "God, I keep kicking myself for shanking that easy little approach on the seventh." Or "That was some drive you hit off the first tee, straight as an arrow and bouncing right in between the traps. What a way to start out!" Or "You really had bad luck back there on the twelfth, when your drive fell into the trap just short of the green and buried itself under the lip. Three more inches, and you would have been in birdie position!" Or "I'll never forget how you way over-hit the seventeenth and your damn ball bounced off that tree trunk straight back onto the green. Boy, Someone was really watching over you then."

This may not seem exactly the kind of stuff from which legends are made. Certainly it seems more like fun than work. Yet it is the essence of the work of closure. I believe that work, in its modest way, to be important, and I am glad that the nineteenth hole is there to sanctify it.

But what about this book? How do we gain "closure" on it? Although I have used an imaginary round on an imaginary golf course as a literary vehicle, the book has been about much more than a single round of golf; it has been about golf itself. How do we achieve either intellectual or emotional closure in regard to an entire sport? Particularly a sport that, I have suggested, is the most complex game on the face of the earth? On a sport some literally see as Heaven, some literally as Hell, and some as both?

On one level we can't. This is hardly the world's final book on golf. Many, many more will be written. Throughout I have urged readers to envision golf as an integral part of their spiritual growth. One of my earlier books is subtitled *The Unending Journey of Spiritual Growth*.[2] Your journey began well before you ever heard of golf (perhaps even before you were born). And it will hopefully continue after you are too decrepit to play the game anymore, when you are playing the game of dying with dignity—a game even more challenging and for higher stakes than any golf game—and quite possibly your journey will continue far beyond even that supposedly final game.[3]

A friend of a friend of mine was a decent man who loved golf but mostly worked diligently for decades at a job he loved the less. He eagerly looked forward to his retirement. It was his fantasy that when he got to retire, he would play golf every day of the year as long as he was fit. At the age of sixty-two, he was able to fulfill his fantasy. With plenty of money and an agreeable wife, he settled into a retirement community that centered on a very fine golf course, which was open all year. True to his intention, he played eighteen holes every single day, rain or shine, for thirteen months. But by the end of those thirteen months, he had become bored by unending golf. He did not quit the game. Still physically fit, he continued to play it two or three times a week. But the rest of the days, he turned his attention elsewhere.

I honor that man. Knowing nothing more about him, I do not know whether he considered himself to be on a journey of spiritual growth or whether the activities he began to substitute for golf had any spiritual merit for him. Yet I suspect that his growing boredom with golf was a God-given emotion,[4] and his decision to cut back on golf represented for him not only a spiritual crisis but one with a positive outcome. Unlike the golfer I humorously described on the previous hole who went to Hell, this man was able to put golf into its proper, paradoxical perspective. Having the courage to take up golf at one point in your life may be a great spiritual achievement. Laying down golf at another may be an equally immense achievement.

Once again, there is more to life than golf. While I consider golf to be potentially a spiritual discipline par excellence, it is not the only spiritual discipline. In other words, the spiritual journey is far grander than the grand game of golf. And in recognizing this, we have begun to arrive at a certain kind of closure.

This is my thirteenth book. I have a far lower tolerance for boredom than the man who finally cut back on golf after playing it every day for thirteen months. Consequently, I've never been able to write the same book over and over again. I've always felt that I was writing something new—most often something very new. Yet in retrospect I can now see that each and every one of my books has had the same essential subject. Yes, that subject has been addressed in most different ways, including a children's book and a murder mystery. But the single underlying concept of all my books has been life as a spiritual journey.

It is interesting that I refer to this as a concept. *Concept* is defined as "an opinion or certain way of looking at things," implying that there are other ways to look at things. For me personally, there is no other way to look at life than as a spiritual journey. Yet the fact of the matter is that mine is distinctly a minority viewpoint. Others have different visions. For instance, we may look at life with a Darwinian outlook as a process of the survival of the fittest. This vision has at least enough coherence to see value in breeding and child raising and in making money. Yet I suggest that even this is a minority outlook. My experience is that most of the time most people have no coherent vision. For them, "life is just a bunch of stuff that happens, and then you die."

So for most, golf is just a game. It may be a game they love or detest. They may see it as fascinating or dull. But either way it's still just a game. What I have been saying throughout, however, is that golf can be something more. The vision of life as a spiritual journey can infuse golf—and everything else—with meaning, even potential glory. In this book I have been using golf to attempt to transmit that vision. Indeed, one of the many virtues of golf is that it can be so used. Play golf, and it may—only "may," only possibly—teach you that there is more coherence to life than just a bunch of stuff that happens.

I do not mean to imply that golf is the only—or even the best—way to teach the concept of life as a spiritual journey. The concept is a strangely hard sell, and in my experience it can be taught by intensive psychotherapy better than by any other route. When it works. If intensive psychotherapy is successful, the patient grows; that is, she changes for the better. With this change comes a sense of movement; she has moved from here to there. Of even greater significance, it may begin to dawn on her that she can keep moving, keep on growing and progressing; that the conclusion of her psychotherapy need not be the conclusion of her healing; that she can now be her own therapist and embark upon a lifetime journey of growth.

This sense of movement, of journeying, may also be gained from travel to foreign lands and experiencing new cultures. It also may not be gained that way. Travel may be mere literal movement. The traveler will move from this town to that, from one hotel to another, from America to Europe to Asia, but if there is no resulting change within himself, he will have gained nothing. Such is often the case. When I speak of life as a journey, I am referring to an inner journey, to an inner movement of the soul. One man may make enormous strides on his inner journey while staying in his home and office, whereas another may travel the world over without enlarging his psychospiritual horizons in the least.

And so it is with golf. Golf is full of outward movement: swings and putts, traveling from the tee to the green to the next tee to the next green, traveling fairways all designed to be different, moving at least four miles on an average single round. But if nothing *happens* to you in the meantime, all you will have done is moved away from the clubhouse and back again.

"But of course things happen to you," the average golfer might retort. "You land in sand traps or behind trees. Good luck happens and bad luck happens. You botch this hole and birdie that one. And it's not just external. As you've pointed out yourself, the golf course is a cauldron of emotions. Aren't emotions internal? And isn't golf the ideal stimulus for emotional turmoil: for movement from elation to depression, depression to elation, shame to pride, pride to shame, joy to rage, and rage to joy?"

"All true," I must acknowledge. Golf is indeed the ideal stimulus for emotional turmoil, and that is precisely why I see the golf course as an ideal laboratory for spiritual growth. As life condensed, golf is likely to cause you more emotional turmoil yard for yard than any other human endeavor. But the key issue is what you do with that turmoil. If you simply bounce back and forth between depression and elation or rage and joy the same way you have on a hundred previous rounds, then in essence nothing has happened to you. Your handicap may have gone up or down a stroke or two, but *you* haven't changed. There has been no movement in your soul. The spiritual journey has to do with deep learning, real learning, and hence much more with inner than outer change. There must be kenosis, the emptying of old patterns of thought and behavior, so that new ones can be adopted.

I have suggested that the vision of life as a spiritual journey is not only uncommon but a difficult concept to teach. Yet it is hardly a new vision. It dates back at least three thousand years to some of the earliest recorded human literature. Perhaps one small group bespoke the concept more clearly than any other in our relatively recent "Western" heritage. I am referring to a group of radical early-seventeenth-century British Protestants who so deeply believed they were on a spiritual journey that they named themselves "Pilgrims." Suffering from persecution and fleeing oppression, a portion of them in 1620 landed their ship, the *Mayflower,* at Plymouth Rock and established the first successful British colony in the Americas.

Ask almost any U.S. citizen today who the Pilgrims were, and he will quickly tell you about Plymouth Rock, the *Mayflower,* and the first Thanksgiving. Ask why they called themselves Pilgrims, and he will likely either scratch his head or answer, "Well, they called this the New World. I guess they may have seen it as the Promised Land. I suppose they thought of their dangerous sea journey as a pilgrimage to the Promised Land. Yes, that must be it."

It is a sign of how alien the concept of spiritual journey is to most of us that only a very tiny minority of citizens could answer the question accurately. The Pilgrims did not call themselves such because they were making a sea journey from Europe to America, a mere geographical move from there to here. They called themselves Pilgrims long before they ever contemplated that move, because they envisioned life as a pilgrimage, as an unfolding and unending, mostly internal journey of spiritual growth. And because I have preached that same vision so constantly in all my works, one might say that I have been in the business of "pilgrimage education." But mostly I preach to the choir, to the already converted. Still, from time to time some members of the majority get the message. At that moment it is as if their eyes are suddenly opened and they see a previously prosaic world as filled with deep meaning—even, perhaps, the world of golf. They will never again be the same.[5]

One is highly unlikely to envision the frustrating game of golf as a potential spiritual discipline unless he has first been captured by the vision of the whole of life as a journey of spiritual growth, as a pilgrimage. Once he has been so captured, however, he can begin to see golf as a particularly lovely stretch on the journey where great movement is possible. Again, I do not mean outward movement from tee to green to tee; I mean inner movement of the soul.

This inner movement, like all of the spiritual journey, like the essence of golf itself, is nonlinear. One does not get from here to there in a straight line. This is reflected in the matter of score. As every golfer comes to learn, no matter how much she plays or practices, her score does not decline at an even rate of one stroke a round or one every three rounds. She will go through long dry spells, months in duration, where her score declines not at all, where it may even seem to be increasing. But if she keeps learning the game, a day will come when suddenly, for no apparent reason, she will score three strokes better than she ever has before. Then she will probably level out again, lower now, but only to stay there for more months until another magical day of dramatic improvement. In this way golf may indeed give one a sense of progress, however erratic, as she moves from breaking 100 to breaking 90.

I have hesitated to use this simple example, however, because while an improving score may reflect significant inner growth, it also may not. Many learn how to play better golf but learn nothing about themselves in the process and nothing about life. Conversely, aging and elderly golfers may helplessly watch their handicap inexorably drift upward at a time of life when they are actually enjoying the game more and learning more from it.

Hard though it may be for golfers to grasp, score is not the real point of the game. There are many points to golf, of which I believe soul learning and growth are the greatest, and score the least. Score is at best a reflection of something hidden. The Buddha once said to his followers: "I am a signpost pointing the way. You look pretty silly bowing down before a signpost." It is similarly silly to worship a reflection. Indeed, it can be a fatal attraction, as it was for Narcissus. The worship of score is the second most diabolical temptation of golf, even worse than the temptations to swing too hard or to look up too quickly. These are more easily subject to correction. An obsession with score is a form of idolatry because, like all forms of idolatry, it misses the point. It is the worship of a substitute for God, of a reflection for the Reality.

The single temptation of golf greater than the worship of score is the worship of golf itself. Golf too is but a signpost pointing the way. I do believe that golf can be a wonderful spiritual path of growth toward God—but only if one chooses to use it as such. And it is hardly the only such path. There are many ways toward God. To say that golf is *the* way would be as ridiculous as to contend that some other particular variety of meditation is the way. Or to contend that some exclusive church membership is a more valuable path than that of marriage, parenthood, business, or monastic life.

In closure, then, let it be restated that this has not been a book about how to lower your golf score. Indeed, it has not even ultimately been a book about golf. In it I have used golf as but an example of a path of spiritual growth that one might choose to use as such. Choice, however, is of the essence. I would like to think the book has encouraged some to take up golf who otherwise would not have, and some others already engaged in the game to go deeper. But it's all a matter of choice fermented out of our own God-given free will.

So ultimately the point is not score. Nor is it even golf. No matter what means or clubs we may pick up, it all strikes me as a matter of choice—specifically one of vision. The real point is whether or not we choose to see ourselves as pilgrims.

NOTES

1. My spiritual director, the Christian nun, is fond of pointing out to me that through the celebration of the Mass, Christians every single moment of the day, somewhere on the globe, are engaged in breaking bread together. Despite all of its immense flaws, the Christian church might well be just about the most successful "company" on the face of the earth.

2. M. Scott Peck, *Further Along the Road Less Traveled* (New York: Simon & Schuster, 1993).

3. See M. Scott Peck, *In Heaven as on Earth: A Vision of the Afterlife* (New York: Hyperion, 1997).

4. When I am feeling bored, it is not unlikely that I am also boring God. And as one of my spiritual mentors once put it, "As far as I'm concerned, the greatest sin is to bore God."

5. See the chapter on pilgrimage in my *In Search of Stones: A Pilgrimage of Faith, Reason and Discovery* (New York: Hyperion, 1995), pp. 205–23. And see John Bunyan's classic *The Pilgrim's Progress* (New York: Penguin Books, 1987). The seventeenth-century Bunyan also wrote a hymn, "Who Would True Valor See," one verse of which suggests how those who suddenly comprehend life as a spiritual journey will never be the same thereafter:

> *There's no discouragement*
> *Shall make him once relent*
> *His first avowed intent*
> *To be a pilgrim.*

INDEX

Page numbers set in *italics* refer to illustrations.

slope of, 34, 205, 216*n*
staff of, 176–78
Zen Buddhist, 123
golf jokes, 293, 294–95
golf rules, *see* rules of golf
golf teaching professionals,
    150–52, 154–55,
    161–63, 164
golf widows, 243–44
good golfers, bad shots by,
    41, 73
grace, 26
Graham, Billy, 297
gratefulness, 265
greenies, 208
greens, 8, 90–92
    ball marks on, 193
    blind, 55
    and rules of civility, 192–93
    slope of, 94, 95
    speed of, 94–95
    staff and, 176
grieving, 180
gross play, 201
Groundhog, 203

H
habit, 43–44, 72–73, 80, 230
handicapping, 34, 203–7,
    208, 209
    sandbagging and, 205–6

harmony, with unseen order,
    95–98, 125, 285
hazards, 14, 34, 37, 53–54,
    61, 62, 283
    sand traps, 14, 34, 103–7,
    108, 110–11, 112, 193
Hinduism, 122
history, 142
hitting all out, 14
hitting the ball too hard,
    69–70, 72, 73, 75, 79
Hole 1, *2,* 3–16
Hole 2, 17–31, *18, 29*
Hole 3, *32, 33*–48, *36*
Hole 4, 49–64, *50, 57*
Hole 5, 65–83, *66, 77*
Hole 6, *84, 85*–100, *96*
Hole 7, 101–16, *102*
Hole 8, 117–31, *118, 121*
Hole 9, *132,* 133–45, *135*
Hole 10, *148,* 149–64, *158*
Hole 11, 165–82, *166*
Hole 12, 183–99, *184*
Hole 13, *200,* 201–17
Hole 14, *218,* 219–37
Hole 15, *238,* 239–58
Hole 16, 259–73, *260*
Hole 17, *274,* 275–89
Hole 18, *290,* 291–302
Hole 19, 303–13
hole play, 202
holes, 8, 10

ABOUT THE AUTHOR

M. Scott Peck, M.D., is the author of many best-selling books, including *The Road Less Travelled,* which has spent more than twelve years on the *New York Times* best-seller list. He lives in northwestern Connecticut.